Pers]

A Journey from S

By
Beverley Anne Freeman

Copywrite © 2019 Beverley Anne Freeman
All Rights Reserved

"In the depth of winter, I finally learned that within me there lay an invincible summer."

~ Albert Camus

A Word From The Author

I have longed to write a book ever since I could remember. At seven years old on a school outing, we went to see Roald Dahl at the local library. After reading a few chapters of James and The Giant Peach he asked if anyone had any questions, confident and eager my hand shot up immediately. "Mr Dahl, I want to be an author when I grow up, do you have any advice for me?", I glowed with enthusiasm as I asked. His reply not only rendered me speechless but also made an indelible mark in my mind. "Don't ever attempt to write a book until you are well into your forties because will not have had enough experience of life", he replied, not realising he had just imprinted a watermark on my life plan.

So here I am in my forties writing books…. In this respect, he was quite right. The past forty years I have been collecting material for this book. Material which will shock you, hopefully, make you laugh and probably, make you cry. I need to thank all those that have unwittingly given me much of that 'material', both good and bad, happy and sad.

I have changed the names to protect the innocent and the not so innocent. Some close friends asked that I used their real names and I honoured their wishes. I realised whilst writing this autobiography that you can't possibly include every little detail of your life; it would be too much! Therefore, there are times, places and people who I have not mentioned. It doesn't mean that those events weren't important, every event is an accumulation of the person I have become and the message I wish to convey.

I dedicate this book to my mother; my partner in crime, my teacher and my student. The love of my life and my soulmate.

I would also like to thank everyone who has touched my life in any way, whether as a lesson or as a comfort. Every experience has made me who I am, has allowed me to gain the love, courage and wisdom to help others. I hope that by exposing my vulnerability, dysfunction and craziness, it will help you heal yours.

A huge thank you to Sandra Downie who has patiently and encouragingly edited this book for me. Thank you, for all your help and lifelong friendship. Thank you to Janet Hodcroft for your love and honesty always and helping me shape this book into some kind of accomplished work, suitable for general sale.

perspective
noun (1)

Definition of *perspective*

1*mass noun* The art of representing three-dimensional objects on a two-dimensional surface so as to give the right impression of their height, width, depth, and position in relation to each other.
'the theory and practice of perspective'

as modifier 'a perspective drawing'

2 A particular attitude towards or way of regarding something; a point of view.
'most guidebook history is written from the editor's perspective'

2.1 *mass noun* True understanding of the relative importance of things; a sense of proportion.
'we must keep a sense of perspective about what he's done'

'though these figures shock, they need to be put into perspective'

3 An apparent spatial distribution in perceived sound.

Taken From oxforddictionaries.com

Contents

"You are born naked, everything else is just drag."

~ RuPaul

Introduction

I Saw The Light

I started working in a cocktail bar in my hometown of Bolton, Lancashire when I was sixteen. Not a glamorous cocktail bar; this had sticky carpets, leery men and sold double shots and cocktails at one pound fifty a go. Nevertheless, I thought I was super glamourous with my long, dark, curly hairpiece, false eyelashes, red lipstick and a fake beauty spot drawn on with eye pencil. I wore the tiniest black velvet hot pants and little satin bra tops, fishnet tights and knee-length, leopard print platform boots. My sense of dress and self-expression was at that time an ostentatious mix of my idols; Marilyn Monroe, Madonna and Scary Spice. I was a real hit with the boys and known as 'the best-looking barmaid in Bolton', a crown I wore with pride in those days.

The owner of the bar, Pat, was born Irish catholic and an 'altar boy' who wanted to join the priesthood, somewhere along the line he slipped off that path and joined the 'Bergerac's' wagon train. That was the name of the bar; Bergerac's Wine Bar. Although to be fair there was not much wine drank in there, most people came into the bar early doors to get as drunk as possible, as cheap as possible before going out on the rampage to a local Bolton nightspot. The girls who worked in the bar, including myself, were not far behind them and most evenings turned into one big alcohol-fueled party.

To be fair Pat was one of the kindest people I'd ever met. He passed away in his early forties from cancer and liver failure and left a huge gaping hole in my heart. Pat 'saved' me many times, from scary landlords, over-enthusiastic punters, stalkers and often, from myself. Despite those days being my most dysfunctional, my Bergerac's evenings were some of the best times I've ever had. Fond memories come back as I write this as well as hellish encounters with men who wanted sex and very little else, and landlords wanting money I didn't have. The whole of it remembered through blurred lines and compromised vision onset by vodka and orange.

At this time, I had dreams of becoming a fashion model and joined a model agency in Manchester. There wasn't an awful lot of paid modelling work at the agency. Every Sunday I and about twenty other girls would arrive at noon and very seriously slap on ten inches of foundation. There was this 'make-up artist' called Rita who taught us how to do our makeup for the photographs. She insisted we finished it in six minutes, and it consisted of exaggerated eyebrow's, lips and cheeks on a base of extra thick foundation that was never the right colour for your complexion (but Rita insisted you went two shades lighter for the camera). We were assured this was the best look for the photographs.

Downstairs Beula dressed us in some crazy outfit and then the owner of the agency Roger would take the photographs. After that, we would practice catwalk for two hours with Esther. The following week we would excitedly get our photographs and usually, I would stand there in total bemusement wondering why I didn't look like Kate Moss. What followed was a humiliating consultation with Roger as to why I didn't look like Kate Moss and the obvious suggestion was that I eat much less the following week, although I was already down to five and a half stone. And for reasons I never really understood, his photography skills never came into question, only my perceived weight problem. I can make light of this now, but that time in my life triggered twenty-five years of yo-yo dieting and hating of my body.

At the model agency, I met this tall thin, gorgeous blonde girl with the widest smile and different coloured eyes. What followed was a twenty-eight-year friendship of two girls who turned into women and continue to support each other to this day. Sonia and I hit it off immediately, not only was she from my hometown, but she worked at this super cool sounding bar where they paid you top rates of pay, cash in hand and didn't ask your age or for your national insurance number. So, it was Sonia that introduced me to Bergerac's Wine Bar. I was sixteen when I started behind the bar and getting paid twenty pounds a night plus tips, four nights a week meant I could afford all the wigs and platforms I wanted!

Sonia was also one of the 'models' at the agency but, there was a higher purpose to our meeting. For one, she gave me the book "Out On A Limb" by Shirley MacLaine to read, which was my first real introduction to the concept of spiritualism. Although I had been to the Spiritualist Church a few times already and bought myself a pack of tarot cards, it was still only an interest for me rather than a 'knowing'. I had read Doris Stokes 'Voices' trilogy and the autobiography of local medium James Byrne but I was very nascent in my understanding. It was through this book that I learned about past lives, that there was another version of God other than the version we were taught at school, and the possibility of aliens.

When I was nineteen, I had left yet another office job and was doing some day shifts at the wine bar, in addition to my evening shifts. I had been involved in a difficult relationship with a married, Asian taxi driver who was now in prison for non-payment of speeding fines. I was feeling very low and down on myself, I had been through a series of upheavals, heavy and sometimes frightening sexual encounters with men, I drank too much, too often and was in a miserable place. I was living in a beautiful flat alone (I always had great taste and although I couldn't afford the rent, mostly lived in fabulous houses in and around Bolton) and had decided to take time out to do some soul searching. Even then I instinctively knew to retreat into my higher self and search for truths when I felt low.

I had been reading Out on a Limb, the Bible and the Koran searching for meaning to life. Out on a Limb was a new way of thinking for me and had introduced me to the work of Edgar Cayce and reincarnation. The Bible was all I knew growing up about spiritualism and the Koran was introduced to me as another form of spiritualism by my married, Muslim boyfriend who was now in prison.

It was a Wednesday afternoon, having finished my shift I went back to my flat and lay on the sofa a little tired. I closed my eyes and started to relax, drifting into a kind of daydream. Within what seemed like a few moments of sitting down I began to see the brightest light I'd ever seen. I cannot explain how beautiful and loving and amazing this light was to me. All I can say is that it was not of this physical world. The light became brighter and brighter and I remember thinking, *my eyes should be hurting right now* but my eyes didn't hurt. I drew nearer and nearer into the light and became the light. I was lifted out of my body and into another realm where space and time did not exist. I wasn't my body anymore; I was just me. I was the true version of me, the total, complete and more relevantly; the pain-free me. This was pure unconditional love before me, it was God and spirit and everything that it encompassed, it was all there is and all there could ever be, right before me. As I moved closer and closer, I was the light. I was love. It was the most breathtaking, amazingly incomprehensible experience I have ever had. I was so happy and loved and fulfilled in the light and had no intention of leaving this place, it was pure utopia. Suddenly, I saw a hand, the hand looked like a physical shape but was also just light. It was most definitely a man's hand in shape and size and although it was made of light, I could see lines on the hand just like a human hand. Next, I heard a man's voice that said, "you must go back". I remember thinking I don't want to go back, but it was too late. Within a split second of hearing the voice I was back in my living room, in my flat and in my body and the light was gone. I looked at my watch. What seemed like only moments was three hours gone. I was vaguely disbelieving of what had just happened but at the same time, I knew it was real. I understood what I experienced was God; showing me the answers that I had been seeking in the books I'd read.

My immediate reaction was to try and get back there. I closed my eyes, visualised the light returning and willed myself to see it or feel it again. Asking the light to come forward, desperate for that unconditional love to return. I knew it wasn't coming back. I knew the next time I saw that light it would be on my death bed. A strangely familiar and yet stark contrast to the life I was living, I felt it was the naked veil of spirit imploring me to trust in the process of life. Yet, in my juvenile mind, I did not know how to process the information. Nor did I fully understand why I was seeing this or why then.

After having this experience, I read of other people having near-death experiences who described the light exactly how I had seen and felt it. Years later, my mother bought me a book by medium James Van Prague who described a strikingly similar experience to my own. What was difficult to comprehend, was why me? Why was a barmaid from Bolton having this experience, an experience, that other people literally must die to encounter? Or in the case of James Van Prague become a world-famous medium? Yet, here I was, there in Bolton sat on the sofa seeing God and understanding what happens when the physical body leaves the earth plane.

Of course, at that time I did not know how my life and spiritual work would unfold and that many times whilst teaching mediumship in the future I would tell people of this experience. Even so, there was no hallelujah, glory, glory moment, no gospel choir and no sudden spiritual enlightenment. I didn't suddenly become at one with The Buddha or download the wisdom of the Tao Te Ching. My life was still the same. I was still a dysfunctional, borderline alcoholic and broken child.

I often revisit this moment when I feel fear creeping into my life. I remember that light and what it felt like for me. A euphoria that is not describable with words of the physical. It says in A Course in Miracles that we 'only see the past', meaning that we can only recognise something in our present moment by our past experiences. So, if I can recognise the light as being God, then surely, I must have had past experiences of it. For me, it felt like it was that light 'from whence I came'. The light was a validation of the existence of spirit and although I had little understanding of it at that time, it was a gateway to stopping the pain, moving into a new chapter. It was a matter of weeks after having this experience that the married, jailbird boyfriend left my life and my future husband entered.

"Life is a strange thing, as soon as you think you've learned how to use it, it's gone."

~ Shakespeare's Sister

1.
Growing Up

My mother Jacqueline, a tailor and my father Joseph, a professional side car champion share the same birthday, the summer solstice in fact. They met in a pub on their birthday, marrying a few years later. My Mum was pregnant with my half-sister at the time and she was legally adopted by my Dad.

My Mother had become pregnant with a Portuguese student who had returned to Portugal not knowing about the child. My Mother too proud and too stubborn refused to tell him; determined to get an abortion and join the RAF. She was refused an abortion by her GP and was advised that adoption would be the only solution. However, she fell in love with the little girl once she was born and ended up keeping the baby.

My mother had a harrowing childhood. Being the product of an extra marital affair during world war two, she would marinate in the womb in the guilt, shame and fear of her mother and eventually took on these attributes herself.

My Mother's father is today only a perception of a Chinese sailor; and she only has the word of her late grandmother as to who he is. The story goes that her mother and older sister met a pair of Chinese sailors. Lonely with their husbands off at war they both got pregnant very quickly and all four of them moved to Liverpool to live in a flat (I'm sure it was more like a couple of whores hitting the town). It didn't work out (anyway) and her Mother returned to Bolton and my Mum was born towards the end of the war in June 1945. Before they left, they apparently left a gold locket each for the babies, my mother still has hers and it houses a lock of hair, which was my sisters first curl.

Her Mother's husband returned home as the war ended and seeing a half Chinese, new addition to the family he was enraged and horrified; subsequently and not surprisingly he rejected the child. Her Mother chose to stick by her husband and my Mum went to live with her Gran who brought her up from age two years. Her Mother then went on to have another two children, in addition to an older sister that she already had. They all lived a few streets away with their parents and Mum could visit on Sundays. It must have been a confusing and heart-breaking situation for a young girl, knowing she had two brothers and a sister who she was not allowed to live with. Always the outcast, she grew up with a perception of isolation and unworthiness. In addition to this she suffered infantile paralysis and half of her face became paralysed at the age of three. The only help the doctors could offer at the time was a wire that hooked from the inside of her mouth over her ear, even more humiliation and ostracisation. This, together with looking Chinese, produced a heavy dosage of school bullying and a busted lip each evening on her way home from school. The bullying continued throughout her early school years.

Not surprisingly, she felt isolated having to live with her Grandmother whilst her siblings grew up around the corner with their parents. Feelings of total rejection mixed with bullying because of her Chinese appearance created a sad child and a damaged adult. As a result, my mother suffered from depression from her early teens right into her thirties.

She tells me stories of her Gran, as she calls her, though with fond memories. Her Grandparents were both tailors and she inherited their ability with talent and skill. Her grandfather unfortunately, lost his right arm in World War One and passed away, probably of grief from losing his craft. Her Gran came from good stock, being the daughter of a Victorian Inventor and had a graceful elegance and refined taste; something myself and my mother have both inherited. Her great grandfather William Wilding invented the bobbin for the cotton mills and received one thousand pounds royalties in 1900. Her Gran said, "he squandered it all on wine, woman and song", he passed away quite young and her grandmother was brought up by two maiden aunts.

When Mum was born in 1945, her uncle Dick had just returned from fighting in France, he suggested they named her Jacqueline, after a little French girl who would run errands for the soldiers. She was shot by the Nazi's at just five years old, a brave and heroic death at the end of a small life. My mum often says, "no wonder I'm bloody cursed".

My father on the other hand, came from a secure loving home born of parents Joseph and Kathleen. Both, my grandparents, were very special to me and I often feel their love and energy around me in my everyday life. My father tried to do the best he could by my mother but coming from a simple home he never really understood her depression or feelings of total abandonment that she carried from childhood into adulthood. It was an impossible marriage, two equally strong people coming together with very little knowledge of how to deal with Mum's deep-seated emotional issues. They did try though, with the adoption of her current baby and then they planned my birth.

When I was born, my mum was badly torn and had to have stitches, the nurse put me on a metal table while she dealt with my mum and forgot about me. I went blue and nearly died, I was put in an incubator and came back to life. So, it seems I came out fighting and God had a plan for me. I am glad I didn't go back home so soon, as I got to do lots of exciting things here; like write this book.

They were both happy when I arrived and tried to make a go of things. They bought a small terraced house which Dad turned into my mum's dream home. Dad worked at a large firm making boats, mum as a window dresser for Richards shops. They clashed at every milestone, even though my Dad was relatively happy, mum wasn't. My parents got divorced when I was four years old and it was mum who instigated it. Despite my Dad opposing the divorce and wanting to gain custody of my sister and I, it was one of the best things to happen. I truly believe I could not have become the person I am today, had they not gone their separate ways. My mother gained custody of both myself and my sister and after seeking healing at her local spiritualist church started to heal her depression in her thirties.

Growing up in Bolton was full of fun and laughter yet raw and gutsy in its northern, rustic charm. Bolton is colourful with a real mix of races, classes and ideals. It gave me a base I am mostly proud of; a Lancashire town which was originally built on textile mills and coal mining, all held together with a strong cup of tea and a good homemade pasty. Until I was four years old, that was my life. Bolton, my mum and dad and my older sister.

My sister is five years my senior so we kind of missed each other at every important event. She was at school for my entire pre-school years, then when I started school, she was too old to be playing with the first-year pupils and when I started secondary school, it was the year she left. This meant play time was more like being an only child. I spent a lot of time with my mother pre-school. My mother wanted to go back to work after I was born so my Dad's mother looked after me. My mum would drop me off at nursery and Nana Curly, as we would call her, would pick me up to take me to her house. I absolutely hated nursery and would scream the place down until they would call my nan to collect me. In the end they gave up and I just stayed with my nan until mum finished work.

I loved it at Nana Curly's house, it was full of toys and games, music, crafts, cooking smells, stewed tea and other children. I had so many cousins and now second cousins and third cousins I can't even count. I couldn't tell you all their names. Those days spent at Nana Curly's house were happy times. She would sing country and western music, read the bible and Jehovah's witness magazines she bought for ten pence when they knocked on the door. She always had a giant jigsaw on the table she was piecing together. When she had finished one, she would put lines of cellotape on it to hold the pieces in place and sometimes put them in picture frames.

My nan chain smoked constantly, drank tea, planted marigolds and cooked from morning till evening. She was as thin as a bean pole and always looked old, wrapped in something knitted or second hand from the rag 'n' bone man. She had so many toys in her toy box; nearly all the dolls had an eye missing, but no child was ever bored at Nana Curly's house.

She taught me how to read the tea leaves while we listened to Dolly Parton records. We would sit drinking tea together, mine was in a blue plastic baby cup, with milk and two sugars. Nan's was in a cup and saucer; loose tea provided the basis for these tea leaf readings. I still have my nan's Dolly Parton records and Mum took me to Dollywood in the Smokey Mountains for my thirtieth birthday. A holiday I will never forget, I know my nan was with me the whole time, dancing with us at 'Tootsie's Bar' in downtown Nashville. Dolly was part of my formative years, my grandad would pop in and out of the living room from the garden whilst Dolly sang like an angel.

My grandad was a lovely man, named Joseph (my Dad is named after him). His army habits stayed with him, long after he left. He would wake up before anyone else, polish his boots and go for a walk to get a paper. He always smelled of Old Spice aftershave, was well dressed, a real gent of a man who I loved spending time with. His birthday was the day after mine, which always makes me feel like we have some sort of unspoken connection.

When I wasn't at my Nana Curly's house I was at home with Mum whilst Dad was out at work and my sister was at school. We would watch black and white movies together and marvel at the glamourous dresses worn by screen goddesses like Bette Davis, Lana Turner, Marilyn Monroe and Grace Kelly. We would sing along with Jean Kelly, Doris Day and Sophie Lauren and hide our faces at 'the king of horror', Bela Lugosi. Sometimes, Mum would cook in the kitchen and bake gorgeous pies, cakes and scones. If I wasn't helping her, I was watching these old movies on my own in the living room. Marilyn Monroe became my idol, and while all the other girls at school were sticking up posters of Duran Duran, my walls were covered with photographs of Marilyn. Her glamour and beauty astounded me, and I wanted to dress up like her and sing 'diamonds are a girl's best friend' from the age of four years old. I still have the whole of her movie collection and know every line and every song by heart.

I always loved music from the day I can remember. It started with those films and I loved all the songs from Gershwin and Bacharach, not to mention other films. I remember one day watching The Jolson Story about a black and white minstrel called Al Jolson. I went into the kitchen with shoe polish all over my face and mum's red lipstick, dancing expressively and singing a painful rendition of the song Mammy "…I'd walk a million miles for one of your smiles…. mammy". I declared right there and then I was going to be a black and white polo when I grew up, my mum replied, "you mean a minstrel?", "oh yes, I knew it was a toffee". My mum laughed and told me I had a wild imagination. I would dramatically fall forwards and say, "I'm being Bette Davies, falling down at the end", my mum would ask, "at the end of what?" …. "every film!" I would reply. She would roll her eyes at me and secretly laugh at my expressive portrayal of these starlets. Later, my love of music would shape my self-expression and dress sense, until I was able to separate myself from my idols and just appreciate their creativity.

I loved those days at home with mum, she would make these gorgeous pies on a dinner plate. She would hold the plate in the air with one hand and trim off the pastry with a knife. I was allowed to make jam tarts out of the pastry that fell off. I would roll out the pastry in the shape of a square, cover with jam and then make a lattice pastry top and glaze with milk. Mum would bake it in the oven for me and I always burnt my mouth on in, too impatient to wait for it to cool down.

Alas these days had to end, I had to face the grim reality that I was to start school. I couldn't get away with it like nursery, Mum said it was compulsory. I was so nervous and sad about starting school. I needn't have worried though, within a few hours of starting I met my very best friend Sarah. We are still best friends today, we always try to make time to get together, even if we are in different countries.

My first day of school is still very clear in my mind. I remember that it was PE on my first day and Sarah and I sat next each other. As neither of us had ever been to school before we had no idea of the protocol. We were sat at a large table in front of about fifty small white drawers, all of which seemed empty. We decided to play a game where we took it in turns hiding our PE knickers in the drawers, the other having to guess which drawer, they were in. It turned out we weren't supposed to do this, so we had to stand in different corners of the room with our fingers on our lips as punishment.

It didn't really deter us; we giggled constantly and haven't stopped for over forty years. School days filled with rapturous laughter over nothing that made any sense to anyone else. Summers playing in rivers and ditches, on monkey swings and weekends swimming at the indoor swimming baths. We attended ballet class in tutu's, pointing our toes with butterfly wings attached to our back's. Later in our twenties, we would have endless alcohol fueled nights in Bolton Town Centre and Fanny's Wine Bar. Standing on tables singing, falling in the snow and hailing taxi cabs with our shoes in our hands. In our forties we became 'ladies that lunch', busy with work, homes, families and lives that we shaped from those early childhood memories.

School sports day would prove just how much of an angel Sarah really was. I was totally unable to run any length and at any speed which mattered in the eyes of winning a race. Sarah would wait for me, holding out her hand and ignoring the pleas of her mother to run. Subsequently, she came second to last, and I came last; in every race.

At school I was terrible at anything that was either physical activity or mathematical (I found numbers so incredibly boring). I was good at art, English and anything that involved performing on a stage. Although I couldn't sing, I loved to dance and was very dramatic and expressive. I always wanted to be a writer or an actress when I 'grew up' but I must admit that becoming a medium, never really occurred to me. I had often wondered if I had past lives in the singing or acting industry because for me, it was just so natural to love all things theatrical. Later, when I trained with Dr Brian Weiss and had a variety of past live regressions, I would link up the connection.

I was also very psychically and spiritually aware from an early age, I would read the palms of girls and boys in the school playground, pretending I could see into the future. I would also use leaves and rose petals to make pretend spells. Not the most normal child in the world, but I didn't worry, I always had this unbelievable confidence to be myself, even if this was a psychic child with very strange tendencies towards all things occult. I've not always been the best ambassador of my authenticity and at times demonstrated insecurities but, I have always done what I wanted and had no time for critical peers.

Although Sarah was my first friend and we remained friends, I had many other friendships. I had a few good friends that I never forgot, I was a bit of a social butterfly in some respects. There was another Sarah who came into my life at around eight years old. She came to our school in the middle of the school year and was very shy. It is unclear why I was chosen as her mentor, but it turned out well, we were like chalk and cheese, somehow blended and spent many memorable times together. Later in my teens I would become close to a girl called Charlotte, I loved her individualism and creative style and we would get up to much mischief. I pretty much got along with everyone and have a story that I remember with most of my school friends. We had scraps, argued, fell out, took sides and were children and teenagers together. We keep in contact via social media and many of them still live local to where we grew up. Our school reunion when we all turned forty was a blast! There wasn't any animosity between any of us, which just goes to show what a good lot we really are.

Between my mother and father, I grew up with two completely different perceptions of life. There was my Dad's family who were all out-going, loved a party and lots of singing, they had a 'make do and mend' mentality. At any given Christmas we would be round at Nana Curly's licking glue to make paper chains which we hung from the ceiling like a multi coloured washing line. Nana would make trifle and rabbit pie, open packets of bourbon biscuits and Wotsits, scattered on a big table in her tiny living room. Everyone would sing, and someone would play the guitar.

Then there was my Mother, estranged from her family who liked things she couldn't afford, had refined taste and always looked beautiful with her dark curly hair and red lips. She always made sure we had the best quality socks and wouldn't buy us anything from the jumble sales. When she got dressed up to go out, she looked like a super star off the telly, I think I thought she secretly popped out to join the cast of Dallas when she went to work. At only five foot tall, she had a tiny waist, shapely legs and always sported six-inch stilettos.

I have a vague recollection of my Mum being diagnosed with cancer and having a hysterectomy. I remember making her a get well soon card with my Dad and sister. I chose pink glitter, but the glue turned it brown which made me extremely upset. There were other times when Mum went into hospital too and sometimes, we stayed at my Aunty Viv's house. It was big and to me then, very posh, she was my posh aunty. We loved staying with Aunty Viv because everything was elegant, she had a big garden and orange and turquoise bar stools in the kitchen where we could eat breakfast. She wasn't my real aunty, but my mothers' best friend who she met at the of age sixteen. They are still friends today, going for days out and driving each other nuts with humor and grouchy comments.

So, my childhood was mainly a happy one. Any challenges in my mother's mood swings (which were down to the depression she felt), were more character building than challenging. Even when my mum and dad got divorced, at the age of four I was able to see the positives in this life change. I can't really explain it, I felt my mother was happier, lighter and somehow, I just knew everything would turn out ok in the end. Regardless of their differences, mum always told me that my dad was a good dad and, for the most part, a good husband. She was just in the wrong situation and needed to be single for a while to figure things out. I got to see Dad most weekends and life carried on.

"The wound is the place where the light enters you."

~ Rumi

2.
Tom

My mother has always been a strong person with a fierce execution of her plans and ideas. After the divorced she struggled financially but healed emotionally. She worked hard and slowly built up the money she needed to run the house and get her life on track. My dad was bitter about the divorce and refused to help her out financially, figuring that he would make it as difficult as possible for her to move on. A few months after her divorce she met some local ladies who were also single, they started to go out to a local nightclub called 'The Touch of Class'. Later it would change its name to Monroe's, and I would party in the very same place. That's where Mum met Tom.

He was short and stocky, and although he was younger than my Mum, he was going bald. He was funny, cheerful and liked Rod Stewart. She brought him home one night after a few drinks when my sister and I were still awake. I sat there asking him questions about himself, being cheeky and making him laugh. Mum sent us up to bed after a few minutes of interrogation, but he would continue to come over more often until he became her official boyfriend.

I took to him immediately, which pleased my Mum and we settled into a new way of life as Tom moved in with us. Tom was cocky, worked in a food wholesaler, loved football and horse racing and used to put on an annoying cockney accent (a la Chas and Dave). He came across to everyone as friendly and amiable but not the sharpest tool in the box. He lived with us for around five or six years.

My Mum was head over heels in love with him at first, they did argue quite a bit, but my mother is a very strong person and will not be told what to do, so I didn't see this as out of the ordinary. They argued a lot less than my Mum and Dad had done previously. To be honest it was my sister that he argued with more. They seemed to clash at every event, always sharp with each other and full of contradictions; we never knew why. I always thought that my sister was just on my dad's side and she missed him being around. She told me many times that she wished Mum and Dad were still together, but I could never reciprocate these feelings because I just felt mum was happier after the divorce.

Tom was always nice to me, buying me gifts, showing lots of affection and generally being playful. He had a daughter who was a year younger than me who would come and visit at weekends. I was also aware he had an older stepdaughter who didn't seem to like him much and never came to visit.

I spent quite a bit of time with Tom at first and I became good friends with his daughter. His affection was flattering, I'd always had a great bond with my dad and saw this as the same thing. He could get a bit grumpy sometimes and when it came to a choice between me and his 'real' daughter there was no competition. There were highlights of a nasty, sadistic side but when someone show's you something like that you try to pretend you didn't see. That's what happened really, we didn't see him. Not him, not what was coming and not his past.

We got close in the first couple of years and I had no problem with him babysitting me while Mum was at work. My Mum worked in a department store, so this included late nights and Saturdays. It was normal for Tom and me to have the day to ourselves on Saturdays. I would walk to the village near my house to get sweets at the local shops while Tom would go to the bookies to watch the horse racing. Later we would cuddle up on the sofa together and watch the telly. There was a connection and a trust between us that was obvious, I felt like he was my friend.

We had got back to the house and were lying on the sofa; match of the day music was playing as it was just about to start. I was lying next to him as I had done many times before and was comfortable and relaxed. It was then that his hands started to go up my skirt and into my knickers. His fingers touched the folds of skin between my legs and I flinched as he continued to push his fat stubby hands inside me. I just lay there, frozen, not knowing how I was supposed to react. My world was changed forever, as he forced my hand onto his penis and started to rub it up and down. A penis my mother had touched a hundred times, my world spiraled like a kaleidoscope of love and fear, all producing patterns which made no sense. My eight-year-old life was gone and replaced with those words 'sexual abuse', words which would haunt my life and create 'my story' for years to come.

I was upset because I was wearing my favourite red dress with a little house embroidered on the front, after that day, the first day, I never wanted to wear it again. My favourite red dress splashed with his white ejaculation and my shame. I never again wanted to hear Match of the Day music or a Rod Stewart song.

I avoided him like the plague after that, walking around the village all day, not coming home until I knew my Mum was about to arrive home or that my sister would be in. Although my sister was never in the house unless Mum was home. I didn't find that strange to be honest, because she was really into her boyfriend at the time and I thought she was just getting on with her teenage life. There were those occasions when I couldn't stay out of his way and similar proceedings prevailed, each time he tried to push things further but by this time I had found my fight and pushed him away. I still didn't hate him though, I continued to be his friend and put on a façade. However, the relationship became silted and the atmosphere in the house became heavy and laced with blind poison.

How did any of us not see what was going on? How was it that, this man was perceived to be Mr Nice Guy, when there were so many girls hating him, avoiding him? Why was it all just business as usual? We all pretended, every day that life was fine. That sexual abuse was not part of it, that the monster lurking in the wardrobe was not in the wardrobe but living in our house, eating our food, sitting on our sofa and using our toothpaste. It went on for a couple of years like a game of cat and mouse. Avoid, Hide. Win. Lose.

I wanted to tell my Mum; I really did. I watched Esther Rantzen present Childline and memorised the number in my head, 0800 double 1, double 1. It would ring in my ears like that inevitable bell which was out to get me. I stood in the red telephone box at the bottom of Ainsworth Road in Little Lever and dialed the number at least ten times, always putting the receiver down the minute someone answered.

I tried to reason with myself, I think he loved me, it was what adults do when they love you. I knew they did that with each other, I saw it on TV, heard it through the wall. I decided to tell my friend at school, Jane. I told Jane what happened, and she went mad at me, I got all defensive then and started saying it was only because he loved me. The truth was it felt wrong, very wrong and I knew I had to do something. Jane told her Mum and she said her Mum was going to call the police. It was a total mess. I was frightened of what was going to happen if I told someone what he did to me. I thought social services would come and take me away, that I would have to eat beans on toast in a children's home for the rest of my life. Added to that was the shame and guilt I'd have to wear like a badge on my forehead.

I decided I would be brave and tell Mum everything, so I started crying and telling my Mum something was wrong, something about Saturdays, something about Tom and men. I wasn't sure what to call it, was I being sexually abused like the children on Childline? I decided that wasn't it, it was nothing like that. At the end of the conversation, it was decided I would go to my Dad's house on Saturdays. I have no idea how that came about, but I failed completely at trying to tell my Mum about what Tom was up to.

Around five years into this relationship, arguments between Tom and my mother became more frequent, more aggressive and more frightening. I remember one occasion when he was punching her in the living room. She was tiny and he was fat, the weight of him flagellating with every strike. My sister was out, and I was screaming for him to stop, I ran outside and knocked on the neighbour's door, "please help, someone call the police" I shouted. The police were called but went away again and nothing changed.

I'm not sure if my Mum had a sixth sense about it all but a few days later we were all sat in the living room. Me, Mum, Tom, my sister, and her boyfriend. My mother asked my sister why she hated Tom so much. It all came out then, my sister told my Mum he had been sexually attacking her for years. Mum asked him to leave and dialled 999. I remember the last words he said as he left the house forever, "come on, Jack, you can't believe her, can you?". Then he was gone. He never returned.

The days that followed this are a bit of a blur. A policewoman came to interview me, my Mum sat on the sofa assuring me it would be ok. Saying, I could say anything, and she was right there beside me. It was tense, and the silence was so loud it deafened me. The atmosphere was thick and meaty, unable to drive through, not even the chain saw of my mind could cut through the solid wall of silence. I was so confused and young and frightened of what was happening.

I tried to get the words out, things going over in my mind, things I saw adults do on TV, what did they call it? Sex? Abuse? I couldn't find the words, so I said nothing, I did nothing, all I could do was cry. It was like a vice around my neck, choking me with words I did not know. The eyes of my Mum, the eyes of the policewoman whittling their way into my brain, my heart, my core. Still, no words came. I was like a slaughtered animal, defeated and broken, ready to be made into mince for worthless sausages. I think those words are still stuck in my throat today, in my thyroid, not working properly. Stuck in dysfunctional torment of a moment in time where things could have been so different. Suspended in time, feelings of regret and shame, my shame and guilt created then at that moment. Shame which haunted me, taunted me for years to come. Every sexual encounter for the next twelve years and sometimes beyond would be shaped by this very moment of my life.

Endless questions, why did you do that, why did you not do that? Who? When? How? How many times? Secrets revealed and lies uncovered. Painful and heartbreaking confessions from young girls who never willingly participated in any of it. All embroiled by Tom. Tom, the overweight, balding football fan with the fake cockney accent.

It was said that he was abused by his father. He had a mentally handicapped sister who lived at home her entire life. Tom told my mum that his father had been having sex with her since she reached puberty. Yes, of course, because hurt people, hurt people. A pathology presented in a monstrous package.

After that, all I got were snippets of overheard conversations, hushed telephone calls, and hidden court documents. I understood later than my testimony would have meant a definite custodial sentence. He was tried for years of sexual abuse of two underage girls. My blocked-up effort was not used in the case. He was found guilty on both counts but given a suspended prison sentence of eighteen months. Justice was not served on my behalf, my fault. Now he was free to re-offend and there was no closure for those concerned.

After that, everything spiralled out of control. The family faced the worst of it. Suicide attempts, photographs representing the last six years cut into shreds. His possessions placed in the wheelie bin, memories wiped out, deceit shredded into a Tom shaped mess. How do you carry on, knowing that he's out there, free and guilty? Mum had lost her relationship, her pride, her sanity. I felt that my sister became angry at the verdict and all hell broke loose in the house. Three women, completely lost at how to carry on with life, because it was never going to be the same again. Like the secret held us together but the truth tore us apart.

I was ten years old after the verdict and just tried to carry on, pretending that it was ok that Mum drank brandy and cried almost every night. That my sister was never there, and I was the only sober member of our three-band family. I think they didn't know what to do, so they momentarily buried the feelings that existed and tried desperately to carry on with life. Quickly turning over the channel on the television when Match of the Day started, no one mentioned Rod Stewart and cockney accents were banned.

A couple of years later and life was 'back to normal', I laugh as I type that because it was a big dysfunctional mess. A cover-up job. A plaster and some TCP in the shape of alcohol-fueled party nights, barbeques, arguments, fighting and crying. Years and years of surface skimmed healing in which three women never really recovered. No matter what we did, it was always there, like the 'hooded claw' – 'eighteen months' probation.

My mother tried everything she could to make things difficult for him, she rang the wholesalers where he worked and told them he was a convicted paedophile. The man she spoke to said, "I sympathise with you Mrs Heys but he's a good worker so there's nothing I can do.", she wanted him to get the sack, but they wouldn't hear of it.

Years later, I heard that some men had gone around and roughed him up a bit but whether that's true or not I don't know. I saw him once on a bus, he stared at me empty and smiled. I just got off the bus and ran home as fast as I could.

When I was about thirty-five years old, I found out he was living with a woman in Bury (a town not far from Bolton), who had two small daughters. The person who informed me of this decided to knock on the woman's door and tell her that her boyfriend was a convicted paedophile, but the woman said she didn't believe her and told her to go away.

Sad to think she could have saved her children, sad to think I could have saved her children.

"Sunflowers growing through a crack in the sidewalk, have what it takes to survive,
Tough times pass,
The things people do Just to stay alive"

~ David Wilcock

3.

The Next Chapter

So, life carried on. We kind of settled into a routine of 'forgetting' what had happened. Mum went through a period of depression, she lost loads of weight, drank her body weight in brandy and cried late at night when she thought we were asleep; then there was the odd attempt at suicide. I don't think my mother ever wanted to die; she simply wanted the pain to go away. There were the guilt and shame but there was also this realisation that the man who'd shared her bed, her life and had been her 'everything' had betrayed her in the worst way possible. However, because she was strong, she carried on. She was the sole breadwinner in the family and had two girls to look after, including paying the mortgage and the bills. Mrs Thatcher (the British prime minister at that time) made it legal for people to buy their council houses with a hefty discount depending on how much rent they had paid. This allowed Mum to get on the property ladder. Even in her darkest times she still got up every morning, put on her make-up and went to work. She still went through the motions of life and little by little the depression turned into a dark cloud which sat surreptitiously behind her, she couldn't see it, but it was always there.

Around the summer of 1988 mum started having weekend barbeques at the house with a regular entourage of willing participants including her brother and his wife, my sister, me and some random others who would turn up on Saturday around midday and eat and drink till Sunday evening. Next door would join us and sometimes next door but one. This became something to look forward to and everyone made food and brought drinks with them. We would buy this popular white cider called Diamond White by the crate load and go through at least three crates each weekend. We bought a karaoke machine from Woolworths and boy did we have some fun. Those fun times in the back garden were a way of returning to some perceived normality.

By the time I was thirteen I was slim and fully permed, painting on make-up and dressing like Madonna (an updated version of Marilyn). I had found a partner in crime by the name of Lucy. Lucy and I were in the same year at school, but only became friends by chance, when one of our teachers rang in sick and two classes were merged for music class.

Born just a few days apart under the sun sign of Aries we hit it off immediately and are still good friends today. We talked over endless cups of tea sat by her bedroom window waiting for the two boys who lived across the street to make an appearance. We did each other's hair and make-up, got dressed up and shared our deepest thoughts as we fantasied about boys, music and parties.

Lucy and I would join in with the weekend barbeques at my house often getting a bit drunk and generally having a good time. As time went on, we no longer wanted to sit with the adults and started drinking at my house before venturing into the village to a pub where we blended in and our youth overlooked. We chatted up boys, drank Diamond Whites, danced and generally acted like young girls, experiencing the middle-class social life that Little Lever offered.

When I met Lucy, she was a lot younger in her mind than I was, she didn't wear make-up, had dishwater blonde permed hair and dressed in accordance to her age. I was way beyond this. My mother was always super glamorous wearing full make-up, a perfectly petite figure of a shapely size eight and wore enviable clothes for every occasion. Being a dressmaker, she copied the styles from Vogue magazines and was always in the latest fashions.

Having an older sister everyone said was beautiful and was just starting out as a fashion model only added to me wanting to look much older than my years. It seemed to be a general opinion that we were a good-looking family of girls and even at a young age I always cared about how I looked and what I wore. The sexual abuse, court case and drunken parties meant I grew up fast and not much shocked me. I thought I could handle myself.

Lucy was a willing accomplice to growing up fast, she loved the freedom my home offered and was quick to pick up hair and makeup skills. Her mother and father were conservative, and I think they saw me as a bad influence. Although we didn't know it at the time, her parents were having some marital problems that would end in divorce when we turned sixteen. Distracted, many of the things we got up to went completely over their heads. We inevitably got up to a lot of mischief, oftentimes finding ourselves in a spot or two of trouble but generally having great fun.

When we went out on the weekends, we both borrowed my mother's and my sister clothes to make us look older and fashionable. We backcombed our already permed hair and made up our faces, showing out at every opportunity. Lucy dyed her hair red which made her look older, more sophisticated and edgy. We were ready to play with the boys….

"The two most important days in your life are the day you are born and the day you find out why."

~ Mark Twain

4.
Mrs Alexander

Around the age of thirteen, I saw an advert in the local newspaper which read, "Spiritualist Church meeting, Queen Street, Farnworth 7pm to 9 pm". I'm not sure exactly what made me so determined to go. My mother had talked about the spiritualist church with fondness and said many times how spiritual healing had healed her depression and cancer.

She had talked about having a hysterectomy after cervical cancer and then going to see a transfiguration healer. Transfiguration mediumship is when the healer goes into trance and (in this instance) a doctor guide comes through to do the healing, at the same time a fine layer of ectoplasm forms over the face, making the medium look like the spirit healer which is coming through. Well, Mum had the operation and the stitches were all bandaged up. The healing lasted twenty minutes or so and then she was sent on her way. The miraculous thing was that when she went to the hospital the following week to have her stitches removed, there was nothing there! Not and stitch nor a scar to be seen. The nurse said there must have been some mistake and called for the doctor who performed the surgery. The doctor confirmed he had performed a hysterectomy and that there should be at least ten stitches. It was an enigma.

With this in mind, I set off with my twenty-four pence bus fare to Queen Street in Farnworth. When I arrived, the building was not as expected. It was a small white, non-descript looking corner of a street. I went to the door and a lady smiled at me and asked me for fifty pence, to which I replied that I had only brought my bus fare. She let me off and I took a seat on the front row of a five-deep circle of chairs.

I watched, mesmerised as an older lady with a Zimmer frame introduced herself as Mrs Alexander, the medium who would take the service that night. She approached the stage and said, "now, if I come to you this evening please answer me nice and clear so spirit can hear you".

Mrs Alexander came to speak to me second that night, her first words being "don't be afraid love because you will be stood here one day where I am….", my goodness, I was petrified.

The dialogue went like this:

Mrs Alexander: "you have a little grey and white rabbit sat on your knee"
Me: "yes that's my rabbit, Bunty"
Mrs Alexander "I have a lady here called Kathleen, she's playing snakes and ladders and has board games all round her"
Me: "I don't know anyone by the name of Kathleen"
Mrs Alexander "she said, tell her it's Curly"
Me: "Oh my God, that's my nan"
Mrs Alexander: "Well she's sending love to your dad. There is also a lady here called Alice who was very close to your mum, she is holding a gold locket with a lock of hair in it."
Me: "Yes that's mother's gran, and I know the gold locket with the lock of hair in it".

Mrs Alexander was riveting from the moment she first spoke to me, she gave me so much evidence, including my uncle's dog that went senile and my mother's stepfathers' name. She told me I would work as a medium on the platform and help many people. She described two guides for me, a woman who was small and plain, she described her as "an oracle woman of Romany descent" and a native American Indian who was strong and wise. Her prophecy of platform came true for me many years later. When I left the church, I felt like I was walking on air; that I had purpose and I never doubted what she said was true. I felt I would be a medium someday.

Not long after this, I purchased my first deck of tarot cards from Camelot theme park in Chorley on a day trip with my mum. I played with them endlessly and did readings for nearly everyone I knew to practice. However, at the time I did not know the significance of what I was doing, nor that it would become a big part of my life. I had already spent time reading books about astrology, dreams, numerology and fortune-telling. I had a propensity to all things spiritual from around eight years old; it just seemed so natural to me. Regardless of all the mayhem in my life, it's always been there like some perennial intelligence, just waiting to surface at the most crucial times.

I continued to go to the spiritualist church on Queen street for about three years after this, before the conundrum of boys, make-up, parties and life engulfed.

"Even through the darkest phase,
Be it thick or thin,
Always someone marches brave,
Here beneath my skin"

~ k.d. lang & Ben Mink

5.
More parties, more boys….

Lucy and I continued to dress up and play out, so to speak. Neither the local village pub or the boys across the street were enough to keep our attention and we started to venture into the town centre for nights out.

We got jobs so we could afford clothes, make-up and nights on the town. We worked at Bolton Wanderers Football Club at Burnden Park selling pies on match days and was lucky enough to be farmed out to Maine Road (Manchester City Football Club) for music concerts. We worked at major music events like The Rolling Stones, Fleetwood Mac, Prince, Lisa Stansfield and others. We loved them because as soon as half time was up, we were allowed to go and watch the rest of the concert for free. Once this job ended, we worked in an aquarium on the weekends and then a butchers and greetings card stall in the Market Hall in Bolton town centre. I worked from being fourteen years old, we had to in those days. My Mum wasn't going to hand out money for booze and make-up to me.

We spent this money frivolously, buying vinyl from Vibe Records, a trendy music shop on the high street. Flower power was making a comeback and we drew flowers on our jeans, caught the bus with no shoes on and declared ourselves vegetarian. Saturday was the highlight of our week when we would get dressed up in hot pants, boob tubes, stilettos which cost a fiver off the market, sun shimmer tanning foundation, purple eyeliner and Avon amethyst pink lipstick. We probably looked horrendous, but we thought we were the bee's knees and we got the boys and the men's attention both in our local village and in the town centre.

At the weekend we were sophisticated ladies who drank cocktails and went to the best nightclubs, flirting with twenty-something young men who thought we were the same age. In the week we hung around with the boys across the street who by this time had become our unofficial boyfriends. John and Dylan were blood brothers, three years our senior and kept us entertained until the weekend.

At fourteen and fifteen we had so many great nights out in Bolton. We would start the evening by drinking a few Diamond Whites at my house while getting ready; curling our hair and putting on the outfits we'd bought that afternoon from Chelsea Girl Clearance shop in Bolton Arndale Centre. Mounting the bus with under sixteen bus passes but looking more like twenty-five and hitting the bars.

We would start the night at Yates Wine Lodge, the manager had taken a shine to me and I thought he looked like Marti Pellow, so I wasn't going to argue! Then on to Sam's Bar where there was a friendly but slightly creepy guy called Paul who used to wink at me and serve me before it was my turn. Towards last orders, we had a regular crowd that met up in this bar called 'Cork's Wine Bar'. It was by far the most sophisticated of the bars in Bolton at that time and with our fashion statement sexy clothes we fit right in. If we had enough money for a taxi back home, we would go over to Maxims or another nightspot till midnight where we would dance the night away to ninety's pop tunes like Pump Up The Jam, Ride On Time and anything by Bananarama.

We met these two older guys called David and Darren who wore beautiful suits, drove expensive cars and bought us drinks all night. I had this line when a guy asked me what I would like to drink, "Cointreau poured slowly over ice", I thought it made me sound dark and mysterious. I usually got my drink anyway.

On a few occasions, we told our parents we were sleeping at each other's houses so we could go to a night club with David and Darren and the others who were all in their twenties, really hoping we could go back to their houses. However, this never happened, and we ended up walking the streets until it was time to go home, saying that we'd got up early for a morning jog.

Lucy and I started going out on Friday's and Sunday's as well as Saturday night. Staying in was not an option and if we didn't show up, we were missed by the crowd in town. We started to get rather well known and we both had our favourite guys to flirt with when we were out. Occasionally there were snogs in doorways after the bars with these guys but nothing seedy. We had so much fun and stuck together, flirted outrageously but sex with random guys in town wasn't our scene. We were more likely to get drunk and dance all night.

Meanwhile back in the village, we were seeing John and Dylan almost every weeknight. When we were fifteen, we both went to doctors together and asked to be prescribed the contraceptive pill. The doctor gave it to us without batting an eyelid and we started sleeping with John and Dylan.

John was my first proper boyfriend, he was the first guy that I went beyond a kiss with, in my juvenile delinquency I thought it was love. He had this thing about brunettes, and I was all about being a brunette. Despite loving Marilyn Monroe and Madonna at the time, I never wanted my hair blonde. I copied the makeup, the clothes and the poses but never the hair. Besides everyone told me I looked like the model Marie Helvin and I soaked up the compliment easily. John was the first guy to make me feel special and he told me I was beautiful. In private he said he loved me and yet when we were all messing around in his house, he could be evasive and non-committal. He made it clear that he would not be faithful to me and that I should do the same.

John was tall and thin with long brown hair; he loved music and had a wicked sense of humour. He used to wear flared jeans, T-shirts with a music icon on the front (he loved Rochford and Living Colour) and soft shoes. He was a good laugh and I liked him a lot, but he never respected me, and I couldn't see it at the time. It was the start of a long reoccurring pattern with men.

Lucy and Dylan were pretty much on the same page at this time, until things got more serious between them a couple of years later. So even though we were sleeping with our 'home sweet home' boyfriends we still saw ourselves as single. We let David and Darren think that they were exclusive and buy us drinks, but we were having too much fun to be serious with any of them, after all, we were fifteen and still at school.

School was a bit of a drag because we thought we were older and wiser than the rest of the girls in our year. To some extent this was true because many of our school friends were hanging around on the canal side, drinking cider, smoking weed and losing their virginity in a bush. We were lucky enough to miss the drugs scene completely. Despite living for the weekend, I somehow managed to pull through my exams and achieve some pretty decent results. I passed all my exams except mathematics (an exam I fell asleep in). Walking away with five GCSE's at grade B or above and bagging a high achievers award at the end of year student awards ceremony.

Dysfunction at home continued, my sister got involved with some dodgy married, drug dealer who made life very difficult; always banging the door down and making wild threats. There were many times when we barricaded ourselves in the house because he was outside, threatening to blow us up and we were afraid to leave. On and on, went the break-ups, the make-ups and neither of them seemed to have any respect or consideration for anyone else in the street. I didn't know it at the time, but this was how her self-sabotage started to manifest itself. The weekends were always a deranged mess of alcohol, music, arguing and brutal catfights. Lipstick, perfume, dresses, anger and bitterness, instigated by

Tom's sentencing that seemed to come up every time we had too much to drink. We were like passing ships, each getting on with our own thing and only getting together if we had to.

My sister became obsessed with Lucy and I and the boys we were seeing, and she followed us around the village in her white XR3i convertible. In some misguided protective 'older sister' pursuit, she was always looking for ways to break up any involvement I had with any boy, especially the older ones. I think her failure to protect me from Tom made her feel like she had to do something. Unfortunately, this just made my life hell.

Some salvation came when my mother got a job as an area manager of a large bridal company, overseeing more than forty shops in the UK and Ireland. The weekend barbeques fizzled out and Mum threw herself into her job which paid her a whopping twenty thousand a year salary. The most money she'd ever been paid, which to her was an amazing achievement. Mum's life was on the up. She travelled for work, re-mortgaged the house and renovated it, making it look less like a council house and more like Buckingham Palace. There it was again, that taste which came from the Victorian inventor's daughter (my great grandmother).

She stripped the floorboards and varnished them in an oak stain, decorated the walls in opaque colours and expensive wallpaper. She had a twenty-foot conservatory built at the back of the house which she decorated with driftwood lamps, a newly restored

Victorian chaise longue and a table made from an old Spanish door. The kitchen was turned into a shabby chic, rustic array of duck egg blue and whitewash, hops reaching out from the top of the cupboards akin to a farmhouse. Outside she had a willow cover built which afforded a large built-in barbeque, honeysuckle and wisteria plants languidly draping in the prettiest of decoration. When she had finished it looked gorgeous and together with the new paved driveway, I think the neighbours thought we had won the lottery.

I got offered a place at an upper-middle-class sixth form college and studied art, English and drama. My dream at this stage was to become an actress. I felt my best way into this was through modelling and TV extra work, which I did part-time as often as possible whilst at college.

Lucy wasn't interested in college and got a job working at a travel agent and started to get serious with Dylan. We sort of just drifted apart after that. We stayed in contact, but our days were so different and since I had long since broken up with John and her with Darren, we were just taking different routes in life. Not long afterwards she got a job with her long-time childhood friend at a holiday village in Wales, so our heart filled teenage nights ended soon after she left. It would happen that she would meet her future husband there and the father of her two children. She ended up leaving my life for quite a long time, dipping in and out like a bag full of fun memories and laughter.

I had carried on seeing David and we went out a few nights a week. He was always nice to me and a perfect gentleman, picking me up and taking me to some classy bar. I think it's possible he spent his days looking up the most obscure place he could take me to for a drink. He came in and introduced himself to my mum, promising he would take care of me. I was sixteen and he was twenty-eight, even so, we didn't sleep together as he thought I was too young and wanted me to be ready. Ironically my mother had met a twenty-six-year-old Italian waiter whilst working away in London, making my boyfriend two years older than hers. I also carelessly forgot to tell him I'd already been sleeping with John for two years.

David had thick wavy hair just passed his shoulders, he was well-spoken, stocky and about five foot nine. He was always tanned with just a hint of tinted foundation and mascara, he wore brightly coloured shirts, ostentatious ties and expensive suits. He was immaculately turned out, polite and had a dry sense of humour which is one of the things I loved about him.

David loved it when, everywhere we went people came up to us and said, "my goodness you look like the model Marie Helvin". She was a Hawaiian model who was married to photographer David Bailey and popular at the time; I think that rubbed his ego enough not to worry too much about the sex. I wasn't interested in sleeping with David anyway. I enjoyed his company but didn't feel sexually attracted to him. Plus, there were rumours about him being gay and the 1990's were filled with news of the AIDS crisis and I didn't want to risk it. I don't think he was gay or at least I never saw any evidence of it myself, it was the make-up and the suits which set the tongues wagging.

College was super boring, and I couldn't connect with other girls at all. Many came from privileged backgrounds and were in bed by nine pm every night. A far cry from what I was used to in my own social life. I would roll into assembly late with a hangover, having been out the night before. At this time, I would go to the local night club called Ritzy on a Tuesday for student night, over twenty-fives on a Wednesday and out with Dave on Thursday, Friday and Saturday to whatever obscure, flashy place he wanted to show me off in.

To add to this, I wasn't interested in the classes either. It was more like school than school had been. In art class I had chosen to major in ceramics, to this day I have no idea why when I loved to draw and paint so much (and still do). The drama studio was lush with the latest sound and lighting technology. I partnered with the only other girl that was not originally from that school, now popular DJ Sarah Cox. I was excited to get stuck in as I felt this would be the start of my amazing acting career. I was still doing TV extra work, modelling and started to look at other areas where I could get experience in the film industry. I was bitterly disappointed though when we started the classes which involved Swan Lake, Mary Poppins and Romeo and Juliet. Everyone seemed to be able to sing and since I was (and still am) absolutely tone-deaf, I got cast as a tree.

I eventually left the posh sixth form and tried a metropolitan college. For some reason, which is now a complete enigma to me I signed up for English and sociology. Sociology was hilarious I had no clue what any of the lectures were about but regardless of what the subject matter was this forty-year-old woman would stand up and say "I'm divorced with two kids…" then rattle on about something I was completely lost by.

Between sixth form feeling like kinder garden and the local metropolitan being like a divorcees club I quit education. I spent about three weeks working in an Italian restaurant as a waitress, getting drunk all night and then staying in bed till midday, followed by a day of watching MTV. This was working out well until my mother kicked me out of bed and told me if I wasn't going to college, I had to get a job. Knowing that she meant it I proceeded to go and look for one.

At first, I had an interview with a local businessman who was looking for a junior secretary. Mr Merna was a rotund man with broad shoulders, thick black hair and a slight twitch. I wasn't used to interviews and was nervous but always determined and tackled everything with gusto. I wore a cream sailor-style jacket with gold embellishment, and a little cream chiffon skirt to match which swished as I walked. I teamed this with a pair of gold stilettos, big hair and red lipstick.

The office was a shop window in the very centre of Bolton with a couple of desks, telephones and an electric typewriter placed on one of them. It was painted white and otherwise, very sparse. I arrived at 11.30 am as instructed and Pat (Mr Merna) was there to greet me. He was friendly and asked me to take a seat at the desk with the electric typewriter on it. He asked me if I knew how to type, to which I replied "yes, a bit", "ok well if you could just type me a letter on here and I will be back in ten minutes.", with that he disappeared through a door at the back of the room.

So, I thought, *this can't be that difficult*. I'd always prided myself at writing and English and knew exactly how to set out a formal letter; where to use 'dear sir' and 'yours sincerely', etc., how hard could this be? Problem was the typewriter was switched off and I couldn't find an 'on' switch. I followed the lead to a plug socket, and it was plugged in, but find a button or switch I could not. *Shit, shit*, I thought, what am I supposed to do now. I turned the typewriter every which way I could but still couldn't find how to switch the thing on. Ten minutes later, as promised, Pat returned and asked how I'd got on, "erh, how do I switch it on?", he looked at me slightly amused and said, "come on kid, let's go for lunch I want you to meet Beryl".

We went to a local Italian restaurant called Toscana's and there was a slim brunette in her 50's waiting for us, I guessed this was Beryl. It turned out Beryl was Pat's senior secretary who needed an assistant (possibly me?). Pat talked about his *businesses*, although I never really got to grips with what they were and he told me what I'd be expected to do; typing, filing, answering the phone, attending business lunches and taking the post to the letterbox each evening. He offered me a decent junior salary then proceeded to give both Beryl and I copious amounts of red wine. I was bladdered by the time the lunch was done, and Pat flagged down a black cab and shoved a ten-pound note in my hand for the fare, not before offering me the job and telling me to start on Monday morning at nine am.

Meanwhile, I'd also been offered a job as a junior secretary at a large solicitor's firm called Garstangs which I figured most definitely had better prospects. I decided to take the job in the solicitors and started in two weeks.

So, Monday morning came, and the phone rang, my sister shouted through to my bedroom "Mr Mooney is on the phone, he said are you going in or not?", "Mr Merna, and no" I answered. That was a short conversation which years later would be become extremely significant.

"Her heart's as soft as feathers
Still she weathers stormy skies
And she's a sparrow when she's broken
But she's an eagle when she flies "

~ Dolly Parton

6.
Wild Child

I started the job in the solicitors and was farmed out as the office junior between working for the senior partner in the criminal department and working with a lovely legal cashier in the accounts department called Mags. I loved my job at the solicitors and spent all my wages on gorgeous suits, always looking the part in my high heels, makeup and perfectly primed hair.

I also worked at an Italian restaurant called Tiggis, which was situated underneath the solicitor's offices. At five-thirty I would swap my suit for a waitress outfit and work till midnight. Thursday, Friday and Saturday nights (and sometimes Tuesdays and Wednesdays) I would usually go the local night club with one of the other girls who worked at the restaurant and proceed to roll in for work at Garstangs with a cracking hangover. Starting all over again the next day. It's a wonder I wasn't exhausted, but I was sixteen and the thing I did best was party.
I'd met a lovely waitress at Tigg's called Andrea and we had great times together after work.

I'd been working at the Italian restaurant since I was fifteen and I loved it. It was a busy job and we got on like a family. I was always getting phone numbers and fifty quid notes pressed into my hand by older businessmen which did make me feel good. By this time things had fizzled out with David and I was single, getting chatted up nearly every night. Some of the men were super good looking and I was on a different date every other week. When I look back,

I'm amazed at how trusting I was. These guys always picked me up from my house in a car and I just got in willingly, allowing them to take me to a restaurant for dinner, wanting nothing more than a snog and a feel in the car before dropping me off home. I looked like a twenty-year-old but underneath I was still a frightened child. If any of them had pushed it would have probably given in, thinking that was what I was supposed to do, luckily, they didn't, not at that point anyway.

I was still pursuing the modelling and TV extra work and got a few castings for popular soaps; Brookside and Coronation Street. I also sent my photographs to a few top London glamour agencies who offered me a place on their books. The trouble was that they expected me to move to London, I simply couldn't afford it and I didn't know a soul there, so it was out of the question.

In the end, I signed up to a model agency in Manchester who ran a 'modelling school' every Sunday. This was run by a hairdresser come wannabe photographer by the name of Roger. He was an unapproachable guy who walked with an air of superiority and was only nice to you if he liked your photographs.

The girls were great though, all different ages and backgrounds and came from all over Manchester. There were four of us who travelled from Bolton every week, usually catching the bus together on Sundays, all of us hungover from the previous night's partying. I'm still in contact with the other three girls and we laugh about how we thought we were going to make it big in the modelling world.

One of them was Sonia, my darling friend who I still hold dear today. She told me she worked at a bar in town called Bergerac's Wine Bar and that you got paid twenty pounds per night, cash in hand. It sounded just what I needed and much more money than the restaurant wages with less hours, starting at seven pm instead of five-thirty, giving me time to go to the gym and get ready for work before my shift started.

Who owned the bar but the one and only Mr Patrick Merna! The guy who had interviewed me for the office junior position getting me very drunk in the process. Pat was a sucker for a pretty face and offered me the job as soon as Sonia introduced us. This introduction started a platonic love affair which lasted seven years.

We were expected to wear 'something sexy', smile at the punters and when it was quiet, we went out ticket touting in the streets, offering people discount vouchers for one pound fifty double shots with mixers thrown in for free. The bar was a disgustingly grimy place, and everything was covered in stale beer and dried up, fruit flavoured alcohol. It was underground so the entrance was down some carpeted steps. This carpet was fitted throughout and although we hoovered it every Sunday, it was soaked with spilt drinks, cigarette butts and sometimes vomit. Pat played light pornographic videos with the volume turned down and there was a DJ box at the back of the large room where Oliver Harrison and Dave 'double decks' would play tunes each evening.

Pat would go to the wholesalers before we opened and then we were expected to haul all the booze down the steps in our miniskirts and heels. Something we learned to do artfully. A few leery men would turn up around 7 pm when we opened, then from about eight o'clock every night it was packed ten deep at the bar with just about everybody in Bolton. There were usually about five or six girls who worked behind the bar and Pat collected glasses because he didn't want the girls getting manhandled by punters in their sexy outfits. Big Debs was considered the manager and about ten years older than most of us. She was a tall, stunning redhead with a wickedly dry sense of humour and a no-nonsense approach to management. But we all loved Big Debs and if you didn't you probably didn't work there for more than a week.

We had such a giggle working there, all the girls got along like sisters, serving large orders of cheap cocktails, necking vodka and orange behind the bar all night long. Looking back I have no idea how we managed to calculate the cost of drinks orders since the till didn't do any of that, mostly we were so drunk we made the cocktails up. We were barely able to stand up, but oh how we could dance and sing behind that bar (think the Bolton version of Cayote Ugly). When we went out 'ticket touting' it was via another pub where we would neck a couple of diamond whites before heading back to drink more vodka and orange. At the end of the night, when we'd finished and the bar closed, we would go on to a local nightclub where we became pretty famous as 'the

Bergerac's Girls', known for being the best-looking bar girls in town.

Still working at the solicitors and with my wages from the bar, I decided it was time to get a place of my own. So, at seventeen I got my first ground floor flat in a smart stone cottage in an affluent area of Bolton. It was sixty pounds per week, but I reckoned it was better than being at home where there was always a weekly argument between me, mum and my sister, not to mention my sister's crazy boyfriend threatening to kill us all at regular intervals.

The flat was owned by a lady in her seventies and she insisted on meeting my mother before I could move in. It had one bedroom, a living room and kitchen, with a launderette and phone box across the road. I couldn't afford a landline and mobiles were not invented at that point so that phone box became my personal line, I gave the number to everyone to contact me. If it rang, I would race across the road to answer it and it was always for me.

Sonia was now working fulltime as a model for a reputable agency in Manchester called Boss. She had invited me to a big model agency party which was to be held at Athenaeum, a stylish venue in Manchester City Centre. When we arrived, there was a black girl stood at the door and Sonia threw her coat in her direction thinking it was the cloakroom attendant. This was met with a vicious scowl and we realised the girl was actually Heather Small, the lead in singer in the popular band M People. Undeterred, we sauntered passed and ended up learning how to dance the butterfly with two African dancers and three transvestites. Later we went back to my flat, played Roger Waters legendary album The Pro's and Con's of Hitchhiking and Sonia rolled a joint. My first and last as it knocked me sick.

As time went on the nights at Bergerac's became more alcohol-fueled, the outfits got more risqué and the men got friskier. I became more confident in my body but unaware at the time that I was leading with my sexuality and this often gave off the wrong signals.

Most of these nights blended into one hedonistic shindig, different faces, different names, smiles, phone numbers but always onset by my friend… vodka and orange. The nights would start off pretty much the same. I would be dressed up like a drag queen with wigs, eyelashes, thigh length boots and the tiniest outfit I could find with the most amount of glitter possible. I had a tiny twenty-inch waist, a C cup bust and long legs, a figure I was more than willing to flaunt in the direction of anyone who was willing to look. Attention seeking became my signature, it made me feel special, wanted, loved and the thing I craved the most…famous. Like most celebrities, the false personification gave me an erroneous sense of security. I would start my shift behind the bar, drink, serve, drink, dance, serve, smile. Go to the Ritzy night club, dance, drink. Smile.

Smile at some hot guy, kiss, getting hot and sweaty and wanting more, finding a cab and back to theirs or mine. They all ended the same, having meaningless, unrewarding sex with a stranger before kicking them out or getting a cab home. If they were lucky enough to stay until morning they would have to sit and listen to my drunken ramblings about being abused when I was a child and Tom only getting eighteen months' probation for the abuse of three girls (and god knows how many more).

On and on it went, more nights, more men, more sadness. They weren't all one-night stands, some I liked and attempted to forge a relationship with. These never lasted very long as I was completely incapable of having any kind of meaningful interaction with a man. Like all abused children, when you get older but have not healed you cannot understand the meaning of sex. I learned through my spirituality, that sex is a gift from God that should be used as an expression of love for another. That through the body, two souls can become one in a beautiful entanglement, often ending in the making of a baby. However, when you don't know who you are, you lead with sex. This is because the example of sex you had was abusive, non-consensual and with empty promises of love, love unrequited. It would take me many drunken nights, lots of self-sabotage and many men (and women) to learn that sex is not a toy but something to be revered. On it went….

Regardless of the wild nights I always turned up for work at the solicitors and I enrolled in a legal executive course at Wigan College with some of the other girls who worked there. This sent me right to sleep every week. It was laughable really as I didn't have the slightest interest in any of it and never really knew what we supposed to be doing, nor did I ever do the homework we were set. I did learn quite a lot through working at the solicitor's especially working with Mags in accounts.

Mags was a petite bubbly girl from Wigan who was engaged to a young rugby player, unlike me she loved numbers and wanted to become an accountant. Another Aries, we got on immediately and laughed most of the day at work, sometimes I would go and stay at her house in Wigan and we became close friends for a while.

Back at Bergerac's the nights continued, I would go out with whoever was up for it. Either the girls from behind the bar, Sarah my friend from the first day at school or alone. I was fortunate enough to be able to walk into any bar or night club in Bolton and know at least someone. In addition to this being a 'Bergerac's girl' meant that the manager of any place in town would generally give me free drinks all night. Pat was also well known in Bolton having previously owned an elite nightspot called Clueso's which housed a casino, in most cases he was well-liked, and this meant his 'girls' were treated with respect.

Big Deb was in a relationship and had a ten-year-old son, so she wasn't always able to come out but when she did, we became the best partners in crime. One of these nights we decided (for whatever reason) to go to a night club after work which was on the same street as Bergerac's. It was a heavy metal bar called Sparrows and was probably one of the worst nightclubs Bolton had to offer. It was full of goth dressed men and women, mostly spaced out on class

A drugs and the music was hard mental and thrash. I think we thought it would be funny to go there, we were neither interested in drugs or metal music.

We went in and ordered two vodka and oranges, although we were already fully intoxicated from working behind the bar. We started headbanging on the dance floor and I went up to this girl also in full head bagging mode and said, "you're a great dancer". She wasn't a great dancer at all, and I still have no idea what I was hoping to achieve by this comment. Suddenly she lunged forward towards me with a knife in her hand. Simultaneously I lost my balance off my multicoloured six-inch platform boots and fell backwards, she missed me and landed on someone else. Within minutes the doormen had arrived, and she was out the door. Debs knew the manager and he asked if we wanted to go and sit in the office for a bit in case any of her friends tried to cause trouble with us. We took a couple of drinks with us and laughed hysterically about what had just happened.

The next thing I remember was waking up in a toilet cubical, my head banging like one of the heavy metal bands was in there, my tongue feeling like a mohair jumper. I moved slowly as I was stiff and screwed up on the toilet seat. I shouted Debs and heard a grunt from the toilet next door. "Debs, we must have fallen asleep," I said as she groped around trying to straighten up. "What time is it?" she asked, "no idea but it's very quiet out there" I replied. We pulled ourselves together, black rings of mascara around our eyes and red lipstick smudges all over our faces and went back into the bar area which was deadly silent and empty. We managed to switch on the lights and tried all the doors, which were locked. There was no way out through any of the doors, nor could we find a phone. There was a payphone in the foyer, but the inner door was locked, and we couldn't get to it. We were still drunk and thought it was hilarious that we were locked in a night club, neither of us remembered a thing about how we ended up asleep in the toilets. We decided to help ourselves to a drink from behind the bar while we thought about what to do next.

The bar was in a cellar and when we went back into the toilets, we noticed a long thin window which opened onto the pavement. We took a chair from the bar and climbed up to the window, rolling ourselves out onto the pavement above. It was Sunday morning at six am so luckily there was no one about. We got taxis home then, giggling about the insanity of it all. I could fill a book on its own about some of the crazy things Debs and I got up to.

Around the same time, a nightclub opened called Bliss in the centre of Bolton. It was a small venue but there was an incredible amount of hype about it. The owners which I think were a consortium of business investors went all out to promote it and there was this exciting buzz around the place. The frontman was a British/Italian guy called Simon who was probably in his forties and (so I thought at the time) oozed charisma. On top of that, he drank champagne and sat in the VIP lounge. A place I wanted to be.

From the opening night, I made a beeline for Simon, I got to know all the staff and even knew a couple of them from the other bars in town, like Paul the creepy guy from Sam's Bar. I made Bliss my regular haunt. Taking liberties, free entry, free champagne and sitting next to Simon every chance I could in the tiniest of lycra dresses, like a hooker on the arm of a gangster. At the time, this to me this was glamour; I was still trying to get modelling work and by now had dropped the idea of fashion modelling in favour of topless modelling and lingerie work. I was attending castings and doing photo shoots with photographers to build up my portfolio. All this whilst balancing working at the solicitors, Bergerac's and paying bills and rent on my apartment.

Sometimes I didn't pay the rent on my apartment. I remember one time getting paid from Garstangs and seeing this amazing corset style black dress with mesh netting for the skirt. It was love at first sight but cost two-hundred and seventy pounds. I absolutely couldn't afford it, so bought it anyway. This left me short for my rent and after few months of begging and pleading with the landlady to let me catch up, she saw me out on my ear. This happened more than once and if Pat didn't bail me out, I just moved, leaving a string of bills and unpaid catalogue debts behind me. Between the years of 1992 and 1995, I lived in seven different houses.

Behind this barrage of inconsistency in my life I always turned up for work. I was asked out and given phone numbers regularly behind the bar, I used to shove them into my tip jar with the coins I collected. I would double or treble my wages on a busy night with tips from men and women who came in as I flashed my winning smile. Some of the guys were super good looking and I was giving them a call, but most of them were going in the trash with ashtray debris.

A guy came in who was blonde, blue-eyed and tight t-shirted showing super pumped up flexed muscles. He had beautiful bone structure, a chiselled jawbone and the sexiest smile I'd ever seen, baring perfect white teeth. He gave me his number one night and I found out he was a model called Lee. He asked me if was going to be in Bliss that weekend and if so, would I like to meet him there after work. If there was such a thing as Play Girl, this guy was centrefold stuff.

That weekend, I wore my sexiest outfit, which consisted of a little velvet bra studded with gold beads, tiny black velvet hot pants, flesh-coloured Woolford tights and thigh length leopard print boots. I probably looked like a caricature, blatant and desperate. Madonna had recently released her Sex Book together with the release of Erotica and it had a major influence on my dress sense. As my idol pushed boundaries and became more daring so did I.

I arrived at Bliss and Lee was there looking hotter than a Mexican beach. He bought me a drink and we sat and chatted, we danced and kissed in a quiet corner, getting hotter and hotter under the collar. He asked if I wanted to get a taxi back to his and I did. And we did. We started kissing passionately as soon as we got through the door, at one point I noticed a huge framed photograph of him on the chimney breast, completely naked stood under a waterfall. The photograph was beautiful but come on, a naked photo of yourself on the living room wall, I had to stifle a giggle. We started to have sex on a sheepskin rug which sat on top of a cream carpet. He penetrated me and we were both so turned on it was a while before we noticed I was bleeding all over the cream carpet. My period had come. He jumped up and ran into the kitchen to get a cloth and some carpet cleaner. He started rubbing at it frantically, I started to giggle uncontrollably whilst apologising. He then turned around to me and said the most unbelievable thing I'd ever heard, "keep quiet will you, my wife's asleep upstairs", "what??" I was floored. The gaol, the cheek, the disrespect he had for his wife astounded me and you can bet your bottom dollar she wasn't asleep either. Having been a wife myself now, I know she would have stayed up listening for the door, waiting for him to come home, as I have done many times. Lee's wife was awake, and she did file for divorce eventually. We would end up meeting periodically after that, but it was just sex and he never meant anything to me.

There was this other guy who gave me his number called Adrian. He was tall, handsome with chocolate brown eyes, dark hair and a lovely suit. He asked me if I wanted to go for a drink with him, Thursday night. He was in luck as it was my night off. We met in the Pack Horse, which was a busy central pub I knew well. I had chosen a tight black figure-hugging dress, black stockings and black stilettos to wear. It was a sexy mid-week assemble and I thought I looked nice but not too keen. He was already there when I arrived and went over to sit with him, he bought me a drink, and then pulled this little white card out of his pocket. He said, "I'm epileptic so this is what you need to do in the event of a fit". It was literally the very first thing he said after, "what are you drinking?". I was seventeen and quite honestly had no idea how to react to this, but the thought that it was important enough to tell me right at the beginning of our date terrified me. I thought, *please Nan in spirit - save me!* I think she was listening. I always told someone where I was going to meet any guy that took me on a date and a few minutes later the bar women came over and said "excuse me are you, Beverley? there is a telephone call for you behind the bar". It was in the days before mobile phones and telephone calls were by landline. I went to the phone and it was Lucy. "Hey, I am home from Wales, I'm getting a taxi there now and we are going out" she shouted down the phone from what sounded like a payphone. "What? I'm on a date, how did you know I was here?" I asked, "never mind that, just get rid of him". I did what she asked, making some lame excuse as to why my friend needed me and we went to Ritzy together for a great night of dancing and booze. Needless to say, I never saw him again.

At the end of the night in a drunken frenzy, Lucy and I kissed. It was a deep passionate kiss that we both participated in fully. It had never happened before, but we just read each other's mind as we locked lips. In the morning we tried to pretend it hadn't happened, but things were awkward, and she went back to Wales with a bit of a cloud hanging over us. It would be fifteen years before we could laugh that off and to be honest, I regretted it a little.

Madonna became my mentor and as she started her Blonde Ambition Tour with her pointed bra's, pinstripe suits, short curled hair and red lips, I tried to emanate her style. I bought a navy blue pinstripe suit from a charity shop and altered it to look like the one Madonna wore in the concert, I bought a corset from a lingerie shop, making the boobs pointed and cut slits in the suit jacket for them to peep out of. I wore fishnets and hot pants; Madonna-style bra tops were in the high street shops and I loved them. I had been copying Marilyn Monroe's makeup for years, so the makeup was already there, it was simply a matter of moving the beauty spot from my cheek to just above my lip. I already had two beauty spots naturally in both places. Madonna was really in her most controversial at this point, there were rumours of her sleeping with Prince, Michael Jackson, k.d. lang and Sarah Bernhardt. Forever the attention seeker, I thought it was marvellous. I had the Prince symbol tattooed on my back with 'erotica' written in Japanese down the side. I started to flirt with women as well as men. There was this gay girl who worked in Bliss who loved Madonna also, she would come up to me and admire my Madonna-Esq outfits and we would flirt outrageously with each other. I'd always been attracted to women but because of my childhood experiences I had been conditioned to sleep with men. I remember coming home from a club late one night, lazily flicking on the TV and there she was… k.d lang in concert. I was completely mesmerised. It was the first time I had ever seen a butch gay women and the feelings it created floored me. I wasn't quite ready to act on those feelings at that time but they were there, sat in a fragile box waiting till I was brave enough to look inside.

In Bliss, I met a guy called Bruno who was young, Italian and good looking. We dated for a few weeks. when Madonna's new song started playing, he always sang it to me in his thick Italian accent "bad girl, drunk by six, kissing some else's lips". I think he got me spot on.

Some nights after work and if he felt like it, Pat would take me out to somewhere glitzy or expensive. We would get a taxi to Brasingamens or The Millionaire's Club which was always lavished with decadent looking men and women and he would order champagne. We would talk and he would tell me stories about when he was younger, joining the priesthood and outrageous nights in Clueso's, his former nightclub and casino. There was this story that made me laugh so much the way he told it. The story was of a very large woman who sat on the toilet upstairs in the club, the floor gave way, forcing the toilet to drop out of the floor, through the ceiling into the casino below. The toilet became lodged in the ceiling, the woman stuck in the floor. Pat said, "all you could see were her legs with her knickers around her ankles dangling from the ceiling". He had to call the fire brigade to get her out and it took them four hours. I said, "oh my god, what did you do Pat?" His punch line… "I gave her a vodka and orange kid".

Pat and I got on so well, he became my friend and savour. It was completely platonic; he was more like a father figure to me than anything else. I think with the girls behind the bar and the soft porn that played on the TV's people thought Pat was a dirty old man, but he just knew what sold and what would drag the punters in. He was a businessman at the end of the day. He always looked after me, lent me money if I was short on my rent and protected me from men who got a bit too friendly in the bar. Despite being an alcoholic, he gave me some great advice on life and much of that wisdom I still hold dear. He told me you would only ever meet a few people in life you could depend on and that if you could count them, on one hand, you were very lucky. I didn't appreciate that advice at the time, but I now know he is completely right.

During the seven years that I worked at Bergerac's pat sometimes had a girlfriend and many of these girlfriends were super jealous of our friendship. When his girlfriends were around, I steered clear of Pat as I knew they felt threatened. Having said that, he didn't make a secret of which of the bar girls were his favourite and I was one of them. I think my provocative dress sense and bubbly personality made me stand out though and a couple of his girlfriends tried to start fights with me.

There was this older woman called Freida who Pat was seeing, she hated me and glared at me constantly whilst I served the punters, her, propping up the bar next to Pat. One night, just as we were cleaning up, she shouted loudly to me "I don't know how you can work behind that bar you, your so pissed up", I turned around and said "Oh shut up, you old slag", she lunged over the bar at me, blocked by Pat shouting "no one calls me old", "oh so slags' ok then is it?" I retorted. Freida was promptly thrown out by the doormen and we never saw her again. I apologised to

Pat afterwards and he told me, "you were right anyway, she is an old slag".

I didn't realise it at the time, but Pat had a serious alcohol problem. It seemed normal to me that we all got drunk in the evenings, but I wasn't fully aware that Pat also drank in the mornings and the afternoons. He could hold his drink most of the time, but there were times when he didn't. He would fall asleep on the toilet and me and big debs would have to lift him off, pulling up his trousers and getting him into a cab. Not an easy thing to do with a big man. Girls came and went from behind the bar but there was a core group. I moved in with a girl called Vicky, sharing a flat, some of the other girls moved in together too across the road from us. We had some great nights together, alone and sometimes with Pat in tow.

I was looking for a serious boyfriend. In my mind, I was looking for love, a husband, someone to have a romantic love story with. To act out the black and white movies I'd watched as a child. That's why I went on so many dates and pursued so many lost causes. The main problem was that my clothes, my job at Bergerac's and my drinking wouldn't allow for the nice guys to take me seriously. Some of the guys were good looking and we had some great conversation, but they were not looking for anything serious, just to sow their oats and have a bit of fun.

"'All things are lessons, that God would have us learn.'"

~ A Course in Miracles

7.
Lessons for Life

I didn't realise it at the time, but I was falling into a downward spiral of drink, men and danger. I don't think I realised what a reputation I was getting for being the party girl, no one took me seriously but put up with me because I was good looking and bubbly. Pat cared and helped me out whenever he could, but I don't think until I looked back on things, I could ever comprehend what a mess he was mentally. He was the older father figure and had some wisdom, but most of the time, was in no position to give sensible advice.

One night after work I went into Bliss alone. I was wearing velvet hot pants, and a top made of black elastic which looked like a load of crepe bandages, this was teamed with fishnets and over the knee black stiletto boots. I had my hair pinned up in huge curls, eyelashes and red lipstick on full lips.

The moment I walked in, smiling and saying hi to everyone, I noticed a very good-looking man I had never seen before. He had dark blond, wavy hair, a pumped-up body and chiselled features. He was watching me from the side-lines as I made my way to the dance floor. Madonna's Erotica started playing and he came over to me, gyrating his hips in time with mine. "Wow, your great dancer" I squealed, with my most winning smile. He had the most perfect teeth I'd ever seen and these unnaturally blue eyes (probably contact lenses). He told me he was in a popular men's dance troop which travelled around the country and was there because the manager was considering booking them.

We spent most of the night chatting and flirting and then he asked me if I wanted to go to his car for a break and a cigarette. I agreed as it was a particularly hot night and the club was sweltering, it didn't seem like a strange request and we went outside to the nearby car park. When we got there, he started kissing me furiously like I was the only woman in the world. He sat in the driver's seat and offered me to sit next to him. He asked me if I would "fuck his gear stick", which I laughed nervously in reply to. I started to think that maybe I shouldn't be there. Just at that moment, this big black guy, who was also exceptionally well-groomed jumped into the back and we sped off. I asked where we were going, he said he was giving me a lift home and asked for my address.

We drove for what seemed like ages and I repeatedly asked if he knew where he was going because I didn't recognise any of it. After a good forty-five minutes, we appeared to be going into a dark lane covered in trees and overgrowth. The guy sat in the back started to put his hands on my breasts, I started to get frightened then, telling him to leave me alone, saying that I was with his friend and not to touch me. I started to open the car door as we drove, "shut the fucking door, you stupid bitch" was the angry retort from the blond-haired driver, and he promptly flipped the central locking button which meant I was trapped. At this point, some headlights behind us started flashing at them. "I think they want us to pull over," the black guy said in a suspicious growl. "Oh, shit," they said to each other. With that they moved over, waiting for the lights to pass, but they didn't pass. As though I had some higher purpose and a guardian angel watching over me, it was a police van.

A few minutes after they both got out of the car, a policeman came and asked if I was ok, "No! please get me out of this car" I screamed frantically. I heard a lot of talking but couldn't hear what was being said, I was ushered into the back of a police van where a policewoman sat with me. She was very friendly but also firm about the fact that I had been very lucky. I told her exactly what had happened, I was still shaking, scared that I had done something wrong. She said I was very stupid to get in the car with them but was also sympathetic, I think because I was underage.

I was sat in the back of the van for a couple of hours before a police officer came to explain to me what was happening. He said the two men were in a hire car which would have been untraceable, that it was all too well planned for it to have been a first time but since I was left unscathed, there was nothing they could be arrested for. They told me I was in the middle of Blackburn forest, some twenty miles away from home. He said I was very lucky. He told me that since the two of them were both models and in a famous dance troop, they had decided to rough them up a bit as punishment, making sure they marked their faces. Then they drove me home.

It was unbelievable that two such good looking guys who would have been every girls' dream boys, would have to go to those lengths to get their kicks. Some might think I was asking for it and maybe I was an easy target, but I was also seventeen and very naive about just how dangerous men could be. They never got booked to perform at Bliss and I didn't bump into them again.

After this I was more careful about the company I kept but continued working at Bergerac's and the provocative clothing, the drinking and the nights out continued. However, my self-worth was on the floor, I started to doubt that I would ever make it as a model or an actress and just resigned myself to be the 'best looking barmaid in Bolton'. I was getting fed up with men who were always asking me out and feeling as though I was never going to meet anyone who took me seriously.

I had moved again from living with Vicky and was back living alone, this time in a three-bedroom terrace house. It was a lovely spacious house and I enjoyed living there, even though it was only for a short time. Again, not being able to meet the rent and this time with a cat and three kittens in tow. If I could type the monkey with his hand over his eyes emoji here I certainly would.

I had started spending more and more time in Bliss after work. I felt safe there because I knew the bar staff well and taxis came right to the front door so I could always get home in one piece. Even after quite a few vodka's I could get a taxi and get home, I somehow always managed to sober up enough to pay the cab driver and get my key in the lock. There was this mystery cab driver who always seemed to turn up when I was desperate to get home. He was an older Pakistani gentleman called Ibrahim with a grey beard and grey hair and he drove a black cab. He would turn up in the most obscure places for years, like my guardian angel and he never charged me a fare even though I offered to pay him.

There was one night when I was in Bliss, Simon was being exceptionally nice to me, plying me with free champagne and asking me if I would come into his office. I loved being with the manager, he was good looking and smelled of expensive aftershave and wore wool suits. It was the status symbol for me though, I liked to feel special like I was better than the other girls because I was with Simon. Once in his office, he started kissing me and taking off my top. I started to take his shirt off, but he refused. I got suspicious then, got dressed and left. I later discovered that he'd had hundreds of girls in that office and filmed them, many of them in more compromising positions than I had allowed to happen. Apparently (so I heard), the consortium of businessmen who were investors in the club all gathered together to watch these videos of unwitting girls. How sad that grown men had to do this to get a thrill.

One Sunday night when I was seventeen, I'd finished at Bergerac's and gone to Bliss. I wasn't in the mood though and just sat there, at one of the tables getting more and more drunk. Paul the barman that I'd known since I was fourteen in Sam's Bar came and sat next to me. He said he was worried about me that I was drinking too much and was becoming a borderline alcoholic. Paul was thin and sickly looking, he had a mass of black curly hair and dark eyes. I wasn't sure if he was entirely of British heritage as he looked like he had a bit of foreign blood in him. I had always been polite to him but never fancied him in the slightest and although he was always friendly, I didn't get a great vibe from him. I started to cry when he told me I was a borderline alcoholic and started to spew out the story about how I'd been abused as a child. I will never forget his next sentence, "you know what you need? A friend." I smiled then, he asked me if I wanted to go back to his flat for a cup of tea. I agreed feeling very lost, not wanting to go home alone and desperately in need of that 'friend'.

His flat was just a bedsit in a rough part of town. It was a room with a bed, a wardrobe and a small table. He explained that he shared a kitchen and bathroom. I went to the bathroom and he asked me how I took my tea. I told him milk no sugar. He said he was going to ask his neighbour for some milk and would be back in a minute. I sat on the bed and waited for him to come back. He came back with the tea and, starting to sober up I drank it gratefully.

The next thing I remember is waking up with the absolute worst headache I think it's possible to have. I was completely naked and in Paul's bed. He was there watching me as I awoke. I looked at him puzzled the last thing I remembered was drinking the tea he gave me. My head was spinning and confused. My vision was blurred, I knew I'd had sex because I could feel it, but I didn't remember a thing. I knew I would never willing sleep with Paul, I just knew it in my heart. He looked at me and said "don't you remember? You begged me to have sex with you. You were wasted". I wasn't that wasted Paul. I threw my clothes on, grabbed my bag and legged it downstairs.

I flagged a taxi down and went home, stinking of booze, of Paul and of absolute shame. I had a quick shower and got ready for work. I looked an absolute state and felt like someone had hit me over the head with a harpoon. It was no normal hangover; Paul must have put a drug in my tea which had knocked me out and then raped me. There was no way I would have willing ever slept with him. I found him grotesque. I also had many drunken fueled nights with men, and I remembered most of it, this was a different feeling.

When I got to work at the solicitors, I went downstairs to the archive cellar, claiming I had some filing to do and then I just cried, buried beneath the files. I thought about going to the police and reporting him. Back then, little was sensationalised about the date rape drugs GHB and Rohypnol so I thought it must have been a strong sleeping pill or something.

The office manager Jennifer came down to see me in the cellar and I told her everything, sobbing inconsolably. She told me that going to the police would be a waste of time because it would be my word against his and that no one would believe me. She told me to go home and she would cover for me with the partners, telling them I was sick.

Looking back now, I think she gave me the completely wrong advice, I wish I had reported him to the police. I think the not knowing what he did to me was both a blessing and a nightmare. It would be twenty years before I could forgive and let go of that night. Paul not only violated my body, but he betrayed me in the worst possible way, offering the hand of friendship and then taking it away with a brutal and cowardly attack. One of my only regrets is that I didn't report this to the police. Even if they didn't prosecute him, I know he was a coward and it may have deterred him from doing it again to someone else. It was certainly calculated so I can only think he may have done it before or after. It must have been the only way he could have got a girl into bed.

I went home that day and slept it off, knowing that life goes on and giving in was not an option. I decided that I needed to get my life together at this point. Bliss closed down soon after and I didn't bump into Paul again (not for many years anyway).

As I approached eighteen, I was due to be paid four thousand pounds in compensation from a car accident mum and I had a few years back. It was a drunk driver who hit ten cars as he was being chased by the police. I only had a scratch on my chin, but we must have had a good solicitor because the compensation ended up at four thousand and was put in a trust fund until I was eighteen.

The Royal Exchange in Manchester was a beautiful old building with a variety of shops on three levels. The ground floor was elegant with a selection of expensive shops that sold, cakes, cigars, a hairdresser and a very expensive leather goods shop. Upstairs was full of smaller designer shops like Vicky Martin, Red or Dead and Destroy. The basement had more creative shops like this vintage shop called 'Arsenic and Old Lace'. At the back of the basement was a small circular section which had been closed for many years. Here, were six empty units to rent, each with an incentive of a six month rent-free period.

I decided to use the money to set up my clothes shop. So, I handed my notice in at the solicitors after two years and they all wished me well in my business venture. My mum, being a tailor had taught me how to sew and I had a tiny electric sewing machine. Mum had loads of fabric she'd collected over the years and so I used it to make little bra tops with matching A-line skirts. I made a few other dresses and Sonia made some jewellery which we called the Utopia Collection. I had an antique tailors dummy, a desk, a chair and my dad came and fitted me a rail and made me a changing room in one corner.

Next door was a fashion designer called Richa Mau and on the other side, a rocker girl called Tanya, also selling clothes. We all got on well and a couple of the other units started to fill up. I had called my shop Dylema, looking back it was quite apt!

Sonia had continued modelling and had been sent to Japan with Boss Models. I remember when she got the news. We were in Bolton together, she had to call the agency at a specific time to find out if she had been selected to go to Japan. We both huddled into a red telephone box outside the post office. When her agent said she had been selected we both screamed and jumped up and down in that telephone box. She would write me ten-page letters which I would shove in my pocket as I left for work and read on the train from Bolton to Manchester.

The shop did ok, and I was still working at Bergerac's at the time, so I wasn't desperate for money, although it was a good job, I had been given the rent-free period. A few celebs came in including Elaine Paige and I was pleased when she tried on one of my outfits. I bought stock from wholesalers in Manchester including bags, purses and accessories, together with a few bits of lingerie. Barclays gave me a business account with a credit card, and I was off. The start of my very first business. The first of many.

At eighteen I was still very young, but I was growing up a little. I had a business; I didn't go out quite as much as I had before, and I was paying my rent and bills on time.

Around this time my mother had also set up a business in Manchester City Centre doing clothing alterations for House of Fraser and a few other shops, as well as walk-in customers. She was doing well and had a team of tailors working for her. I would close my shop up at lunchtime, buy a pasty from Greggs bakery and eat it at my Mum's place whilst chatting to her staff.

I met an Asian guy who owned a taxi firm in Bolton, I found him intriguing. He was thirty-seven, five foot ten, medium build and wore a black hat with the Malcolm X symbol on it. He had a good sense of humour and liked to talk to me about his culture and his religion. It all started when he took me home one night after a shift at Bergerac's, I was sober for a change and we chatted all the way to my house whilst he was driving. We ended up talking for two hours before I would go inside. This became a regular occurrence, whenever he was my driver, we would just stay in the car chatting for hours. He told me about his life, his arranged marriage at eighteen, his five children and how his wife and he lived next door to each other because they couldn't stand the sight of one another. He was quite serious about his religion and I wanted to learn more, so I bought myself a copy of the Koran in English from WH Smiths. It was a bit hypocritical, to be honest. He'd left his wife at one point and got together with an English girl having two children with her but got back together with his wife after ten years. It was a crazy story but all I saw was this cheeky guy who was kind and gentle and seemed to know a lot about life (compared to me anyway). One night after many evenings of long talks we kissed. He didn't set my world on fire or anything, but he was older and a bit more stable at the time.

The biggest problem was his jealousy, he was paranoid that I was seeing other guys. I was faithful to him, he knew so many people in town I wouldn't have dared to go there anyway. For a while, I was besotted, and it progressed into a relationship that would become argumentative and difficult. It lasted about twelve months and during that time he got sent to prison for non-payment of road traffic finds. The case was going ok until he started shouting at the judge that the British raped and pillaged his country (Pakistan) and why should he pay the fines. He got sentenced to six months in prison. He called me from prison and told me to forget about him, that when he came out, he was going to go back to his wife to try to be a better father to his children. It would have been a great idea, but I could tell that he was just stoned out of his mind *he would never change*.

I was heart-broken by this phone call and went into a bit of a depression. I started to study more about religion and spirituality. I had closed the shop down after the six months free rent period, as did everyone else who rented those units because not enough customers shopped there. I was free most days and started doing a few extra daytime shifts at Bergerac's. This gave me the time to read more, I read books on reincarnation by Edgar Cayce, Dr Brian Weiss and Shirley MacLaine in addition to reading the bible and the Koran. It was a deeply personal time of reflection. I would do this often in my life, hideaway whilst I worked things out.

I had also moved again. This time I was in a beautiful one-bedroom flat that was situated in a Georgian manor house. It had an ornated oak door, a large living room with floor to ceiling windows and a spacious bedroom. The kitchen was also quite big and decorated in a country style. The manor house was situated in an affluent area of Bolton near a beautiful brook and natural beauty where walkers would stroll.

This was where I had my moment of going back to the spirit world; of seeing 'the light'. I had been living my life in total chaos. From the outside, I looked like I was having fun, but I was playing out my childhood distress whilst looking for love in the wrong places to catastrophic consequences.

 I was seeking male acceptance, love, trust and instead finding hard lessons, ruination; a reflection of the total lack of self-worth I had at that time. There was a distinct shift in energy when that happened, it was as though spirit were willing me to move on with my life purpose, I didn't know it, but a new chapter was about to unfold. I now know that spirit wanted to use me as a medium between the two worlds and I would help many people, just as Mrs Alexander had predicted. I didn't know of any of this at the time, I just knew that God showed me that there was unconditional love there, just waiting to be tapped into. That I didn't need love from men, nor did I need acceptance from anyone. That it was time to forgive, let go and move forward.

I decided at nineteen that it was necessary to forgive Tom, to let go of that chapter of my life and find a happier version of me. I also encouraged my mum and sister to do the same, a suggestion that was met with disbelief and malice. It would be weeks before meeting my future husband, a huge turning point in my life. It was by no means a path to perfection and self-love (that would take many more years) but I was starting to heal. I had seen and felt God, I had seen and felt love beyond the sentimental love of the earth plane. In a sense I was reborn, but I was also about to embark on different challenges.

"Being deeply loved by someone gives you strength, while loving someone deeply gives you courage."

~ Lao Tzu

8.
Getting Married

I now found myself single again and was determined never to go out with an Asian guy again; it was too complicated with the religious aspects.

That night I went out with a couple of the girls from Bergerac's to Ritzy, which had undergone a total refurbishment. I was just stood there at the bar when this gorgeous Asian guy walked past me. He was slim, five foot ten with jaw length silky dark hair and was wearing a smart suit. I went up to him and smiled my cheekiest smile, "Hi there, what's your name? Imran Khan?" I said, he eyed me suspiciously and stammered "yeess, how did you know?". I didn't know at all, I was just trying to be funny, at the time the famous Pakistani cricketer (now politician) was in the press a lot and I just made it up. It was his ACTUAL name. I asked him if he wanted a drink as I was leaning on the bar waiting to get served. He said he wanted a diet coke, so I promptly ordered him one, shoving it in his hand and signalled for him to follow me to a quiet table. We sat down then and chatted easily; I can honestly say it was love at first sight. My heart was pounding out of my chest and I felt like he was the man I had been waiting for all my life. He told me he had dreamed about meeting a girl who was British with Chinese looks many times, dreamed about my face. Later he would tell me that he felt the same as me, that he fell in love with me instantly.

We were so smitten with each other he came back to my apartment that night and didn't go home for two weeks. He told me he was an artist but was asked to do a computer programming course which was offered to him by the government in an attempt to get him into some kind of job. He explained that he had been dedicated to badminton and being offered a place on the England team, it was his dream. His strict father had other ideas and promptly packed him off to Pakistan for an arranged marriage as soon as he turned twenty-five. Imran wasn't up for it and refused to marry the girl, returning home and living on the streets to escape the nightmare of his fathers' traditional ideas. He told me of a kind lady who had taken him to a refuge for the homeless and they had got him a flat in Wigan through a housing association. The agreement being that he would attend a vocational training course. Since his interests were painting on large canvasses and badminton, both careers that were not on the government's education list, he plumped for computer programming. He knew nothing about the subject but told me he was enjoying it and had been offered a placement at a local company where he was getting some experience.

Imran was softly spoken, shy and a gentle person. He giggled rather than laughed, flipped his hair in an embarrassed manner and looked forlorn through long eyelashes. He didn't drink alcohol at that time and didn't seem to know an awful lot about people or the world. He described his childhood growing up in Pakistan as free, playing outside and spending all his time with his older sister and mother. He explained his father had got a job working for British Aerospace as an engineer in Manchester. He had waited several years before saving enough money to be able to buy them a suitable house in England and bring them over from Pakistan. He was ten years old when he was brought over and didn't speak a word of English, this together with his stammer, made for a shy child. He was still shy when I met him at twenty-five, but he was intelligent and caught on to things quickly. If he didn't know something he would ask and not forget the next time. As far as I could see he was gentle and kind and needed a bit of navigation to get him through life. I was outspoken, sometimes harsh, unafraid of anything, and just what he needed.

After two weeks of being at my apartment, eating all my home-made vegetarian curries (I'd always been a decent cook), making love whenever I was home from work and talking endlessly about everything, he said he should go back to his flat in Wigan. I agreed to go with him, not wanting to leave his side for a moment.

When we arrived in Wigan, his flat was a brand-new block fully kitted out with a new kitchen and bathroom suite. His bedroom was a mattress on the floor with large canvasses of the most fantastic brightly coloured artwork I'd ever seen. He had a brand-new sparkling credit rating and had been accepted on HP against a Volkswagen Corrado VR6, which was bright red and gleamed in the car park outside.

That evening we went out to Wigan town centre; he brought his friend Ged with him and we had a hoot. Ged was tall and slim, a personable character who chatted away freely to me about his work, life and told me what a great badminton player Imran was.

Years later Ged would marry my sister and they would have a little boy named Jake.

The next morning, I woke up in Wigan and Imran was gone, since there were no mobile phones in those days, I had no choice but to just wait till he came back. It wasn't long before he returned with a MacDonald's chocolate milkshake and a kiss. I thought he was the most beautiful, thoughtful and gorgeous man I'd ever seen. I looked at him and said, "will you marry me?", "yes" he replied. That started a ten-year marriage right there and then, two weeks after we first met.

It was a Sunday when we agreed to get wed, so there was not much we could do then but come Monday morning I rang Bolton registry office and set the date for our wedding, 27th October 1995. I would be twenty years old and Imran would be twenty-six by October. Looking back, I don't think either of us had any idea what marriage entailed we were just so head over heels in love with each other. So much for never dating a Muslim again….

Imran was a product of his strict Pakistani upbringing and with that came a set of principles and ideals that he should be the responsible man of the house. Since the placement from Kalamazoo was coming to an end, he promptly got a job so he could support his new bride. I was doing temporary secretarial work in the daytime, with Bergerac's in the evening and my modelling was starting to take off. I was getting castings for big names like Ann Summers and GUS, there were photoshoots with photographers in

Manchester who sold pictures of glamour girls and lingerie models to magazines.

At the time, I was friends with a couple called Suzanne and Jon and Jon was the manager at Staples, a chain of stationery retailers. Jon got Imran a job as the IT technician in the Bolton Store. The job paid him a measly eight thousand per year salary, but we were just pleased he had any job, to be honest. With this, we put a deposit down on a flat and planned to move in on our wedding night.

The wedding was a simple budget wedding, we got married at the registry office in Bolton and then had a meal at Tiggis, the Italian restaurant I had worked at in my youth, later we would have a party at Mum's house.

My dress was a sample Mum had got from the bridal company she had worked at and been made redundant from a few years earlier. I was able to wear a two thousand-pound Andrea Wilkin wedding dress without spending a bean. The dress was a size eight and fit me perfectly. It was ivory silk and love knot lace, Georgian style, straight with a bustle at the back and a sweetheart neckline. My friend Jane, who also worked at Bergerac's by night was a florist by day and did the flowers for me and my bridesmaids' bouquets. The bridesmaid's dresses were simple red satin shift dresses I purchased from Miss Selfridge. I had asked my sister and one of the other girls from Bergerac's to be my bridesmaids.

The rings were purchased second hand from a pawn shop in the Royal Exchange in Manchester and Imran hired his wedding suit from Moss Bros. A family friend who was a professional cake maker whipped up the wedding cake, Mum did the food for the reception at her house, bought the booze and we were all set.

On the day of the wedding, my Mum and sister started arguing and said they weren't coming so I just got in the taxi and left them to it. No surprise there, it was just another normal day in our lives together. They did arrive eventually and so didn't end up missing the wedding. I got there before Imran with my other bridesmaid and was getting nervous that Imran wouldn't show. He arrived with Jon, his best man and all went ahead as planned. It was a fun day; my dad gave me away and everybody bought me a Diamond White. Pat secretly paid for the meal at Tiggis when I wasn't looking, and my grandad (Dad's dad) gave us an envelope with fifty pounds in it and wished us well.

Imran had invited his family, but they chose not to come. I think they were angry at him for refusing their choice of bride and then going ahead and marrying a non-Muslim English girl. He told me he wasn't bothered about their 'no show', but I realised later that he did mind, a lot. He loved his mother dearly and on a subconscious level was still seeking approval from his father.

We had a party at Mum's house, played "Grease" tunes and partied till the early hours. Everyone I loved at that time came to the party and it was a great day. Diamond Whites flowed and even Imran had a little tipple!

That night after the wedding we went into our new
pad with fresh bedding and nothing else. When we
woke up the next morning, I realised I hadn't brought
a change of clothes, we had left the car at Mum's
house because we had all been drinking and got a lift
to the new house. The house was on the other side of
Bolton and we couldn't afford a taxi, so I mounted
the bus in my wedding dress to raucous cheering and
laughter from well-wishers.

"Your task is not to seek for love, but merely
to seek and find all the barriers within
yourself that you have built against it."

~ Rumi

9.
Married Life

I settled into married life, Imran worked at Staples and I did a variety of office-based temporary work whilst still working at Bergerac's a couple of nights a week. I wasn't much of a cleaner, but I gave it a go; washing, cooking, making beds and making love to my husband. We fancied each other rotten and were like a pair of rabbits, having sex at any opportunity we could. We talked and encouraged each other to pursue our dreams. Imran told me of such a thing as a Pentium Chip which would be in every computer in the world at some point. He told me he had a dream of importing the Pentium Chip thingy from Japan and distributing it in the UK. He also told me that there would be something called the Internet, that people would use all over the world instead of the Yellow Pages. I laughed then, saying "don't be daft, nothing will replace the Yellow Pages".

The modelling work was getting better, which is why I didn't get a full-time office job, although I was offered plenty. I reasoned that I needed the money, but that I also had to be available in case of my 'big break'. I embarked on doing temporary office jobs which would take me to many different places, offices, and to meet all kinds of people. I caught buses and trains to destinations I had never heard of, always dressed in a gorgeous suit and high heels, painted with my best face. I was sent to a building society in Oldham stuffing envelopes, a battery factory answering the phone, a warehouse stuffing parachutes into rucksacks and a funeral parlour typing invoices, to name just a few.

Simultaneously, my sister and I were offered a year's contract with a company called Big Bang Management. This involved touring around the North participating in Miss Wet T-shirt competitions, filmed by the Adult Channel production team. The company set up these nights in large night clubs, advertising for locals to compete in the competition, the winner would receive a hundred-pound prize. The company employed 'professional girls' to make the show attractive to watch. It was enjoyable but also an opportunity to make contacts in the industry and get more paid modelling work.

There were other professional glamour models; beautiful, friendly and enthusiastic. The night clubs were spread around the North of England in places like Bolton, Wigan, Manchester, Sheffield, Halifax and Blackpool, there were mostly large chains and good venues. We had to make our own way there, Imran drove us sometimes, but he didn't like watching his wife on stage performing to hundreds of lecherous men. He was learning very quickly not to tell me what to do or to try to stop me from pursuing my modelling dreams; at the same time, he didn't feel entirely comfortable with it.

On arrival, we would be escorted into a VIP room by a big burly security bloke and met by an enthusiastic management team, plied with free Champagne and treated like celebrities. One or two professional photographers would take our photographs, sometimes alone and sometimes with the other girls.

The photographs were mostly topless, and we never had any clue where those photos would end up.

The clubs were always packed to capacity and mainly full of enthusiastic and sometimes impudent men. All the girls had a wardrobe of spangly, glittery bikini's which we were happy to share; dressing each other up. We would rip the t-shirt into a cropped version, halter neck or some flattering variation, the t-shirt was always discarded at the end of the show anyway and the girls would end up dripping wet and topless. We wore high stilettos and stage make-up which we all excitedly applied backstage in our dressing room. We would walk on doing a variety of sexually provocative poses before being asked "what's your fantasy?", to which I would reply "a threesome with Pamela Anderson and one of you guys in the audience", it was always a crowd-pleaser. Then we would do a type of lap dance for the shower cubical, the water would not be turned on at this point, so you were able to gyrate freely, smiling at the TV cameras for the Adult Channel, tossing back your head and swishing your hair. The moment the water came on however, it was a completely different matter. The water was always absolutely freezing, and it took your breath away. You had a millisecond to catch your breath and then smile again, trying to look sexy whilst soaking wet and intoxicated with champagne.

Again, these nights were great fun but filled with alcohol, even illegal drugs flew around at these events, although drugs never interested me. After the shows, we would dry our hair and dress in an evening gown we had brought with us and go out to greet the scores of men waiting for us after the show. Some even wanted our autographs and would pay to be photographed with us. It was a single girl's life and although I was never tempted to stray from my husband who I was deeply in love with, I felt guilty that Imran was home alone during these nights.

So, this is how I was making a living and progressing with my modelling work whilst trying to balance married life. It wasn't spoken about, but I knew Imran didn't like it. He would roll his eyes during conversations about the previous night's events and slope off to a different room in the house when I was on the phone to Big Bang Management. We were newlywed and in love but lurking in the background was bitterness and Imran cocooned himself away from me at times, bubble wrapped in jealousy and self-pity.

My sister was getting offered lots more paid work through this job, but I was mainly overlooked. I managed to get through most of the shows, but I was quite often too drunk to stand up by the end of the night. Had I been single, more mature and not stuck in a quagmire of self-destructiveness I may have been able to turn this into a more accomplished career. However, it seemed as though God had other plans.

The flat we had moved into on our wedding night was a long way from the centre of Bolton and with me still working at Bergerac's and Staples located in the town centre also, we decided to move a little closer. We moved into a small 1st floor flat in a pretty rough area of Bolton, but it was affordable and much closer to town. Money was tight then and we made decisions without really thinking things through, neither of us had any experience of living with another person, of compromises or marriage. We sliced through the first part of our life together, cutting out patterns that didn't fit together, like pieces of different jigsaws; some fit, others didn't.

Not long after the move and because of the low wages and long hours, Imran had decided to open his own business. He built custom made PC's and developed computer programmes for clients. We hired some offices in the centre of Bolton which consisted of two offices for fifty pounds per week. He got a few good clients and the business was ticking over, he was also learning more computer languages and started to teach kids badminton. At this time, he was painfully shy, he spoke with a stammer and used to jump when the phone rang. Making a call was even more traumatic, in those early days I had to coerce him into speaking to just about anyone.

It was not long before I wanted a piece of the pie, so I rented the office next door and opened a model agency. I recruited models, making use of the contacts I had accumulated whilst pursuing my modelling career. I held grooming courses, showing the girls (and one boy) how to apply make-up, walk on the catwalk and organised photoshoots to build up a portfolio for them. I got index cards printed up with all my best talent and set about finding companies who needed models. It worked out well and I took the standard 25% cut of the fees charged, as well as charging for the grooming courses and photoshoots.

At one point, my sister and I organised a topless

dance troop with a few of the girls we had met through the Adult Channel, we called it 'The LA Teasers'. We choreographed dance routines, sewed costumes with stars and stripes sequins and took bookings for local nightclubs. We rehearsed the scenes and I took promotional photographs, getting flyers printed and doing mailshots to clubs. However, we all had our ideas about what was required and there were more arguments than in the House of Commons. As the manager I felt like I was in 'The Commitments', we axed the idea after only one gig.

Through the agency, I developed an interest in photography and purchased an expensive Canon camera from the catalogue. I had always been creative, so it was just a natural progression for me. I began taking photographs of the models myself. There was this tall, slim seventeen-year-old blonde girl who I took out to photograph in the cobbled street behind the office. I did this total fluke, an action shot of her turning around to face the camera. I had the film developed at a lab in Salford and had used a 110 film which gave a grainy effect. It was a stunning photograph. A few years later she wrote to me thanking me for everything I taught her and informing me that she had been recruited by Elite Models in London (think Cindy Crawford and Gisele Bündchen) and that her booker had decided to keep my photograph in her portfolio.

Imran became engrossed with his programming and hooked up with this unemployed computer enthusiast called Steve. Steve gave me the creeps. He lived alone in a three-bed semi that had absolutely no furniture in it, he was a confirmed insomniac and loner. Always unkempt, in the same tatty black trousers which dangled around his ankles and a navy-blue jumper, lined with dandruff on the shoulders. I told Imran he looked like Steptoe from the TV show, which didn't go down too well. He smelled funny and didn't like me very much, I think he thought I was a 'show off' and a snob (and he was right).

Imran stayed up late with Steve, coding for a new computer programme he was putting together (I think to sell to businesses). I was immersed in the world of modelling. Vein like cracks started to appear in our relationship and we argued over small irrelevant things. He flinched awkwardly at any mention of modelling or my world and I scoffed at any mini achievement from him and Steve's efforts.

There were so many occasions when I went out with work or my girlfriends. It seemed like I was an extrovert and Imran the complete opposite. In reality, I was a normal twenty-year-old girl from Bolton with a weighted pool of issues and he was a normal boy from Pakistan who loved the way I looked but was lost in a world that engulfed his life like a grey shadow. These occasions often got out of hand; my inability to stop drinking when I'd had enough and Imran's sensitivity to everything were the main issues.

One such occasion was when I went to a BBQ on Sunday afternoon with a friend of mine called Janet. Imran was submerged in his programming with Steve; I had told him I was going, and it hadn't seemed like a problem. We set out about midday, getting a drink at a local pub before ordering a taxi to take us to the BBQ.

When we arrived, it was packed with people who we both knew from Bolton town centre and everyone seemed to know me from Bergerac's. It was a hot summer's day, alcohol flowed and if there was food, I didn't see it. Janet and I got drunk quickly, it started to get dark around 10 pm and I thought I should call Imran. I rang and rang and but there was no answer.

Eventually, after quite a few attempts, I called and he answered, I was relieved, he started shouting down the phone "where are you?", I was drunk and couldn't get my words out properly, in addition to that I didn't even know where I was. The guy who owned the house came over and snatched the phone out of my hand, slamming it down and saying, "that's enough, get off my bloody phone". I tried to explain that I needed to tell my husband where I was, but he wouldn't listen. I asked a few of the other guests how they were getting home, they said the taxi companies were all fully booked but that they had taxis booked to go to an Indian restaurant in town. Everyone told me to chill out and that my husband would be ok, around ten of us went for a curry. Once inside the curry house, I went to use the payphone to call Imran again. There was still no answer, it just rang and rang. In the end, I thought he must have gone to bed.

I finally arrived home at 2 am and Imran was nowhere to be found. I was frantic then and had sobered up a lot. I went to the phone box and called the police. A lovely female police officer arrived within minutes, took my details and asked me loads of questions before driving me round the streets to look for him. I was sobbing telling her the events of the night and how I had been trying to call him. As we were driving back home, along a street not too far from our flat, I spotted him in the dark. He was wearing the green tracksuit I'd bought him for Valentines and his white Adidas trainers. The policewoman dropped us off at home. When she had gone, he went mad saying that he had walked to Farnworth and back to find the house the BBQ had been at and that it was empty. Yes, of course, it was empty, we had gone for an Indian.

I tried to explain but he just wouldn't listen to me. His viewpoint was that it was all my fault for drinking too much. Mine was that I had tried everything in my power to contact him because I did care about him and I wanted him to know I was coming home - home to him! He had not been brought up to drink alcohol and didn't understand the appeal. I hadn't known anything else. This was going to become a real problem in our relationship.

Not long after this, we moved again, probably so that Imran could get me away from Janet who lived around the corner. This time it was some Pakistani guys who showed us a terraced house and promised us it would be fully furnished by the time we moved in. We handed over one month's rent and a deposit, a total of one thousand, two hundred pounds. When we arrived the beds and furniture were not there as promised, so we had to buy a mattress that night and just crash down on the floor. Regardless of how many times we called the landlord, he didn't reply to our messages. Letters started coming through the door postmarked Halifax Bank in the name of someone else, not the name the landlord had given us. It became apparent something wasn't right, so we opened a couple of the letters and discovered that the mortgage hadn't been paid for months, that the house was about to be repossessed.

We were devastated because we had used all our money to move and the pot was empty. Imran had to go to his parents' house to ask if they could lend us some money to move again, which they did. Despite his parents being angry with him for marrying me and running off to make his own life, they loved him. His mother still wanted to wash his clothes and cook his food and his father would support him financially many times during the early days.

We found a new flat in Farnworth. It was a nice spacious flat with two large bedrooms, a big bathroom, living room and an extremely big kitchen. It was situated above an ironmonger and the owner of the shop, a nice chap, rented us the apartment no problem.

A few weeks after moving, I found out I was four weeks pregnant. It was a complete shock; we had never discussed having children and to be honest we didn't want them. I was quietly happy though; women have hormones which produce an excitement that a man can't possibly feel. We were relatively happy, very much in love and although we had no money, I knew that we would get by. When I told Imran he went berserk, started crying and saying we were too young. He said we had no money; we weren't stable and that a baby would ruin everything. I tried to reason with him that we would survive, that babies come for a reason and that we would make great parents.

It was no good, he wasn't having any of it, but I told him that we were having a baby and he had to get used to the idea. I could see he was in turmoil even then, but he couldn't express himself properly and I was hormonal, confused, twenty-two and felt completely unsupported in this pregnancy.

During this time, Imran was still working on his computer programming and grinding away at his business, spending all the hours' god sent on his computer which was set up in the spare room. Creepy Steve was still coming around and I had dire morning sickness, sequestered in our bedroom while they 'played' on the computer till the early hours.

I was deeply unhappy at this time, I felt abandoned by the man I loved and on top of that, ill with the pregnancy. I chose to close the model agency down because I didn't have the energy to do anything. I remember being alone in that flat during the day, sleeping most of the time whilst Imran was at work, hiding. I had been vegetarian since I was fourteen but suddenly, I was craving bacon, meat and full cream milk. I gained four stone in three months and often walked to Asda for more supplies, carrying heavy shopping bags back to the flat.

I did have my moments daydreaming though about what she would look like. I was adamant it was a girl.

Imran had pale skin and I knew she would be a beautiful olive colour with big brown eyes and thick wavy hair like her father. I thought up baby names and decided on Paige for a girl. I never even contemplated a boy's name; I was just so sure it would be a girl. I found myself wandering through the supermarket checking out the price of nappies, looking at formula and thinking up recipes for my homemade baby food. I would look at prams in the catalogue, visualise the cot and the baby room. I was going to paint it mint green and decorate it with whitewash wooden furniture. Everything would be perfect, and I would show her the black and white movies I'd watched as a child. I would change, stop drinking so much and become a proper mum with all the love in my heart to give her.

Around this time, I started to visit a model called Jo at her home which was close to the flat. She was stunning, blonde thick hair, a wide smile and frequently got stopped by people telling her that she looked like the fashion model Claudia Schiffer. She was witty, fun and a bit wild, right up my street. She was always chasing after footballers and one night she asked me if I would go in town with her so she could meet up with this footballer who played for Bolton Wanderers. I reluctantly agreed but I wasn't drinking, looked huge with the pregnancy and agreed only to stay until he turned up, then I was gone.

I got ready, dressed in black to hide my bump and met Jo as agreed. As we approached the first bar, I started to feel ill, with a heaviness in my groin, pains in my abdomen and I wanted to sit down. I told Jo but she said I was just being soft and bought me a vodka and orange. To my surprise, it didn't smell awful like all the other times I'd been near alcohol. I was worried and as soon as the footballer arrived, I got a cab home.

Imran was in the spare bedroom programming with creepy Steve and was ill impressed that I had gone out. I told him I didn't feel well and went straight to bed. The next morning, I was bleeding heavily, and Imran took me to A&E.

I had missed carried at twenty-two weeks and had to stay in the hospital for two nights, waiting for the foetus to come out. They had given me tablets to induce the birth, but I was in labour for two whole days and nights giving birth to this dead baby. The baby finally came out in a bedpan after twenty-eight hours of labour. Imran sat with me the whole time, holding my hand, bringing me glasses of water and takeaway pizzas. The worst part of it was that I was in a ward with lots of other mothers, giving birth to perfectly healthy babies.

I took the whole thing badly. I was hormonal, approaching twenty-three years old and felt completely unprepared for how this would floor me. The past experiences with men were nothing compared to the pain I was feeling. Imran felt guilty because he hadn't wanted the baby and although he had been amazing throughout the process, I also felt a little angry towards him.

I was told to have a thirty-day break before going back on the pill but less than six weeks later I would get pregnant again. I couldn't face going through with the pregnancy, I was scared, and Imran never really encouraged me to keep the baby, so I had a termination. Imran held my hand through the whole procedure and although it was purely my decision, I did feel slightly resentful at his relief.

"A hundred thousand reasons why I should
walk away,
A hundred thousand more make me stay,
I'm standing in the shadows of this desire,
The longer I wait, the more I'm a liar"

~ k.d. lang

10.
Champagne, Clothes & Money

Approximately two and a half years into our marriage Imran got offered an interview for a programming job with a large pharmaceutical company. He had no idea what the job was for but eagerly attended the interview, nodding in all the right places and agreeing that the code in question was something that he had done before.

He got off the phone to the agency with a huge grin on his face, "I got the job!" he squealed. "Amazing well done! How much?" was my immediate response. He looked at me with the biggest smile ever and said, "three thousand pounds a week". I nearly dropped to the floor when he said that, but instead we danced around the living room singing "*Everything is good, oh, and green, say, I'm red again, and I don't suppose I'm coming down*", our favourite song of the time by popular band Jamiroquai.

We later discovered that the type of coding that Imran had said he had experience of was called 'Biz Talk' and there were only three people in the world who knew it in 1998. He wasn't the slightest bit phased by that and said he would learn it on the job. And he did. This meant that he was now in demand and started getting job offers with serious amounts of money. He took a permanent full-time job earning two thousand pound per week and we were on our way to easy street!

Imran was such a multitude of complexities and contradictions. He had the confidence in his work and wouldn't let an opportunity to make money pass him by, yet he was shy and painfully insecure at times. He was kind, with the most beautiful and sensitive heart and yet critical and unaccepting of things that didn't make sense to him. He was a brilliant artist and a creative designer, whether it was a building, interior design or clothing, he saw something in shape, design and artistry, in a stark contract he was stubborn, naive and indecisive.

After this things moved quickly, it was like a whirlwind of cars, houses, celebrating and clothes. We bought a custom-made purple Audi convertible with bespoke alloys; we each got Nokia banana mobile phones and drank champagne like it was going out of fashion. It's funny how a bit of money could change Imran's mind about alcohol so quickly. It was obvious that champagne impressed people and Imran, lacking confidence and having issues wanted that badly.

He also decided to check himself into the local cosmetic surgery clinic for a nose job. The surgery would cost four thousand pounds in a private clinic in Cheshire and involved cutting out almost two inches of bone and completely reshaping his nose. Little did I know he had taken a photograph of me with him and stated that he wanted his nose to look like mine. This was all fine and dandy except that he never mentioned anything about it to me until the day before the operation. I was completely shocked by this revelation and couldn't understand why he hadn't thought to tell me, weeks of preparation and consultations? This would be the first of many little secrets I would discover.

I had closed the agency down and was relying on my modelling work to make a living, but it wasn't enough. To distract me from modelling, Imran offered to set me up in business doing whatever I wanted. I told him that a ladies wear shop selling clubwear, designer labels and accessories would be my dream. Homegirl was born.

We rented a large two-story shop, in a four-story building; there was a tailor in the attic and a hairdresser in the basement. It was in a great location directly opposite the prestigious and iconic jewellers 'Preston's of Bolton'. It had a huge window right next to a set of traffic lights, women would often get beeped at by the car behind because they were so busy staring into the window that they wouldn't realise that the traffic lights had changed to green.

We painted the shop in purple with everything else silver. Imran designed a counter that he had custom made which housed a sunken computer screen and he designed a programme for the till and stock control. We found these wacky Perspex shelves which we had fitted throughout the shop and a beautiful wooden floor completed the look. Imran was meticulous with design and made sure it all looked perfect for the grand opening.

Buying the stock was my department and Imran gave me six thousand pounds to buy whatever I wanted. I chose ostentatious designs in flamboyant colours which screamed personality and had a message of "wear me if you dare". The lines were glamorous, risqué, often revealing and mostly expensive. I passed my driving test and bought a red Vauxhall Corsa so I could do regular runs to Manchester for the stock.

Having spent so much time in the Royal Exchange with its little chic designer shops I knew exactly which labels I wanted. We had them stickered across the window and it brought some new excitement to Bolton. The stock was delivered, and we were ready to open on the 11th of October 1998. On the opening night, everyone came and bought so much stock we hardly had anything left afterwards. I was happy again, the opening of the business was a new start and Imran and I became close, love sealed our new adventure.

The following month in November 1998 my dear sweet grandad passed away from pancreatic cancer. The service was held at the crematorium in Bolton where (his wife) Curly had been cremated seven years earlier in January 1991. They played Danny Boy as his coffin went through the curtains. Joseph Heys was a gentleman and my grandad. I had the fondest memories of him and was so very sad to see him go. Little did I know at that time that I would see him many times through my mediumship in the future.

Life continued…the shop was a huge success. My wardrobe grew with each new collection and to promote the clothes I went out as often I possible to show them off. I became a mini-celebrity in Bolton then, everyone knew me, and I loved it! Imran came out sometimes but had found a new group of friends by way of his work colleagues so spent most of his time with them. I recruited staff in the shop who all worked part-time shifts to cover the busiest periods.

The tailor upstairs was a simple guy, pleasant and set in his ways. He didn't get me, my clothes or the young girls that worked for me; I think he just about tolerated me. In the basement was Vivien, a petite bubbly blonde hairdresser who was dating the owner of the building. Viv and I got on well, we had such a good laugh and I would often pop downstairs mid-afternoon for a quick trim.

I had a great eye for clothes and fashion and a personality that was able to sell, however, managing money would not be my strongest point. I would take home many of the clothes that came into the shop for my collection and much of the takings went down my neck in the form of champagne. I would venture out in quiet periods and buy makeup from Chanel and YSL, shoes from expensive retailers, lunches for all the girls in the shop and expensive bottles of red wine and champagne. The money came in and went back out again and Imran had to subsidies the buying of new stock with his wages.

A few months into the shop opening we decided it was time to purchase a home of our own. Since I had just opened a new business, I wasn't able to show any income to get the mortgage, so Imran got the house in his name. It was a modest two-bedroom house with gardens front and back and a long driveway. It was in a lovely area of Bolton and we were excited to finally have our own place. We renovated the house to our taste and were happy when it was completed.

Sarah my childhood friend from school moved in with her future husband not far away and she introduced me to her close friend Elizabeth. Elizabeth had bobbed dark hair and sparkly blue eyes. She always reminded me of a young Elizabeth Taylor, she had sharp witty humour that could slice through anyone who she wasn't impressed with. The three of us started to go out regularly. We were all in serious relationships, so it was perfect because we just went out to have great fun. We all had a love for champagne, could afford to buy it and regularly drank copious amounts of it. A couple of new night clubs opened called The Temple and Atlantis and both housed VIP lounges. I was given free entry into both VIP lounges and since the Temple was owned by the previous Bliss owner, Simon, I reckoned he owed me one anyway.

Imran started to grow in confidence, his new nose and the lads he worked with instilled a new sense of credence. He started to buy designer clothes, care about his appearance and the stammer almost vanished overnight. He started going out with these new friends and I started to go out with Sarah and Elizabeth, we were socialising in completely different circles. When it was just the two of us, we were best friends, chatted about everything, made love often and went on lavish holidays. We visited Puerto Banus, Paris, Venice and had weekends in the Lake District.

My drinking still affected him. I didn't eat very much and was still a UK size ten, this meant I got drunk very quickly and my inhibitions started to show after a few drinks. I would get loud, provocative, dance on tables and generally have a good time. Imran on the other hand, although he now drank like a fish preferred to sit at a quiet table discussing computer programming and badminton. Regardless of where I was or who I was with I always stayed faithful to him, not even a kiss or a phone number, always returning home to him at the end of the night. We would wait for each other to get home from the clubs and make love before falling asleep in each other's arms. Despite our differences, we still loved each other.

We also spent time with my family, my mother's business in Manchester was doing extremely well and she now had clients from all the designer shops in the city as well as the TV studios. She had clients like David Beckham, Vivienne Westwood, the cast of Coronation Street and Stars in Their Eyes. My sister had married Ged and life at home was better than it had been in years. We got together for weekend BBQ's and parties and Christmas became a big celebration. With mum's increased income and Imran and I had all-round more money, gifts became Louis Vuitton handbags and Chanel No. 5. Ged worked away a lot on the oil rigs so sometimes it would just be the four of us. We went on holiday to Puerto Banus in Spain frequently and sometimes Imran would stay at home and just let us girls go on holiday.

Life just got a bit fast-paced and we were always doing something that involved other people and left little time for Imran and me. We started to drift apart. Imran became quiet and distant and was often removed from conversations. I didn't know what to do so I just carried on with things, burying my head in the sand, hoping things would get better. We were like a pair of zombies going through the motions, passing, planning yet not committed. Is it possible for two people to both feel unrequited love in the same relationship? It seemed so.

"That it will never come again is what makes
life so sweet."

~ Emily Dickinson

11.
Pat

I still did the odd shift at Bergerac's, more for old times' sake than anything else and Pat was still a big part of my life. He had never been impressed with any of my boyfriends but seemed to think Imran was the best out of a bad bunch, Imran, on the other hand, was jealous of Pat. I still confided in him and felt like I needed that father figure in my life. My father was still accessible to me, but he didn't know the person I'd become. My dad only knew the little girl who would play with his nuts and bolts in his shed and glue pieces of balsa wood together whilst he made model aeroplanes. Pat knew the dysfunctional, needy teenager who had turned into a young woman right before his eyes. Regardless of my new husband, my shiny new shop and all the notoriety I had, I still needed Pat.

Finishing a shift in Bergerac's one-night, Big Deb said, "can you work next Wednesday as Pat has to go into hospital?", "Really, what for?" I quizzed. Pat came over then, he was shifty and unwilling to talk about it. It turned out that Pat had cancer of the oesophagus and would need an operation to remove it. He assured us it was a pretty routine operation and would be back at work in no time. So, in September 1999 Pat went into hospital for the operation. My last words before I went home that night to him were, "see you on the other side..".

I rang the hospital to see how things had gone and were told that the operation had gone well but that because he was an alcoholic his kidneys had packed in under the anaesthetic, he was in intensive care and the next few days were critical. I was heartbroken and not knowing what else to do, I bought a huge bunch of flowers to take to the hospital to see him. I knew Pat was strong and was sure he would pull through; I needed him and couldn't imagine life without him. When I arrived at the hospital, I was told flowers weren't allowed in the intensive care unit. I asked if they could be passed on to his daughter Charlene, the nurse said: "of course, they are beautiful, would you like to go in and see him?" I replied, "no, it's ok I will wait till he wakes up".

But he didn't wake up. I received a phone call at 7 pm two nights later informing me that his liver had failed and that his family had made the decision to switch off the life support machine. I was so sad; thick, soggy tears dripped down my face. Imran was in the living room when I got the phone call and I turned to him for comfort, but he simply said, "I'm going playing badminton" and left me alone. Alone in my grief, feeling lost and devastated. I sat in the silence, with one lamp on wishing I had said that one last goodbye to him.

At approximately 8 pm that evening there was a knock on next doors house, I heard Lewis answer it and a man said to him "is Beverley in?", Lewis replied, "no, she doesn't live here, she lives next door, but, she's in just knock-on". I very clearly heard the man's reply, which was "no it's ok, just tell her Mr Moonie called". That was the name my sister had called Pat when I didn't turn up for the office job that day. I leapt to my feet and pulled the curtains open, to see a male figure in a grey raincoat walking off into the distance, Pat's box-like figure and thick dark hair walking away. I ran to the front door as fast as I could, but he was nowhere to be seen. Knocking on the door I asked Lewis what the man looked like and he described Pat. He came to say a last goodbye.

Even as I write this, it's tearful but I know he is here smiling at me, I know Pat is a soulmate that I was one hundred percent supposed to meet. He has visited me many times since his passing and although I lost a father figure, I gained a guardian angel. Forever in my heart, Pat will remain with me until I meet him again. The song that was played as his coffin went through the curtains was 'Simply The Best' by Tina Turner, a song that was so fitting in many ways, a song that always brings a tear to my eye.

"When truth is replaced by silence, the silence is a lie."

~ Yevgeny Yevtushenko

12.
Deceit, Lies & Heartbreak

The shop was doing really with a particularly flamboyant range called Catwalk Collection, some of the Spice Girls were seen in their clothes as well as other celebrities and we were the only shop in Bolton to sell the range. This range attracted entertainers including transvestites and transgender customers. As they were much bigger than the regular females and demanded a lot more attention when they shopped, we decided to open upstairs dedicated just to these individuals. There was a lot of fun with these gutsy and humorous clients and they spent a fortune on the clothes.

We had opened a bank account in Barclays and had a dedicated banker called Trisha who dealt with all our banking. She was a lovely woman, petite with dark hair and I went to meet with her regularly. On one occasion I went in to see Trisha and was told she was on holiday, so I needed to speak to a different banker. When she logged on to our accounts, she asked which account I was asking about and said that Imran had two accounts. To my knowledge, we only had one joint personal account and the joint business account. When Trisha returned from holiday, I asked her about the additional account, and she told me that Imran had specifically asked that I not be told about the account. I confronted Imran and he said he was saving up and didn't want me to know about the account because he thought I would find something to spend it on. I was hurt and confused but just let it slip because his explanation seemed plausible. I would probably have suggested we spend it on something, regardless; it did seem a little deceitful.

Imran continued to spend time with the guys at work and I continued to go out with my friends. We did try to cross over into each other's social circles, but it didn't quite fit. His friends thought I was snobby, brash and loud. In total contrast to Imran's meek and gentle ways and my friends were too brash, loud and snobby for Imran. In the end, we just settled into different weekends. We continued to holiday together though and spent days shopping and were close.

Not long after Pat's passing and knowing I was struggling, Imran booked us a holiday in Marbella, just the two of us at the Don Carlos five-star hotel. It seemed like a great idea. The travel agent called the shop and said we needed to pay the balance, so I called in to pay for it on Imran's credit card. It was all booked under his name so I gave the girl the details, our regular booking agent was on lunch, so another agent typed in Imran Khan and said, "which booking is it for, Ibiza or Marbella?", "Ibiza?", she smiled nervously and followed with "oh no sorry that was in June, it's the Marbella holiday that requires payment".

It seemed that Imran had lied to me about a work trip earlier that year and had gone to Ibiza with the lads instead. I was dismayed. I never had any reason to doubt anything he ever said to me. I trusted him completely, naive as it may sound, I believed that Imran was a good person and that he loved me regardless of our differences. I went berserk at him, calling him all the names under the sun. I was angry and although I'd failed to see the red flags with the nose job and the bank account, this couldn't be washed over. He bought me a hundred white roses and had them delivered to the shop that afternoon. He attempted to explain himself and I forgave him. There was no good explanation for what he'd done, and I could see no reason why he had to lie. There is no way I would have stopped him from going away with his friends, I trusted him completely with other women. I just didn't get it.

He was always quite secretive, to be honest, sometimes he would just skirt around things, giving me Tony Blair answers, which I always found odd. I can be quite confrontational and direct so I often let things slip, thinking I was coming on too strong. Things started to go from bad to worse, Imran told me he needed some space and that he'd decided to rent a flat where he could think. It didn't work because I was either at his flat or he was at our marital home. We always ended up in bed together, like I said we still fancied each other undeniably and sex never left the relationship. Sometimes we would barely speak but we could still manage to have sex with just as much passion as when we first met. At times there was a smile in Imran's voice but often disdain at the things I said, the things I liked and at ME. His work colleagues were a major influence on him, later I discovered, he was telling them that our marriage was a disaster. As a result, and in support of Imran, they didn't like me and wanted to help get away from me. The problem was, he was leading a double life. He was telling them one thing, and me another.

Imran decided to go to Gran Canaria with some of the boys from work and I had a trip planned with my mum to go to Paris and Reims on his return. I picked him up from the airport and dropped him off at his flat. As I drove away; I noticed he had left his mobile phone in my car. Pin codes weren't popular in those days, so I just browsed through it noticing a Spanish mobile number. I rang it and a girl answered. He had met a girl in Gran Canaria. I was jealous, angry and felt completely outraged.

I didn't have it out with him immediately, I wanted to ask him about the holiday. When I did have it out with him, he never mentioned any girl to me. Yes, he had moved out, but he never broke our relationship off, we were still sleeping together, we were still married. Imran didn't have the expression or ability to tell me what was going on in his head and he was being heavily influenced by his 'friends'. Still, I felt very sad, desperate to save our marriage and so very lonely in my thoughts.

Eventually, he admitted it all to me. He had gone on holiday and met this beautiful girl who was, titled Miss Iceland (not the supermarket, the country). He was flattered by her attentions and had ended up in a bedroom with this girl, sex was on offer, but he explained that he felt unable to have sex with her because he realised, he was still in love with me. He said it had been a mistake that he had left and called me straight away. I had remembered the phone call. He had called, sounding strained, saying he loved me and missed me and that when he got back wanted to make a fresh start. We had a long talk and he still referred to my drinking, saying he felt as though he couldn't handle the way I was after a drink; the abused rape victim that came out to self-sabotage. It turned out he didn't like her much, and neither did I.

Unfortunately, he got too attached to this story of me drinking too much and was unable to see a different perspective. If he could just lighten up a little and realised that I was a young girl who knew no different, we could have worked at things. Instead, he started to tell anyone who would listen to him that I drank too much and he was the victim. It wasn't so much the drinking but the way I acted that he didn't like. After a few drinks, I would dance provocatively on the dance floor and occasionally fall over, never spilling a drop of champagne of course! I was always wearing something outrageous and sexy and would get frustrated because he couldn't control me.

After the argument about Miss Iceland and with his tail between his legs, he moved back home. We reverted to married life and some kind of normality. We went through the motions and tightly smiled through much of the week until my trip away. I had a coach trip planned with my Mum to the Champagne region of France, Reims. We would have an amazing four days there, champagne was so cheap to buy we both bought three cases each back with us.

I got back and was sat on the sofa at home, I noticed Imran's phone on the coffee table. A message flashed up "it was great to meet you last night, love Tracy". Seriously? We had only just agreed to make a fresh start. I rang the girl immediately from his phone. She was all sweetness and like until she heard my voice. I told her I was his wife and six month pregnant with twins and I suggested that she should stay away. When I confronted Imran again, he told me that he had met a girl the night before but that she was irrelevant, that he had been thinking things through while I was away. He had wanted to call it quits on our marriage. He dropped a huge bombshell on me at the same time; he had accepted a new job in Germany and wanted out of the business. He said he was closing the shop down as it wasn't profitable (it would have been if I hadn't spent all the profits). *Shit* was my first reaction. I needed Imran's wages to subsidies the stock and he knew that. His withdrawal from the business was a blow but I knew I would survive and didn't fight it. Instead, I just let him sort things with the landlord whilst I decided on my next move.

The whole thing left me angry and bewildered. He had made all these decisions about our life without even a word to me. I had no idea he had been applying for other jobs. He told me he was leaving that day to see the German managers but would be back the following Monday to sort out the shop. He left me with a huge Imran shape hole and a whole load of questions about my future. Within two minutes I had become single and unemployed.

After he left, I started to plough through the eighteen bottles of Champagne. I opened the first bottle Friday night and the fizz sent me into a gentle relaxed state which released the pain. The next bottle took the pain away completely and I started to forget. By Sunday afternoon, the eighteenth bottle had me in a complete blackout. I pissed all over the sofa.

"If all you have to offer me is tragedy,
I'll learn to live without your charity"

~ k.d. lang

13.
Moving On

Imran gave the shop and all its contents to the building owner in exchange for the remaining money owed on the tenancy agreement. His daughter was to run the business, the business I had built up. It was a cruel blow from Imran, he had filtered money into the business, but I had put my heart and soul into it.

After we broke up, I had heard that throughout the past year he had been contacting my friends asking them if I had affairs with other men. He even asked a blonde model I knew called Jo if I had slept with her. In other words, he was paranoid about both men and women. I couldn't understand him at all. I was flirtatious, flamboyant and led with my sexuality, but I honestly thought that he knew me. When you can pick up a guy in any bar or club the thrill goes out of it, I was happy and in love with my husband. Not only did he not understand me, he never knew me.

I remember right at the start of our relationship there had been this girl we met at Ritzy. We were taken by each other because we were very similar looking and were messing around saying we were sisters. Our respective partners were both with us and we playfully and briefly kissed. I was being playful and thought Imran might find it a bit kinky. He didn't find it kinky; he found it upsetting and tawdry. When I sobered up, I apologised and I never repeated the same mistake, I had never met a man so sensitive before so was a bit lost by his attitudes. He never forgot that night. He clung on to it like a nasty virus, working its way through the lungs of our relationship, until there was no breath left. His insecurity was a cancer that would eat away at the core of our relationship and crush the love, potbound like a plant dying slowing on a windowsill.

He had gone off to Germany and said it was over between us, that there was absolutely no way he wanted to reconcile the relationship, so I just had to accept it and move on. At least I wasn't homeless, staying in our house whilst abandoned for Germany.

Despite everything, Imran and I were to remain friends and he rang me a few times per week to let me know how the job was going. I can't stay angry with anyone for very long and am pathetic at holding grudges so, even though he'd turned my world upside down, I forgave him.

My mother was responsible for doing all the clothing alterations at Emporio Armani in Manchester City Centre. She told me that they were conducting interviews for new sales staff. I was offered a position as a sales associate (shop assistant to you and me), for a measly eleven thousand pounds per year plus commission on my sales. I didn't have many other options and accepted gratefully. I finished the handover at the shop on Friday and started at Armani the following Monday.

Armani was a whole new world for me. The clothes were luxurious, sophisticated and the store was plush and sumptuous. I was put on the ladies wear department, inducted via a training course in the first week. There was another new girl who started on the same day as I called Rebecca; she was a petite brunette, bubbly and beautiful. Also, an Aries, we had an undeniable connection. There was a gorgeous girl named Sarah who was of Korean descent and the three of us became inseparable. I loved working at Armani, the clothes, the celebrity customers, the glamour and all the sales training we had was good fun. I got to meet David and Victoria Beckham, Sue Johnston, Eric Clapton and a host of footballers from all over the world who would shop when they were in Manchester. There were around thirty staff, we went out every night, creating memories and howling laughter. A core group would usually go out together midweek, then on Saturday nights, at least twenty of us would have a big night hitting the town.

Manchester life was just what I needed; it was a new group of people and a new start. Imran would continue to phone me and said things weren't working out in Germany, he had decided to take a new job in Limerick, Ireland. I was getting on with my life and although it was nice to have him there in the background, I did believe things were over between us. I was enjoying myself and at twenty-six was now a newly single gal without the restrictions of boring, sensible Imran.

I dated a few guys, there was this French guy called Fabien, a heavyweight boxer named John and a roofer called Alec. Intermittently, I was also having meaningless, drunk sex with one of the other female sales associates at Armani, Suzi worked on menswear so didn't feel like one of the girls. She was naturally beautiful with long dark hair, dark eyes and a slim figure. We both caught the same train home after work so usually made our way home together. Quite often we would end up leaving the others to get the train but make a diversion via a restaurant, drinking copious bottles of red wine, before falling into bed together. We didn't want to go home alone, both desperately insecure and lost. However, it was Alec the roofer that had stolen my heart, he was becoming very special to me; he had a look of a young Bruce Willis and I fell for him in a rebound kind of way. He was wild, fourteen years older and sexy as hell. His wit was what caught my attention, together with being unavailable, I was enjoying the chase.

I had told Imran I had met some other guys and that life was going well for me. I had been heartbroken by his departure, but I was starting to piece my life back together, slowly like a picture sketched out in pencil, now colour was being applied; things felt better.

I had been given a set of Titania's Fortune Cards for Christmas a few years earlier and with Imran out of the way, I started to practice doing psychic readings with them. I read my own cards and anyone who wanted a reading. I was good. I never read much of the book, they were just natural to me, and they spoke to me in a voice that was clear, precise and joyful. My cards were my friend; I still use the same deck of cards today to do readings. I think with Imran gone, glimpses of the authentic me started to poke through, just a little bit then. Not brave enough to embrace the whole thing yet but it was coming slowly; the girl who fell in love with souls has a natural psychic ability and is never afraid to be herself.

Six months later Imran called and said he was coming home from Ireland at the weekend, and could we meet up for a drink? I agreed, I'd missed him, and it would be nice to see him again. We met up on Friday night after work in a small traditional pub just off the main drag in Manchester. I was wearing a little denim mini skirt and a cropped T-shirt that said Playgirl on the front which showed off my flat, tanned tummy. I had lost a good stone in weight since the breakup and was back down to a size eight.

He was all smiles and happiness when he arrived, still beautiful with his shiny dark locks, wide smile and gentle manner. He got the drinks in and we chatted amicably. He told me that it had all been a mistake that he missed me, he wanted me back. I was surprised but pleased. Imran was home, he was my everything and I had never stopped loving him. I had only gone out with others because I had been rejected so abruptly. I was enticed by the need to feel normal.

His salary was now a lot more than the two thousand per week he had been on previously and came in Armani the next day. He spent thousands on suits for us both; all my friends at the store were suitably impressed (and so was I). He gave me affection, attention and told me he was wrong to ask me to stop drinking. He said he loved my carefree bubbly attitude and would do anything to win me back. I was flabbergasted, to be honest, if not a little weary. I agreed to give things a go on the understanding that we take things slowly.

The following weekend I went to visit him in Ireland, he was really excited by my arrival and went all out to impress me. He had rented a plush apartment and took me to see the sights of Limerick, we went out for dinner and he seemed hell-bent on spoiling me. The thing was, I had lost my faith in him. He had let me down badly and I couldn't seem to get that feeling of love back. I was thinking about Alec the whole time and so I told him that I didn't think things could work between us. I needed to be true to myself and him. I painfully explained that I was with Alec and that he was my choice. I handed him back my wedding ring and said it was over. He didn't take it well at all. He cried like a baby, stole my phone and started texting Alec all sort of things like "I hope you enjoyed fucking my wife". *The wife he had left when he buggered off to Germany, leaving single and jobless.* I returned to Manchester following a series of arguments with a heavy heart.

Following my return home, I was invited to a Malibu beach party at a pub with my friend Jane, who I had previously worked with at Bergerac's. It was November and freezing but we all wore bikini's and grass skirts, drank cocktails and the pub had imported sand and made a fake beach. We had danced and sang all night and we had a crazy but wonderful time.

After the party, I got a taxi home and to my surprise, Imran was in the house. He had packed up all my clothes in bin liners and wouldn't let me in. He was angry and kept saying "I've never slept with anyone else; you have broken our marriage up". I was drunk, wearing a bikini and in the snow and giggling wildly.

145

The police came and sided with Imran as he looked entirely saner than I did. He also showed the police officer the deeds to the house, in his name of course.

So now I was homeless. I stayed with my sister for a few weeks and arranged for a van to collect my belongings which I had arranged with Imran on the phone. When I arrived at the house on the day in question, with the removal 'man and van' organised for noon that day, I was dismayed to find that he had changed all the locks. I was so pissed at him. I smashed the kitchen window, climbed in and passed all my belongings to the driver through the broken window. Before I left, I removed all the light bulbs in the house, threw the remote control for his beloved Bang and Olufsen TV in next doors wheelie bin and didn't bother to cover the kitchen window.

New Year's Eve 2000 we would meet up and reconcile our differences once again. He would apologise, saying he loved me that he couldn't live without me and I would just melt into his arms as if nothing had ever happened. It was fair to say that he didn't have a clue what he wanted, couldn't survive in the world without me, and I was still head over heels in love with him. He was the only man that had ever treated me with any respect and although he was by no means perfect, it meant a lot to me.

Things got a little better then because he worked away during the week in Ireland and London and it gave us the space we needed. He paid to have the house renovated, creating a larger kitchen and living room, and building a third bedroom. He decorated the house with expensive furniture, light fittings and oak flooring. He had bought some expensive, original paintings by Salvador Dali and Andy Warhol and some prints from art galleries around Manchester. It was great that he did that, but he acted like my opinion didn't matter, that his money gave him the upper hand. He decorated the whole house without consulting me about any of it, and I just let him.

When he came home at the weekend, he would buy me lavish gifts from Dolce and Gabbana, Gucci and Armani. We would go for nights out in Manchester to expensive restaurants, meeting new people while he put his black American Express card behind the bar, and everything would go on his tab. He started having his hair cut in Tony and Guy, wearing Vivienne Westwood clothes and all his accessories were by Louis Vuitton. He got a bit cocky then, snobby and pretentious, but underneath he was as insecure as I was scared.

He told me he was buying a penthouse apartment in a prestigious new development in Manchester City Centre called The Edge. This apartment would cost a quarter of a million and he never asked me my opinion about it. He talked about buying properties in Canary Wharf and projects with other people he'd met in Ireland and London. I didn't know who he was anymore, and I think deep down I didn't care because the money, the clothes, and the holidays kept me mute. It was like a glass wall had been built between us, he built it. He'd stopped all the lying but deferred to telling very little about anything. I had a full and happy life and when he came home at the weekends, we went through the motions. Like artificial intelligence on adult mode; sex, shopping, champagne.

During the week when Imran was away, I would meet my mother after working at Armani. She was also doing extremely well financially, turning over half a million per year in her business. This meant we would do the same kind of thing midweek as Imran and me at the weekend. The three of us also went out quite a bit and holidayed a few times per year in Marbella and Paris.

I wasn't doing too badly for a girl on eleven thousand per year, but I needed more income to support my lifestyle. Although Imran and my mother paid for a lot of things, I decided to leave Armani in search of a better title and salary. First, I got a job as the store manager of Daks, a luxury clothing brand with its own house check. Unfortunately, six months into this job, head office made everyone redundant. I was also offered Store Manager of the Body Shop, Manchester flagship store and at an independent furniture shop. I was unhappy in both latter shops because deep down I was fashion through and through.

A recruitment agency put me forward for the manager of the new Zara store in Manchester City Centre, which was being built and would open the following year. I had to attend an interview on Regent Street in London, where they explained to me that I would spend a year training at various locations and assist with the Bond Street store opening. I started there in 2002, initially spending three months at the Trafford Centre and Leeds stores.

In October I was sent to the new Bond Street store which was to be the biggest UK store to date. I would be acting Store Manager until the new manager would arrive in a few weeks and then ladies wear manager until my store was completed in Manchester.

"A woman who cuts her hair is about to change her life."

~ Coco Chanel

14.
London

I arrived at The Selfridge hotel on Sunday afternoon with a merchandiser from the Trafford Centre store called Paul. This hotel would be my home for the next three months. We had to start work at 6 am the next morning, we had three weeks to prepare everything for the Bond Street grand opening. After unpacking I met Paul in the foyer of the hotel, and we decided to go out for a few drinks. Paul was tall with reddish hair and beautiful blue eyes, I always thought he had a look of Paul Newman. He loved clothes and fashion, he was a gay Geordie boy with a cutting wit and undeniable sharpness. Back in Manchester at the Trafford Centre, I had teamed up with Paul and a gorgeous blonde girl who we affectionally called Loula May. The three of us had hit it off and we'd had a few nights out together which were a hoot. Loula May, (who's real name is Louise) would be joining us at the Bond Street store for a few weeks soon, but for now, it was just me and Paul.

Paul and I hit the bars in Covent Garden around four in the afternoon and we wouldn't arrive back at the hotel until five the next morning. We went to this flashy bar where I ordered a bottle of champagne, I was so drunk I attempted to pay for it with my room card key. When we finally returned, we had an hour to get ready and get to work, still drunk. I was to be the temporary store manager but too immature to understand the responsibility.

When I arrived there seemed to be hundreds of staff milling around and some Spanish girl shoved me into a line where there were about twenty people passing boxes from a huge truck outside into the store. I would discover this was 'the Zara way'; twice a week a truck would deliver stock to all the stores and the staff would form a huge line from the truck to the stockroom, passing down each box until it reached its destination. I didn't know at that moment (but I was about to find out), the store was a huge, with three retail floors and three stockrooms, including a ladieswear stockroom the size of Manchester United football pitch. There would be two hundred permanent staff and seven hundred temps for the first three months.

The UK sales director arrived and came up to me, "Bev, Gill.", I swallowed hard realising she was my new boss, she turned to me with a deadly serious face and said, "you're in charge". *Shit, shit, bugger….* was all I could think. I managed to wing it even with the cracking hangover that crept up as the day continued.

It turned out ok though, within a few weeks, and with the help of the nine hundred other staff, it was ship-shape. I worked the hardest I ever had in my life. From six in the morning to midnight every day for three weeks until the store was ready to open. The day of the opening was sensational, people were queuing at 8 am, even though we didn't open till 9.30. By 3 pm on the first day of opening, we had taken a million quid! The new store manager, Louise, had started by that time and I was now the ladieswear manager. I had a message from her via my walki talki to meet her in the downstairs fitting room to do the till reading. When we saw it was £1million we danced around the changing room singing Car Wash in fits of giggles. Louise, another Aries, was extremely professional and knowledgeable about retail, but she was also an amazing human. Although my time at Bond Street was short I will never forget her and all that she taught me.

I was on a great salary, commission on the store turnover, fully expensed accommodation on Oxford Street, laundry paid for and three hundred pounds per week for food. Not many people get the opportunity to live on Oxford Street in that lifestyle, so it was an experience. We worked hard though, I would be the first person in and the last person out (together with a few other die-hard managers). We had great fun and you had to be a little cookie to get through the long hours, energetic environment and hard work. There were quite a few celebs I served in there, including a very charming Bob Geldof shopping for his daughter, looking completely lost and in need of saving, to which I obliged.

There was this great UK sales manager called Del that kind of took me under his wing. He was tough on me though. He rang me up the first week and asked me how many items of ladies wear stock had been delivered and what new styles had arrived. I had no clue, I mean there, were around fifty thousand items arriving daily. When I admitted I had no idea he slammed the phone down on me. There was one occasion when he went ballistic at me because the stockroom was a mess, he told me I had to have every single item in code order and the floor swept by the next morning. I stayed until three am to get that done. When it was finished, I was so proud of myself, it looked perfect. Every item was in perfect order of its barcode. The next day I excitedly waited for Del to arrive, but he didn't show. I called head office and was told it was his birthday and the only day of the year he ever took as a holiday. Gutted. He taught me perfection, meticulous precision and how to manage in a way that got results.

When I did manage to get any time off, I would go to Camden, Portobello Market and Greenwich Village shopping. As Christmas started to approach, London looked beautiful and the boy band 'Blue' would do the annual lights switch on; Loula May and I pushed to the front and screamed like our lives depended on it. I was able to do all my Christmas shopping on Bond Street, in Harrods Department Store and at the various markets around London. This might be normal for some people but for me, it was a dizzy spectacle of glamour, glitz and British culture. I was having fun with money to burn and the shops to burn it in.

I purchased goods from Louis Vuitton for my sister, violet truffles from Charbonnel and Walker for my mother, I got Sonia a vintage Mrs Beaton's cookbook (she had since got married and become a housewife) from Portobello market and Jane who had done the flowers for my wedding; the complete Elvis Presley Collection on vinyl. It was so great to be able to treat those who were special to me and I had a few days off to see everyone in Bolton at Christmas before returning to London for New Year.

Imran was working nearby to London in Reading at this time, we were in touch whenever I had any spare time. He sent me a text message and asked if I would meet him for lunch. We had been apart for some time; he was snowed under with work and I had been working round the clock. He told me he wanted a divorce and said he would give me some money to set up a new life wherever I wanted. I was getting used to these chats by now so just went along with it.

I was still young, successful and attractive. I had never been unfaithful to him, but I could flirt, and I saw men look at me. I knew I would be ok. It wasn't that I didn't love my husband, it was that I didn't feel he loved me. Paying for things and buying me stuff was all well and good but the things that mattered weren't there. We couldn't go out and socialise because he was always cautiously eyeing me to see what I was drinking, who I was talking to, what I was saying to people. I would wind him up by being provocative, daring and outspoken. He would 'tut' at most of my suggestions and was so self-absorbed that I could barely whittle through the solid wall of ego.

I agreed that I would look for an apartment in Manchester City Centre when I got back. That I would still be his friend, his lifeline, but not his wife. I had long ago stopped being his life, but I could be his friend. We both kind of needed each other in a messed up dysfunctional way. The thousands of times I would kiss his soft lips and stroke his hair, look in his dark brown eyes and feel his heartbeat; was all slipping away. We would still be Beverley and Imran, yet different. We would be in the past, gone. It didn't break my heart then though, because I knew in it would never be over. I was there in his head, sweeping through his memory, explicit and obvious. He would cover the love with bad memories, trying to pretend, but first love never dies.

As my time in London was coming to an end, I was sad. I had loved my time there; I had learned so much about fashion and retail and didn't want to go home. I pleaded with the managers to let me stay but they were insistent that I had to go to Manchester to open my store in the city centre. In any case, without the accommodation paid for across the street from work and all the expenses paid, it wouldn't be easy living in London on my salary.

Del came up to me on my last week and said, "Beverley I think you've cracked it, I'm so proud of you. Now, remember, forget everything anyone else has told you and just remember the things I've taught you." I laughed and cried then, he told me not to get soppy on him, as he didn't do 'soppy'.

When I left, all the staff crowded around the main cash desk and presented me with a lavish leaving present of wine, perfume and flowers. They presented me with a card signed by everyone and I even got some individual cards and presents from staff I'd formed a bond with. I shed the tears of a baby on my last day.

"Even with eyes protected by the green spectacles, Dorothy and her friends were at first dazzled by the brilliancy of the wonderful City."

~ L. Frank Baum,
The Wonderful Wizard of Oz

15.
Manchester

On my return to Manchester, I rented an apartment in the city centre, walking distance to the Zara store. Imran gave me the money to move in and I bought some cheap furnishings from Ikea to start with, in addition to some bits from our marital home. One of the girls who worked for me at Homegirl now worked at Louis Vuitton in the city and so she moved into my spare room.

It was an exciting new chapter in my life. I had a fantastic job in a gorgeous store, friends in the shape of Paul and Loula May, in addition to my new roommate and all her friends from Selfridges (where Louis Vuitton was located).

Days were spent slogging my guts out, running up and down escalators, dealing with irate customers and stroppy staff not long out of puberty. I managed to earn the name 'little Hitler' (thanks to Del's training) whilst driving a hard bargain as a manager. It was not for the fainthearted; I would be in the store at 5 am most days and didn't go home till midnight, having swept the stockroom floor and locked up. Loula May was the children's wear department assistant manager and Paul was the senior merchandiser. They, along with a few others, were the people who kept me sane under the pressure of managing this huge three-story shop.

I had a pretty good salary and not an awful lot of time to spend my money due to the long hours in the initial weeks. When we did get a day off, it was spent comatose in bed, every muscle aching with all the running around. When the shop was fully open, things did settle a little, and we were able to get some time socialising.

This chapter of my life started a love affair with Manchester's gay community; Canal Street. It was a buzzing vibrant place where gender, sexual orientation, race or colour did not matter. People were mainly judged on their humour and ability to party; we went together like lemon and tequila.

I had been to Manto's Breakfast club way back when I was around twenty-one. I'd heard that it was open till 6 am and the in place to go in Manchester after a night on the razz, I naturally wanted to go and check it out. So, Imran and I decided to take a look. I remembered talking to a lady in a bar earlier in the evening, telling her that we were going onto Manto's later, she told me that if I mentioned her name, I might get in for free. She told me, "just say you're a friend of Dorothy's", "great!" I eagerly replied, feeling like I already had a foot in the door. So, when we arrived, I said to the guy on the door, "I'm a friend of Dorothy's", he smiled and said, "aren't we all love, go on in". Little did I know that this term 'a friend of Dorothy's', actually referred to Dorothy in the Wizard of Oz. It was a term used to explain that you were gay, in a time when people didn't openly use the expression of being gay. What a plonker!

I first started to venture into this area with Paul and Loula May, we would get dressed up on a Friday night and go for a few drinks before moving onto an RnB club called Gaia. Later, I would meet a lovely guy called Chris who was also gay, and we would share an apartment, having many fun nights on Canal Street.

Manchester's gay village (as it's known), became popular around 1990 when a bar called Manto opened and advertised openly as a gay bar. It runs along Canal street, over to Princess Street, Minshull Street and Sackville Street. There are lines of bars and restaurants, nightclubs and a few watering holes which are adjacent, below and above, all creating a gloriously free and colourful façade. The bars are littered with colour and music, some have transvestites and transgender acts, others are specific to just gay women, many of them open to anyone who wants to have fun. There is a definite seedy side to the village though, where overtly sexual and promiscuous men and women can pick up just about anything (including the clap).

I slotted right into this scene because I was and still am a free spirit. I could wear what I wanted (I once went out in the village on a hot summers night in just an orange bikini), say what I liked, danced how I chose and no one, and I mean no one batted an eyelid. So, I became a dancing queen, right there on Canal Street; many other dancing queens in celebration!

The other thing that I loved about the gay scene was the freedom I felt from men. No men were looking at me as a sexual object, because they were too busy eyeing up each other. If women looked in my direction it was fine because I didn't feel threatened by women. I had visited Manto a few times in my youth, but it wasn't until I started to go there that I felt the full impact of the safety net it provided. At that time, I needed to be free of the eyes of men, penetrating my insecurities and inhibitions.

A sharp contrast to this was the nights out with my flatmate. She mixed with footballers, went to glitzy nightclubs and hung about in VIP areas. She often ushered me along to a multitude of events with her and some of the other girls from Selfridges. Whether it was the England football team party or the opening of a letter, we were there. These events were always full of beautiful women, models mainly and I often felt completely out of place. I no more wanted to date a footballer than I wanted a facial boil, but I got to meet people like David Beckham and Alex Ferguson, people off the telly like those in Coronation Street and Brookside, bigger events would include Boy George and Lionel Richie and the boy band East 17. I would hang around, looking awkward, necking champagne then sneak off, imperceptibly to the gay village for some 'proper' fun.

Imran had written to me several times, asking me to give things another go, I always ended up saying yes to him. I had this total inability to let go of him. I think I just wanted it to work so badly and so did he. He did try towards the end and I attempted reconciliation several times, but it was a lost cause. Maturity teaches you to let go but inexperience encourages you to beat the living daylights out of a relationship until it's so battered there is no getting up. That's what it was like for us; a relationship battered, bruised and dishevelled, no one saying *stop*.

The last time he broke up with me was via a letter he posted from London. It was a nice break-up letter, as break-up letters go, but I was so angry and upset with him. Every time he begged me to give it another chance I did, but it would be him who would eventually give up on us again and again.

Regardless, it was a good time in my life because everything else was going well. Despite the long hours at Zara, I had good friends, plenty of opportunities to socialise and money in the bank. I realised I didn't need Imran and had got married far too young (especially to someone who tried to restrict me). Because of the long hours at Zara, there were times when I would be in work with a cracking hangover and at times, I still had a lot of alcohol in my system. It didn't happen often, but when it did, it was noticed by certain people who weren't my biggest fans.

The shit hit the fan when I went out with Paul, Loula May and a member of staff called Ryan. It was a normal night where we had a few drinks in the many bars on Canal Street and then we went on to a popular night club called Essential. I remember dancing on stage, all three of us jumping up and down to chain reaction by Diana Ross. I looked down and realised I had blood all over my feet and legs. Once outside I could see that the others also had blood all over their legs. When I checked my foot there was a five-inch gash in it. I think I had put my foot down on a nail or some glass. Everyone got into a taxi to my apartment to help me; Ryan was amazing. He got me in the shower cleaning and washing my foot out, God knows what the stuff was that was coming out of it, but it looked like veins and innards. When the paramedics arrived, they took me in an ambulance to A&E at Manchester Hospital. Loula May stayed with me whilst we waited from 5 am till 2 pm the next day to have ten stitches in my foot. Ouch!

Zara was not impressed and as soon as I could walk, I was summoned to head office. I had to take three weeks off work plus all the bitchy rumours of my hangovers and wild drunken nights. It was not acceptable behaviour for a manager, even if it was in my own time and they took the accident as an excuse to make a big deal of it. They offered me three months' salary to leave quietly. So, I accepted without arguing because I was getting fed up of the long hours, nagging from head office and all the pressure. They said the money would be in my bank account the next day.

As I walked along Regent Street in London my Mum called from Marbella. She had gone to Puerto Banus for a short holiday and said that she had fallen out with her friend who she was holidaying with. I walked straight into a travel agents and booked a flight over, leaving the next day. With 12k in the bank (courtesy of Zara) we had a great time.

Next, I took a job at Jeager as the store manager of the Manchester flagship shop on King Street. It was a lovely job with great people. I think some American oil tycoon had purchased the company on a whim and he offered me double the salary I'd been on at Zara. Crazy considering I'd been "let go...". It was short-lived because I was desperate to leave retail and get into something different.

My flatmate and I had moved into a large penthouse apartment in the same building. To celebrate we decided to have a party for her birthday. She invited all her friends from both Louis Vuitton where she worked and Newcastle, her hometown. Amongst the guests that attended was a slim, dark-haired twenty-something-year-old by the name of Chris.

I spotted him immediately as if some invisible auric field brought us together. Again, our birthdays were only a few days apart, he was flamboyant and witty. The thing I remember most about that first meeting is that he was wearing purple trousers, slim-fitting with a slight bootleg, which he wore with a crisp white shirt. He was a gay hairdresser from Cheshire, and I found him warm and charismatic.

In the days that followed, we would text each other hilarious messages and found we had a synergy that sparked a close friendship.

Fast forward eight months and we had decided to share an apartment. We moved into a brand new two-bedroomed apartment in the city centre and had so much fun, there are not enough pages in this book to recount! Chris is an absolute Abba fanatic. There wasn't a day that went by that we didn't act out a rendition of an Abba song or dance in the living room to a video from his vast collection. Chris also has this uncanny ability to do impersonations. There were many nights we just sat on the sofa and Chris would pull off Bet Lynch and Annie Walker from the Rovers Return, Kenny Everett and Freddie Mercury. I remembered this phone-in to a local radio station, doing an impression of Marjory Dawes from the TV show 'Little Britain', it was hilarious, and he won, of course!

I don't know who we thought we were but we both loved good food and fine champagnes. Chris had got a job in a prestigious hair salon in the city centre and I, by now was working as a recruitment consultant at Brook Street. We spent most of our money buying champagne, smoked salmon and caviar from Harvey Nicolls, in addition to nights out in Manchester's gay village, which were nothing less than slapstick.

At this time there would be a small hub, mainly from Chris' hairdressing days, that would meet up for drinks in the many bars that lined the streets of the gay village; Queer, Bar Below, Via Fossa, etc. before moving on to a nightclub. There were a couple of gay girls, guys with razor blade humour and a transvestite called Paris. Most of the younger people at that time loved Essential because it was banging and loud, drugs were rife and testosterone amongst the boys was in full swing. However, there were much cheesier pop clubs like Cruise which were my favourite. I much preferred dancing around to Britney and Madonna than jumping up and down to some innate dance anthem (since I still never had any leaning towards drugs, loving my poisonous friend, alcohol). Sometimes we would go in all of them on the same night and dance and laugh till the early hours.

I was single during this time; Imran was still in the background and had made it clear that he needed a divorce to move on and the wheels were set in motion. We were still good friends though and would go out for a drink together so that Imran could meet some new friends. Imran wanted to find a new girlfriend and I was happy to help him move on. He did meet a girl and although he had some reservations about her at first, I pointed out that he should give her a chance. He did, now they are happy together with children, so that little pep talk did the trick. Although I didn't want to stay married to him, I still needed to know he was there and we talked, confided in each other, had lunch and went shopping, frequently.

I was abstaining from relationships at this time, I unhealthily became quite co-dependent on Chris. We were both co-dependent on each other really, it was like some messed up platonic marriage. Chris was dating and looking for Mr Right and we would have such a laugh with his various dates at the time. There was this one guy who brought his fag hag (female best mate) out to meet me and Chris. They were getting on great for a while, then I and the other girl started arguing and then they both started sticking up for their respective females and bang…" my fag hag is better than your fag hag, on and on". Needless to say, it ended before it had begun.

Even though we did everything together; food shopping, clothes shopping, went to the sunbed together, for days out, Sunday lunch, basically everything you would do with a partner, it was deeply off and out of emotional balance. I knew deep down that it was another dysfunctional relationship, but it became addictive. I had the companionship of a partner without the hassle of the relationship. I can't ever remember us arguing until a couple of years later.

That year I turned thirty and mum bought me a little Smart car to run around the city in and took me to Dollywood in the Smokey Mountains, Tennessee. Thanks to my nana Curly, I had grown up to love not just Dolly Parton but country music as a whole. We stayed in Nashville and took the greyhound bus to Memphis and Pigeon Forge, where Dollywood is located.

The trip was a blast! In Nashville we went to the Grand Ole Opry, the Ryman's Auditorium, the famous Tootsie's Bar, RCA studios and the Jack Daniels distillery. I cried most of the time, as I felt a deep connection to Nashville. When we went into the Ryman's Auditorium, I could see a vision of Patsy Cline singing and swinging her hips on that stage. It felt more like a memory than imagination. I felt sure I had been there in a past life, watching Patsy Cline. In Memphis, we visited Graceland, BB Kings, The Rock 'n' Soul Museum, Sun Studios and the Peabody Hotel. In Dollywood, we exchanged money for Dolly Dollars and bought cowboy hats and T-shirts that said: "save a horse, ride a cowboy" on them. We experienced life on the other side of America by travelling with the vagrants on the Greyhound bus, got lost on the wrong side of the track and met a guy from our hometown of Bolton in Lancashire. A trip of a lifetime and one of the best experiences I've ever had.

The following year Chris and I would participate in an Abba pilgrimage across Stockholm. We visited all the places that Abba used in their music videos, documentaries and to Polar Studios where they recorded most of their tracks. We had such a good time, visiting gay bars, nightclubs and historic places along the way.

For Chris's birthday that year, he said he wanted to invite his friends and family to the apartment to celebrate. So, without him knowing, I bought loads of food and champagne and had a birthday cake made which spelt out ABBA, with very camp yellow and black feathers coming out of it. When he got home from working at the hair salon that night, I flung open the door and shouted "surprise!". He was happy but replied "nobody is coming….", "what?". It turned out they had all let him down, except this one guy who was an old friend. I can't even remember his name, but he did show up, telling us he was really sad because the Pope had died that day. Chris and I just kind of got rid of him as quickly as we could before having a full-on Abba party for two. We didn't need other people to have a party. It was just one of the many crazy but jovial nights we had at this time.

I was enjoying my job in recruitment and felt that it was an area where I could use my natural skills; talking to people, using my intuition, organising and sales. It was fast-paced, people orientated, great hours and I worked with a varied team who I had affection for. I started at the Stockport branch and progressed to the city centre branch which was bigger and busier.

I was also getting quite good at readings by this time and was practising with them more and more.

Things were going well, Chris and I decided to move to some brand-new slick apartments on the other side of town. It was expensive but it had a gym, rooftop jacuzzi and Zen gardens, it was super stylish. My mother then sold her house in Bolton and decided to rent an apartment in the same block on another floor. She wanted to buy a property overseas and put the money in the bank, renting in Manchester whilst contemplating her next move.

It was then, that the energy just kind of changed. Chris and I were somehow disconnected. He had a string of partners while we had lived together but I had remained single; for a time, he was the only man in my life. Although there was no sexual attraction, we did have a deep affection for each other. Any relationship that looked like it was getting serious between him and another man threatened my security. I was completely co-dependent on him, and it was getting to the point of self-sabotage. I was scared of looking for a relationship again, it would be easy to just stay single and hang around with Chris but if I was honest with myself, I needed more. It was time to step out of this false world and realise that Chris was, in fact looking for a man to settle down with. That me and him would have to go our separate ways at some point and that I was young enough to marry again, maybe even have children. I decided to join a dating website and see what the joys of online dating had to offer. This was how Chris had met most of his dates, I thought I would give it a whirl.

The first guy was a Yul Brynner look alike from Manchester called Steve. It was valentine's day and a notification on my computer popped up, "would you like to meet up tonight?" the message said. Well, I figured it was one of the best nights to go on a date so responded, "yes, how about Fat Cats 8 pm?".

I chose a short leather mini skirt, knee-length boots and a cropped fur jacket to wear for the date. As I entered Fat Cats, I was so nervous, he was already sat at the bar, all I could see was this bald head. When he turned around, he was drop-dead gorgeous, he walked over confidently and kissed me on the lips without even a second thought. *This works*, I thought, as something stirred within me and taking a deep breath, sat next to him. He was great company, full of stories and jokes which had me laughing and flipping my hair, fluttering my eyelashes and blushing when he told me I was 'as fit as'. We didn't want the night to end so when the bar closed, we ventured into China Town to a Chinese karaoke bar. I did a tone-deaf rendition of Tammy Wynette's "D.I.V.O.R.C.E", a strange choice indeed for both a first date and valentine's day.

We started seeing each other then, every weekend. Steve being a Scorpio was passionate and insatiable, he drove me wild with desire and I drank him in every time I saw him. He was like heroin. When he wasn't around, I ached for him, when he was there all I wanted to do was surrender everything to him. We had sex anywhere and everywhere. One night we had sex on the sofa in the living room, I knew Chris wouldn't be impressed but as soon as he started kissing me, I would melt into a pool of weakness. Chris went mad, saying he would never have sex on our communal sofa. I was sorry that I'd upset Chris, but Steve just had me in the palm of his hand.

This was the breaking point in our friendship. Chris and I were miles apart at this time. He didn't understand why or how I had changed but he didn't like it. I knew in my heart that it was coming to an end but didn't realise just how abruptly this would come. I liked Steve; it was time I started to look at relationships that could be more fulfilling, but it was hard to accept that it was impacting on the friendship we had together. I knew Steve was never going to be the love of my life, whilst there was sexual chemistry, he wasn't really on my wavelength. I suspected he took drugs, (something which would never sit well with me) and his outlook on life was very different to mine. I needed to meet him at that time though, he taught me that I could feel passionate about a man again, that I needed to connect with another human on a sexual, raw level and to show me it was time to move on. He decided to move to Brazil so things fizzled out, but I will always be glad I met him, he got the blood flowing through my veins again.

Mine and Chris' birthdays were coming up, on the 2nd and 7th of April, so we organised a trip to London. I had paid for myself, Chris and Mum to stay in a five-star hotel, we had Phantom of the Opera theatre tickets booked and afternoon tea at the Ritz.

My mum paid for a birthday cake in the Ritz which said 'happy birthday Beverley and Chris' piped on it. This cost over two hundred pounds as well as all the other extras we had paid for. It was a treat for Chris and a joint birthday celebration.

We were due to set off for London at 6 am, Chris sent me a text message from his bedroom saying he wasn't feeling very well and wouldn't be coming. It had been so strained between us; I didn't go into his room to persuade him otherwise. Mum was so disappointed that he didn't come. She had started to look at him as a surrogate son and I hadn't mentioned to her we weren't getting along. We had a great time in London, but he was sorely missed, and I felt angry at his ungrateful attitude and all the money that had been spent and not enjoyed.

Not long after my return from London, I went into Chris' bedroom to retrieve my hair straighteners which he often borrowed. As I kneeled under his bed to get them, I saw an envelope that said to 'Chris and Beverley' on it. That's how much of a platonic couple we had become, people were inviting us to things together (he was always my plus one). I was confused and peered inside, after all, it had my name on the envelope. It was an invitation to his mother's wedding to both of us. But he'd hidden it from me, I was bewildered and dejected. Why would he not tell me about the invite? It dawned on me then, he was taking this more seriously than just a bit of distance. There had been one argument and a few terse words but to be honest I just thought he would always be there for me.

A few days later, a mutual friend informed me that he was making plans to move out of the apartment and leave me out on my ear; I would be homeless again and unable to afford the expensive rent in the flashy new apartment. I didn't know if it was true and looking back, I guess we should have talked it out. However, we were both too immature to sit down like adults.

I remember the last conversation in the living room. I wanted to say to him that I had found the invitation, that I had heard he was moving out behind my back and ask him if we could resolve things. My ego stood in the way, as it often did back then. Chris was just as closed in any kind of resolve. The conversation ended, perhaps aptly in the two of us singing our last Abba song, Winner Takes It All. The last goodbye.

We were both complicit in the breakdown of our friendship to some degree or another. We were also both Aries; as selfish and pig-headed as one another, immature at times and not fully grown. I agonised at the decision of what to do next. I didn't want to stop living with Chris, I didn't want to move out of the luxury apartment, and I didn't want to hurt anyone. I had spent so many hours with this man, I had poured out every last emotion, feeling and secret. There was nothing we didn't know about each other and yet we couldn't talk to one another now. At the same time, I wasn't about to risk the rug being pulled from under my feet. So, I started to look for a new property pronto. I found a modest two bedroomed cottage in Bolton. My mother had purchased a house in Antequera, a rural region of southern Spain. She was slowly winding her business down in favour of opening something smaller over there and relocate permanently. She was now spending all her time there and so the cottage would act as a place for mum to stay at when she came back to the UK for business trips.

I moved out sneakily while Chris was at work. It was a pretty low move, but it was a case of 'survival of the fittest'. I did feel guilty because, despite everything, I had so much love for Chris. We had met at a time when we were both a little lost and moving into a transitional period of self-discovery. We were two souls that came together to really help each other heal and move forward. That's what we did, we both moved forward and it was time. It was time to let go. There have been a couple of people in my life that letting go of was both necessary and yet painful. Chris was one of those people. So, life continued in a Chris-less way…it was a little bland at first. It would be many years before we would bury the hatchet and speak again, but I'm happy to say we did manage to forgive each other.

"My expectations were reduced to zero when I was 21. Everything since then has been a bonus."

~ Stephen W. Hawking

16.
Spiritual Encounters

From birth to stepping into my mediumship fulltime there were many spiritual encounters. They were not at the forefront of my life until my early thirties, but they were always there. Some of us develop our mediumship over time, but I was born of mediumship. Either way is a natural unfoldment; a special and individual journey. Mine started before I was born, I'm sure. I suspect that a consortium of guides decided how it would all happen for me and have been assisting me from birth. Growing up, you don't necessarily know what it's all about but for me, it felt natural and loving. I never had a bad psychic or mediumship experience as a child nor have I had one since working as a medium. The spirit world is the most kind and gentle, loving wisdom and anyone who feels them is truly blessed.

Spiritualism ran in the family on both sides. My mother's gran would attend the spiritualist church in Bolton from a very early age and my mum was also a great believer and attended regularly, receiving the healing mentioned in earlier chapters. On my dad's side, my nan would teach me how to read the tea leaves and there would be another medium born into that side of the family.

As a small child, of around two or three years old, I would play with plug sockets in the house and mum would say blue sparks would fly out of them. It could be that the house needed a complete rewire, but it didn't happen to anyone else and I never got electric shock. I honestly believe that it was the strong psychic energy that I had as a child that caused these electric pulses.

Growing up I would have visions of spirits who had passed away coming into my room at night. I had no fear of these spirits or the energy that surrounded me growing up. I just lived with it, embracing all that came, each time it came. I would feel loved ones on the other side come close at night and often knew when things weren't quite right in the family.

I was in a pub in my late teens and would see a woman sat alone. I went over to her and just felt compelled to speak to her, saying "your mother used to work in a small hotel?" I wasn't sure if it was a question or a statement, it just flopped out of my mouth, involuntarily. She turned to me in surprise and said, "yes that is correct". I went on to describe her physical appearance and told her that I could see her very clearly *folding crisp, white bed linen*. She confirmed this to be true and I knew it to be in any case, it was just so clear. Nowadays, you would never catch me doing that, but I think there was a dual purpose. It was a much-needed message to the communicator's daughter, that her mother was alive and well and living on in the spirit realms, at the same time, it was teaching me that I could accurately communicate with them.

There would be a few occasions when I would meet a person and instantly, I could see their whole life in front of me within seconds. One such occasion was a man in a bar in town. I was very young at the time, perhaps fifteen or sixteen. He went to shake my hand and introduced himself as Leon, as my hand touched his hand, and within a split second, I just knew everything about him. I told him "you work in sales, you have recently split from your girlfriend, and you lost your father at a young age". I'll never forget that look on his face, complete astonishment as he confirmed it to be correct.

I was chatting to a girl in the gym and she mentioned a local businessman who owned a bar in Bolton town centre. She said he was a horrible, nasty man and revealed some shocking revelations to me. I turned to her and said, "that's awful, I bet his bar will burn down!", I couldn't for the life of me think what made me say that because I am not a malicious person at all. It turned out that the bar did burn down, that very same night. It would also turn out that he didn't have any insurance and would go bust following the fire. I don't know if that was a premonition, but it certainly came true.

There was also a night where Imran and I were driving home late at night from Ritzy and there was an older lady stood on the roadside. Imran pulled over to see if she was ok. She looked distressed and almost as if she was thumbing a ride in some way. When I wound the window down, she said "please help me, my son has been rushed to the hospital. I ordered a taxi, but it hasn't shown up", "Get in!" Imran ordered, "we'll take you to the hospital". The lady got in the front seat, I advanced to the back of the car. As we drove, I said to her, "I feel as though your son will be ok, is he in his thirties and in the army?". She turned around to me, slightly startled and said, "no that's my other son who died". I felt that her other son had come through to reassure her at this time of distress. She seemed pleased with the information and although unexpected, she said she believed in mediumship and that he had been through to her before via a medium she went to see.

I always had this gift of seership, where I could see and predict things that were going to happen, this was especially true when I used my Fortune Cards, the same ones I use today. I used to pretend I was a Romany gipsy in the school playground and that I could read palms. I couldn't read palms at all, but I did roll off information about other kids that were quite often true. When I started to read the cards properly it was so completely natural to me, the information seemed to come from nowhere.

I have been doing readings, one way or another from the time I could talk and the connection to spirit was always strong. However, to get to the place I am today and on this treadmill of continuous development, it seems God wanted me to learn many life lessons before I could fully step into my unique talents. My life lessons involved learning compassion, eloquence and comprehension of different lifestyles and ideals. I learned non-judgment and detachment. I learned we all have problems and we all have our way of dealing with them. I feel these lessons created a deeper understanding of people and life and made me a better medium and coach.

It has been a wondrous journey and throughout my life, I have had many experiences which have confirmed to me that spirit has always been there. People's understanding of the afterlife is quite personal, but I do have complete faith in spirit, working as a perennial process in all life.

"I only drink Champagne on two occasions,
when I am in love and when I am not."

~ Coco Chanel

17.
Spain

My mother was by now living in Spain full time and just winding down the business. A visit to see her would change everything….

The village was a typical Andalusian, whitewashed affair where very few people spoke English. There were a handful of British expats scattered throughout the village, in fact, there were probably more pubs per square mile than there were English people at that time. It was close to the town of Antequera, some ninety miles inland from Malaga. It was a hot summer and in June it was sweltering.

There was a bar right in the centre of the village where most people gathered and this particular day, it was the world cup, Portugal vs England.
I was sat with mum on a table surrounded by chairs. A guy who was tall, slim and wearing white linen kind of sauntered into the bar, an overwhelming feeling passed through my being. I remember thinking to myself *this is trouble for me*. It was like soul recognition, the strongest feeling of a spiritual reflection, that it almost floored me. He walked right over to me and sat down next to me, "you're a northerner" he exclaimed, "how do you know that?", I replied in mock surprise. It turned out his name was Ben and he was born and bred in Manchester, living in the village and building a house.

We talked and talked, all day and all night, I have no idea what the football score was, I was smitten by an undeniable connection. We realised at 3 am that the bar was closing, and he asked me if I wanted to go to another bar where they sometimes played reggae music. I agreed and moving to the next bar, we continued to talk about everything from Spanish expat life to Manchester to the music we both loved and all the things we had in common, including our birth sign, you guessed it... Aries. As we talked the air was electric and I don't think I had felt a link this strong my whole life.

We spent time together for the rest of the holiday as friends, and I planned to go back in a few weeks, hoping to see him again.

When I arrived home, all I could think of was getting back to Spain. To being back with Ben, in the steamy summer of Andalusia and the quirky little village where Spanish life simmered gently and without incident.

I started to browse the internet looking for jobs, there was absolutely nothing in English around Antequera, but further down, on the Costa del Sol there were three recruitment agencies; all were hiring. I got to work emailing the companies and managed to secure interviews with all three for the following month. I had decided to move permanently to the Costa del Sol, a place that held fond memories of the many holidays in previous years.

I thought Ben would be pleased, but when I got over there and told him, he looked troubled. I couldn't understand it, the sexual chemistry and ease of company was unfathomable, he felt it too, so why wasn't he thrilled by my announcement? That summer we spent nights talking over delicious, mature wines, listening to Billie Holiday songs whilst talking about everything and anything. He was intelligent, warm and handsome and I started to fall completely in love right there and then.

The bubble would burst when he confessed, he was actually in a ten-year relationship with his girlfriend who was due to move over when the house was ready. It was an earth-shattering blow and I took it badly. He said he was sorry, that he had got carried away with the feelings that existed between us, not wanting to break the dream. He promised me that if things ever changed, he would find me and we could give things a go, but for now, he was committed to someone else. I didn't believe him of course, but years later he would prove his word was good.

In the meantime, I had been offered all three of the recruitment jobs and plumped for one that was situated in the seaside resort of La Cala, a twenty-minute drive to Marbella.   I had secured an apartment and was due to start in three weeks.

On my return to England, I received a letter through the post, it was my decree absolute. Our divorce came through on the 27th of October 2005, exactly ten years to the day we had got married. I had mixed feelings about it, to be honest. On one hand, it was sad and the end of an era, I saw it as final and absolute (I guess that's where the name comes from), it was a feeling of failure and gut-wrenching heartbreak. On the other hand, it was the end of a chapter and the beginning of something new. I called Imran immediately as I opened the solicitor's letter, and he was in tears. He had received his copy the same day and was inconsolable as he realised the finality of it all. I told him that I was leaving for Spain in three weeks and his reaction shocked me. He came to see me and was completely devastated by my departure. He told me "I thought you'd always be there". I guess that was the problem, he didn't try hard enough in the marriage because he thought he would always have me as a friend. I would always be there for him as a friend, I promised him that, and I have always kept my end of the bargain. Imran would let me down yet again a few years later by cutting all ties with me at the request of his new girlfriend. It was a hard lesson, but one I needed to learn.

I had so many mixed emotions about the divorce. Anger, bitterness, sadness and most of all love. I was the bad guy because I was loud, brash and drank too much. I fell over far too often in public places on a big night out, I was ostentatious, obvious and couldn't hold down a job, an undeniable flirt and a reputation which was hard to shake. I ran a clothes shop, but it was *his* money. We had a nice house in a posh part of Bolton, but my name wasn't on the deeds. From the outside looking in, he had been the perfect husband and me the reckless wife who preferred freedom to the confines of her marriage.

Imran with his soft voice and endearing stammer was the good guy. He had money, wore flashy designer suits, bought expensive artwork and owned a penthouse in The Edge (a prestigious address in

Manchester) and had footballers for neighbours. He carried a black American Express card and bought people drinks and lunch. He drove an expensive car, was polite and kind, always ready to help anyone who could make a martyr of him.

Yet it was Imran who had lied about going to Ibiza with his friends, it was Imran who had met Miss Iceland and ended up in a bedroom with her, it was he who had text messages from other women in his phone and it was him who had been secretive and untruthful the entire relationship. I had stayed completely faithful to him until he ended things. The whole relationship he was reluctant to wear a wedding ring, making excuses as to why he didn't like it, or it didn't fit. He went behind my back to the bank manager, opening a secret bank account with instructions that I wasn't to find out. He hadn't wanted the baby when I got pregnant and was happy when I had a termination, he wasn't there for me when Pat died and left me at my hardest times. At the time I had put him on a pedestal and didn't see him for what he was.

Looking back, I can see that he had no idea how to love. He had deep insecurities that went right back to his father not accepting him, no matter how much money he earned, in his father's eyes he wasn't a good Muslim and that's all that mattered. He constantly told me he wanted me to stop drinking, but couldn't he see? He was doing to me what his Dad had been doing to him. Have an arranged marriage, work in the family business, do this, do that. They say those who are abused become the abuser and this is what he was doing to me; trying to squeeze me into a box of his ideals. At the end of the day, he pretended to respect me, love me, buy me things and decorate me with designer handbags and Gucci shoes (all chosen by him) but, he was no different than any other man I had dated. He only liked my looks and didn't want to get to know the real me, the vivacious lively girl from Bolton who was capable of so much.

On the other hand, if we had stayed together, he would have held me back. He is now settled with children and I think this is the life that he is most suited to. My life has been a myriad of colour, travel and experiences which would not have suited his desire for conformity and security. It took me a long time, but I saw him. I saw who he was and why we would never have worked out longer than the ten years we were married. I forgave him and I let him go. Just another chapter in this book.

Putting the past behind me, I packed everything I owned into my Smart car and headed for the Costa del Sol. I would drive down to Plymouth, cross the water via Brittany Ferries and continue down from Santander, through Madrid and onto mum's little Spanish village, spend a few days there before rocking up in La Cala to start my new life.

The apartment was a large two bedroomed located on the second line to the beach above a veterinary shop. I was pleased with it as it was near to all the bars and restaurants, and within walking distance to my new job and the beach. I unpacked my clothes, lay on my new Spanish bed and daydreamed about this new adventure.

The team at work were a good bunch, friendly and helpful, offering anything I needed as I adjusted to my new life. There was James, the MD, tall and slim with a wide smile, a sharp mind and an Essex accent I could never quite get my ear around. His PA was a young girl from Guatemala by the name of Adriana and we would become good friends. There were two other consultants called Karen and Jeremy and we got along swimmingly. It was a tough job because there was no basic salary, only a hefty commission on successful placements and I was completely on my own with finances. I didn't take anything off Imran in the divorce settlement. A stupid move I know, I was so naive to think that his friendship meant more to me than any money. However, I learned through this that spirit would always provide both financially and emotionally. They have never let me down.

I started to read a good list of self-help books including 'Money and The Law of Attraction' by Esther and Jerry Hicks, 'The Monk Who Sold His Ferrari' by Robin Sharma, 'The Power of Positive Thinking' by Norman Vincent Peel and 'The Power of Now' by Eckhart Tolle. I joined Robin Sharma's 5 am club doing yoga and journaling. I learned the art of Louise Hay's affirmations and started to manifest and create on a very basic level: money, clients and opportunities.

My mum would visit frequently from her house in Antequera but when I was alone, I started to get despondent and lonely. The people I worked with were lovely, but they were all in relationships so there wasn't much socialising with them. I ventured into La

Cala alone a few times but found a tirade of bitchiness awaited me from local girls. They seemed jealous that a single girl with nice clothes, long hair and a good figure had invaded their space. Like a hungry pride, waiting to attack the newcomer. Finding no joy in the local bars I took to meals out alone at the local Indian and Chinese restaurants, often necking a bottle of red wine and taking an extra one home 'for the road'. Days were spent walking along the beach to the next holiday resort, sunbathing and then heading back home, as brown as a sausage. I also longed for Ben, still not over the strong connection and love I felt, I couldn't seem to shake him.

Mum came up for her birthday the following year in June 2006 and we went to a Thai restaurant there to celebrate. We ordered four bottles of Don Perignon and staggered home, happy and broke. The next morning feeling slightly worse for wear, I announced I would go to the local rescue centre and adopt a kitten.

As we entered the room, there were hundreds of cats and kittens, all colours, sizes and ages. They were lined up in cages, sat on the desk, lying in the doorway, sprawling across every nook and cranny, meowing loudly as we walked around looking for my new love. It was heartbreaking to see all these babies needing a new home. I noticed a little grey cat, semi-asleep, languidly stretched out in a cage alone. It was as if she was just waiting patiently, knowing her new mum would arrive when she was good and ready (no rush). I adopted her then, called her Charlotte and loved her for the next fifteen years.

So, I had a new love in my life with four paws and a pink nose but, and, I don't know why, I had expected a multitude of suitors to line up at my door following my move to Spain, but none came. I resorted to a local online dating site and met up with a string of unsuitable males, seemingly more disturbed than I was. I missed the unbridled fun of the gay scene, the warmth of Bolton and the diversity of Manchester. Still, being positive and part of the 5 am club, I soldiered on.

It was late 2007 when my mum sold her house in the sleepy whitewashed village and moved down to the lively Costa del Sol. She rented an apartment and opened a shop doing what she did best, clothing alterations and tailoring. We had broken all ties with Manchester at this point and was determined to make a go of things in Spain.

I started charging people for one to one psychic readings and was asked to go to people's houses to do group bookings as well as a few bars that wanted a psychic event. I was working at the recruitment agency by day, so this all had to fit around it. I was getting good at reading the cards, tuning into past, present and future and there were brief messages from loved ones. My name was getting passed on and I got a few business cards printed to hand out.

Things were good but there was something missing in Spain, a disconnect to life. I couldn't quite put my finger on it. There were plenty of people around to socialise with, the beaches were great, I had a good job with a great team, but something was off. I felt a deep emptiness inside, like a hollow in my stomach that nothing could fill. Around this time, I took a trip back to Manchester, primarily to see Dolly Parton in concert, but also to catch up with old friends. I loved it on my return, I had missed the vibrancy of the city, the sheer normalness of it all and I have to say, I had a good few pasties on my visit. This feeling never left me for the whole seven years I lived there. I automatically went to the same old self-destructive pattern of drinking too much. It was escapism from the parts of my life that weren't completely fulfilling. I acted out, drinking with just about anyone who would keep company with me.

There was a night when I went to a charity ball. I was with a few work colleagues but as it grew late, they disbursed, and I found myself talking to some randoms. There was a mix of girls and boys probably about my age. I had had a lot to drink. One slim, tanned girl with long blonde hair, sporting a glittery dress said to no one in particular, "hey wanna come to a party?". *Hell yes!* I thought as I jumped into the back of a large white 4x4. There were about ten people in this car, including two people in the boot.

We drove for about thirty minutes, music banging, blaring out of the speakers, windows down, wind sweeping with the freedom of party energy. We then pulled up outside a very normal looking white house. It was deadly silent. After a few minutes, someone opened the garage door and led us into a small corridor and down some steps. As the new door opened, I felt like I'd stepped onto the movie set of Star Wars. The whole room was white, white walls, white leather sofas, a white bar and a white DJ console. There were a pale blue light and disco ball sparkles flickered as it spun around the room, my head not far behind it.

The place was packed with all sorts of people, there were beautiful women with long limbs and floaty hair, men in tuxedos smoking, some looking decidedly bored. Two men were kissing provocatively on the dance floor and topless girls with silver body paint holding trays of cocaine and little white tablets in the air, laughingly shouting "narcotics anyone!". My head was spinning and if I could have recognised anyone who I'd been in the car with, I don't think I would have anyway. I smiled timidly at a few people as I made my way to the bar. I asked for a beer and was handed a bottle of Budweiser, there seemed to be no charge.

I staggered around a little and found myself sat on one of the white sofa's, the guy sitting next to me was smiling through me, as if I wasn't even there. Someone started talking to me, but it was just lips moving, no sound. Someone handed me a tray with a huge pile of white powder, and some rolled up hundred-euro notes, I pulled my face and said, "I don't do drugs". Another beer was handed to me, I started flagging then, drifting in and out of consciousness. The next thing I remember is one of the tuxedo clan carrying me outside and into the back of a black limo. I passed out then. When I woke up in the morning I was in my bed, my dress had been removed and was folded neatly on my bedroom chair.

I was wearing my underwear and my door keys carefully placed on my bedside table.

Many crazy nights followed a similar protocol, although not quite as bizarre as that one. I realised that Marbella was full of people who had gone there looking for something and were a long way from finding it. I was one of them.

I didn't want to feel that I was failing at my new life, so I just plodded on. My mother and I went out nearly every night, dining out at overpriced restaurants in Marbella, weekends were spent lazing around in Spanish tapas bars and shopping in the prestigious shops in Puerto Banus. I didn't meet an awful lot of genuine people and found myself in shallow, lack-lustre company, drunk and bored. As I was single there were a few nights when I would participate in one-night stands with men that I had no interest in. The lack of love would become acute and there would be many late-night phone calls to Imran with garbled messages, asking him to take me back. There was absolutely no way I wanted this, but the coldness of the life I was living would do anything for warmth, even artificial warmth. Imran would respond with an angry retort, not realising that I was asking him for help.

Adriana who I sat next to in the office was a welcomed relief from all these empty evenings. We got on well, she was a beautiful, genuine girl and we laughed all day at work. I went to watch Ricky Martin in Antequera with Adriana, which was a great experience, upbeat and fun. A weekend in Ronda together, also created precious memories. I had received a hefty commission that month, nearing ten thousand euros and we had a great time eating, shopping and sightseeing.

After two years working in La Cala, the company was given the opportunity to purchase another recruitment agency situated in Gibraltar. The agency had been successful for twelve years but following the sudden and untimely death of the owner, it was now on the market. All the other members of staff were settled with children in the local area, so I was the obvious choice to head up the new office. Given my success in the job and the management training at Zara, I was eager to progress.

It was a welcomed relief, La Cala never provided me with support, love or inspiration. Gibraltar would offer a fresh start. I was optimistic about the new challenge of managing this office and meeting new people there.

"A man's spirit is free, but his pride binds him with chains of suffocation in a prison of his own insecurities"

~ Jeremy Aldana

18.
Gibraltar

The new office was on the main shopping street that ran through Gibraltar, it was on the second floor of a dingy 1970s looking building. When I walked in on my first day, I was overwhelmed by the smell of smoke that was puffing out of the main office. There was Tony, the widower of the deceased owner. He looked like he had died himself and had been warmed up in the microwave, a small depressed-looking dog lying next to him. I soon learned that Tony would be my office buddy until all the legal documents had been signed and we legally owned the company.

I sat at Sue's desk. You could feel her in the walls, in the index cards, the filing cabinets and the computer system. She had passed away suddenly and I think the community were shocked at her departure. I had some big boots to fill.

There was a receptionist called Jo who I was to discover would stay on as part of the team. I got to work sifting through the hundreds of CV's and client index cards that Sue had lovingly collected over the many years she had built up that business. I felt incredibly honoured to take over from her. All her customers were extremely complimentary and willing to give me a chance.

There were strange occurrences that took place in that office. I would come in first thing and find CV's on my desk that matched exactly the job description I was looking for. Index cards of clients would fly on the floor and when I called them (which I did instinctively), they would have a job vacancy that needed filling. I knew Sue was guiding me, it was almost as if, through me, she was saying a last goodbye to all her good clients and friends. As I rang each of them, they invited me to go and see them so they could explain about their business and the relationship they had with Sue. However, when I got there I was treated to tea, cakes, sandwiches and warm conversations about Sue and her remarkable life.

One of these days I was sat at my desk (Sue's desk) and Tony was sat opposite me reading a newspaper and puffing away like the magic dragon. I heard a whisper in my ear saying, *"ask him about the Ponderosa Hotel"*, I ignored the voice and carried on typing. It came again …. the "*Ponderosa Hotel"*. I felt a distinct poke in my ribs… "*tell him..*", the voice spoke, this time louder and more impatient. So, I cleared my throat and said to Tony, "does the Ponderosa Hotel mean anything to you?", as he changed shades from grey to white, I could see it did. "How on earth do you know about that?", I explained the voice in my ear and told him I believed it to be his departed wife. He explained that the Ponderosa Hotel was the hotel where they had met, she had owned the hotel and he had been hired as a saxophone player, the rest was history. He just got up and left then, in shock.

It was a small piece of information, but it meant so much to him, his grief was inconsolable, and I think it brought him a glimmer of light that she was still around. I wasn't fully aware of it then, but this was the start for me. The spirit world had decided it was time. Time to begin the wonderful journey of mediumship which would change my life forever.

As the weeks passed, I settled into a new routine working in Gibraltar. Tony departed us once the contracts were signed, a new team member was recruited. Kathleen was a stunning looking girl who was strong-minded and passionate about Gibraltar. We would become good friends and together with Jo who worked on reception and a few others, nights out in Gibraltar and nearby La Linea became a regular occurrence.

I had moved into a town about twenty minutes' drive from Gibraltar called Sotogrande. Sotogrande was a strange place that I would affectionately call Stepford (after the Stepford Wives). It is the largest privately-owned residential development in Andalusia. Many of the richest families in Spain and the UK reside there. Sotogrande was established by the couple Joseph and Mercedes McMicking from the Philippines. The McMickings, having seen the area in 1962, acquired five neighbouring farms with the idea of creating a luxurious residential development by the Mediterranean. I moved into a two-bed apartment overlooking the marina, which was plush and grand. The bed was so big in the master bedroom I often got lost in it, the cat had her own space and we never rolled into each other.

I should have been happy. Gibraltar provided me with a great job, some warm companions and a luxury apartment in a beautiful setting. However, I became deeply unhappy. I started to gain weight, became lethargic and despondent. I was uninterested in the job and spent most of my time in the office browsing the internet, instead of what I was supposed to be doing.

My mother had seen an opportunity for her business to succeed in Sotogrande, as opposed to La Cala and acquired both a shop and an apartment in the area. She was happy and doing well, earning money and making friends of her own.

I remembered one of my mothers' customers from Manchester telling me that she had a recruitment agency. She told me if I ever wanted a job, to call her. So, I did. An interview was set up and a friend of a friend said there was some accommodation going in a shared house in Hulme, close to Manchester. I was going home, happy and excited. I left Charlotte with mum temporarily, to see if things worked out before taking her to England permanently.

"To shift your life in a desired direction, you must powerfully shift your subconscious."

~ Kevin Michel

19.
Manchester Again……….

I arrived in Hulme at the small terraced house that was to become my new home. I was told by the owner that there was only one other tenant in the house, a gay guy called Dean. There were two spare bedrooms and I was able to choose either one. There wasn't much between them, so I placed my one suitcase of clothes on the bed and sat down leafing through the interview information I'd been sent by Sandra who owned the recruitment agency.

I mooched around the house, looking in cupboards, switching on the TV and running my finger over the CDs and DVDs in the front room. Around 7 pm a tall, light-skinned young man of Jamaican descent came bounding in through the front door with a big smile and a blast of energy. He said "hi, you must be Beverley, I'm Dean", I smiled at his generous and enthusiastic warmth. "My friend, Duncan, said you drank red wine, so I picked one up at Asda", he said as he threw down bags of shopping and removed his coat. We started chatting away like old friends. We talked for that long, that we didn't realise the time, it was 5 am by the time we got to bed!

Dean was one of the better parts of this return home, we hit it off instantly, and had many profound conversations, nights out in the gay village and shared bottles of wine on the sofa. We would remain good friends to this present day. He was playful and lively but had this serious 'let's put the world to rights attitude' and we both loved a good debate. It was

Obama's inauguration not long after I moved in and we both stayed up to watch his grandstand speech, loving the historic moment of the first black president of the United States, a real triumph.

At one point his boyfriend at the time had come over to the house, I knew nothing about him at all, as I had never met before. I told him that his mother was in the spirit world and gave him evidence of her life and a message of love. My mediumship at the time was getting stronger, but it was still raw and untamed.

After a couple of gruelling interviews, I was offered the job which was located in Didsbury, two buses from Hulme where I was living with Dean. It was part of a global business called the MRI Network and I was commissioned with starting up a new department dedicated solely to aerospace recruitment. The basic salary and commission structure were fantastic and Sandra, who owned the business was a dream to work for. There would be opportunities for travel all over Europe to visit clients at manufacturing sites and airbase camps. It was hard work in the beginning because I had to undergo intense training and learn the industry; something I knew nothing about. It was interesting though speaking to aircraft and spaceship engineers, learning mind-blowing things.

I was enjoying being back in the UK and the city of Manchester again, Dean was a blessing and the job was a great opportunity.

Unfortunately, however hard I tried; I could not get rid of an ache within me. I had left Spain because I felt empty, confused and unsettled. Now I was feeling much worse. The travel to work was getting me down and I was late a few times because the buses were unpredictable and unreliable. I decided I needed to move closer to the job, to gain more peace and took a one bedroomed apartment in Didsbury centre within walking distance to work. It was a modern, spacious apartment above Marks and Spencer's food. Didsbury was a vibrant, buzzing community filled with bars, restaurants and an array of quirky little shops. There was a beautiful park which I passed daily and often stopped by to meditate in the tranquil surroundings.

Nothing I tried seemed to create peace within me. I started to gain weight rapidly, I was eating copious amounts of ready meals from Marks & Spencer's below, washed down with many bottles of red wine. I gained four stone in weight in two months. I started to get large, painful boils all over my face. I later discovered this was adult acne due to hormones, probably out of balance with stress. I was lost. I should have been happy. Things were not at all bad in my life and I had been blessed with a new beginning, but try as I may, I could not achieve that feeling of peace within.

Close to the apartment was a mind, body and spirit shop where I would browse the shelves of angel cards, books, herbal teas and crystals. I loved the energy there, and it was the only place that inspired me.

It was early spring, and I met Dean for a coffee in the city centre and we strolled over to Waterstones to look at the books in my favourite section; mind, body,

spirit. Whilst standing facing the bookshelf, completely out of nowhere, a book fell off the top shelf and landed at my feet. There was no one around as far as I could see. The book was called, 'How To Find Yourself And Create True Happiness' ….
 mmmm, not one to ignore the universe, I bought the book and took it home to read.

The book woke me up to the fact that I was not living a truly authentic life. I realised that happiness was not about where you lived but who you are inside, what your life purpose is and if you are fulfilling it. It took me agonising nights and many bottles of red wine before I gave up trying to step into my life purpose. In the end, I said to absolutely no one, "I have no idea what I am supposed to be doing, I hand my life over to God". It was then that I let go of having ideas about my life and the power of God and spirit took over. It occurred because I meant it when I said, I was open to whatever came in next. I let go of expectations, opened my heart up to a new chapter as I felt completely lost, I figured I couldn't go wrong.

The first thing I did was hand my notice in at the job, realising that this lovely woman who had given me the opportunity needed someone who was dedicated. It broke my heart to let her down, but it was for the best in the long-term, I spent most of my days on google and there was very little 'recruitment' going on. I rang my mum and told her I would be returning to Spain and could I stay in her spare bedroom until it was clear about my future.

It wasn't until I was on the plane back home that an idea came to me that felt so unbelievably obvious, it was like a huge pink elephant that I had unwittingly ignored for a long time. I had been inspired by the little mind, body, spirit shop I had seen in Didsbury. On my return to Spain, my mum asked me, "what are you going to do for a job?", "I'm going to be a fulltime medium and open a mind, body, spirit shop", I replied. And that's what I did.

"I may not have gone where I intended to go, but I think I have ended up where I needed to be."

~ Douglas Adams

20.
The Book Angel

I was nervous as I parked up at the hotel in Sotogrande. Everyone told me that Derek was an astute businessman, often short with people and drove a hard bargain. However, the empty unit was perfect for my new shop and if he was the owner, I had to approach him. He owned this hotel and many other properties in the area and was a bit of a business tycoon, having previously been the founder of a large British bakery. When I entered the hotel, there was a small older gentleman sat reading a newspaper and I just had a feeling it was him.

"Hi, Derek? I was told I would find you here" I said nervously, smiling shyly, "yes, who's asking?" he replied in a curt voice. I explained that I wanted to rent the shop he owned in the commercial centre and he stood up then, fumbled about in his pocket and handed me a bunch of keys. "Here's the keys, speak to my secretary about signing the lease, she's not in till Monday", he said, and turned back to his newspaper; conversation over. *Is he kidding me?* I thought. Wow! I skipped back to my car.............I had a shop! His secretary was a lovely woman she told me that Derek often gave a rent-free period and that she would put something together for me, but in the meantime, I was free to move in whenever I wanted. I could hardly believe it, it turned out to be six months before she came for any money at all.

Next problem was I had absolutely nothing to go in this miracle shop I had acquired. Mum said we could go to Ikea in Malaga to get a desk, chair and some shelves and I could put it on her credit card until the business started to make money. I opened a credit account with a big publishing company and ordered some mind, body, spirit books, gift sets, angel and tarot decks etc. I was so excited as it all started to come together.

Miracles continued to occur daily. A lady came in and asked if I wanted to sell her homemade lavender products on a sale or return basis. Then another with homemade teas, a different person with crystal jewellery, essential oils and homemade bath products. The shop looked and smelled beautiful within a month of Derek giving me those keys. I did readings in the shop and talked endlessly to people who loved all things spiritual. I read many of the books I stocked and started to gain much more knowledge about the industry. I had called the shop The Book Angel, after whichever angel had sent me that book in Waterstones and got me on my new path.

Approximately one month into the opening of the business I decided to ask the universe for some additional income. I had been following the law of attraction for some time and was an avid fan of Esther and Jerry Hicks. *'Ask and thou shall receive',* I thought to myself. A lady about the age of seventy walked into the shop and introduced herself as Dorothy. She told me she owned a second-hand bookstall, selling English books on the local flea market. She said she wanted to retire and had no one to pass the stall on to, did I want it? She explained that it was every Sunday from 8 am to 2 pm and usually took about four hundred euros per week. Did I want it? Miracles were occurring by the bucket load. I now know that this is what happens when you hand your life over to God, to divine guidance. When you trust and let go, God steps in with better ideas than you could ever imagine. It says in A Course in Miracles "Miracles occur naturally as expressions of love. The real miracle is the love that inspires them, in this sense everything that comes from love is a miracle".

So, for a good few years, my mother and I got up at the crack of dawn and worked on the Sotogrande Sunday flea market selling books to English expats. That additional income became invaluable to my survival in the early stages of the business.

Whilst dabbling with 'The Law of Attraction' I also inadvertently manifested my next relationship. I read that you should make a list of the qualities you would like in a new partner. So, I wrote down: fun, friendly, likes animals, creative and with a strong connection, just to make sure I knew when they arrived, I wrote, dark hair and green eyes. It was unlikely that I would find all those qualities since Spain had offered me very little choice of any standard, but it was worth a shot.

One book that helped me at that time was a book that still sits on the bookshelf next to me as I write. It's called 'Opening to Channel: How to Connect with Your Guide' by Sanaya Roman and Duane Packer. This book taught me how to open my channel and connect with my guides.

In my first meditation, as per the instructions in the book, I became aware of a lady who was reading a deck of oracle cards. Next, I saw a native American Indian with a bright red feathered headdress, I asked for a name, hearing the name William. I thought it was an odd name for a Native American Indian, but I went with it in any case. I didn't know if these (so-called) guides were my imagination or real spirit beings from another realm, it was fun discovering the many aspects of connecting anyway. I remembered what Mrs Alexander had told me all those years ago in the spiritualist church and wondered if I was seeing the same two figures in my meditations.

It took a little time and a lot of patients, but I gently started to feel authentic communication with the female I had seen. She told me she had lived a life as a Romany Gypsy, travelling the world and telling people's fortunes. She told me that she had been working with me for many years and helped me read the cards and see the past, present and future during my readings. I could never get a clear name for this woman, so I called her a name that just popped into my head one day, Samsara. I talked to my new friend, who was my old friend, all day long, every day. I chatted away to her asking questions and making conversation like she was a solid person in the room. The Native American Indian only came a few times in the beginning but he always felt loving, strong and powerful. Knowing I had this dynamic duo by my side made me feel encouraged in my readings, I became more confident and the information clearer.

There was one day when I had been reading a very interesting book about Edgar Cayce, the famous medium I had first been introduced to in my teens. I had a full day of bookings and felt I needed some extra lift, so I asked (without expectation) if Edgar would come and help me with my readings from spirit. I completely forgot about it by the time my first customer arrived. It was a young girl of eighteen who sat nervously in the chair opposite me. Immediately, I got the vision of her sat on a large, pale brown horse. I was acutely aware that this vision was not of her current life but a life many years ago. I explained what I was seeing and told her I felt she would start to work with horses in the very near future. She told me that she was a trained ballet dancer and had been since a very small child, a talent which her mother had before her. She told me she was very much 'expected' to continue her career as a ballet dancer at university. The only problem was, very recently, she had become confused and had started to desire a career in equestrianism. I saw that in a previous life she had loved and trained horses but due to a bad accident that left her a cripple, she was forced to stop. I was given the message, that, in this life, she would work with horses again and heal the karma of the past life. She would write to me a few years later and tell me that she had decided to drop ballet and follow her heart, she was now working with horses.

All-day I saw past lives that made absolute sense to things that were going on in their current incarnation. I knew that the wonderful medium Edgar Cayce had answered my call and helped me with my readings that day. He was known for his insight into the past lives of his clients and the wisdom he passed on regarding their life path and purpose.

A woman named Janette came to see me on this day also, she had worries over her current relationship. She had fallen in love with a married man, who was in the process of a divorce and taking steps to be with her. The process was taking its toll on her emotional wellbeing and she was seeking confirmation that they were supposed to be together. She told me that when they met, she had a deep feeling of soul recognition and wondered if they had been together in a past life. I tuned in to see what light spirit could shed on this question for her. I was taken to Mexico in my mind, where I saw a soldier going into battle. I knew that this man would not be returning home to his love and the woman who was waving him off would remain a childless spinster in grief following his passing. I was given names and dates of the solider and told her that I felt, she was the solider and the young window was the married man she had fallen in love with. She said it felt right but being a practical woman, wanted to do some research on the information I'd given her. The email received from her a few weeks later, confirmed the names and dates of a solider in Mexico. This man had risked his life to save a school of children and a small monument was erected in the village where this had occurred. She was thrilled that she was able to confirm the past life information and overjoyed that the stressful situation had some karmic reasoning.

Many occurrences that were both surprising and wonderfully reassuring occurred during my time in that little shop. It was guidance from a higher power, taking me on a magical journey of spiritualism. One such occurrence was when I approached the door of my shop there was a book on the doorstep. Since opening the store, that doorstep had become a shangri-la of mysticism and this morning did not disappoint. It was a copy of the Bhagavad Gita, to most people, this is the Hindu equivalent of the Bible. I never found out who left the book there, but I knew it was for me, perhaps it was my book angel again. The Bhagavad Gita is a wonderful book full of wisdom and spiritual insight, a book of love that I still study today.

"I'm selfish, impatient and a little insecure. I make mistakes, I am out of control and at times hard to handle. But if you can't handle me at my worst, then you sure as hell don't deserve me at my best."

~ Marilyn Monroe

21.
Meeting Emily

As I worked in my little shop in Sotogrande, filled
with books and love and gorgeous stuff... I began to
gently heal. The adult acne started to clear up
revealing smooth glowing skin, I lost weight and I
started to smile, I was becoming ME as I stepped into
service of spirit.

It was a beautiful spring day when Emily walked into
the shop. She was just over five-foot-tall, slightly
overweight with sparkly green eyes, an olive
complexion and thick, short, dark hair that was a little
too harsh for her round beautiful face and high
cheekbones. She was wearing cropped denim jeans, a
baggy t-shirt, black fabric flipflops and on her wrist
one of those fabric bracelets you find in every
souvenir shop. I also noticed a silver pendulum
necklace around her neck. She kind of bounced in,
almost comically with an air of confidence and
humour. She was selling advertising for a local
newspaper and got me to sign my life away within
minutes, but that wasn't the real reason she had
manifest in my life.

She browsed the shelves and told me that she loved
all things spiritual, was developing her psychic
abilities and believed in reincarnation. I had got pretty
used to people telling me things like this on a first
meeting by now, my shop had become an open
invitation for people to reveal all and bare their souls.
I can't remember what she said to me exactly, but she
made me laugh and I liked her instantly. That day she

bought from me the book 'Dear Fatty' by Dawn French and when she left, I found myself thinking about her.

Over the coming weeks, I started to look forward to her visits, to her sparkly green eyes and smiling face making an appearance at my door and always having me in stitches of laughter. We talked about everything, from Spain to spirituality, pendulum dowsing, wizardry and reincarnation. She even said she liked Marilyn Monroe. Although Marilyn is an icon it's not that often you meet a person who is as curious about her as I am.

She told me about her past relationship and how it had broken up badly and that she was still bruised by the repercussions of it. I plucked up the courage to ask if her ex was a man or a woman, to which she replied he was a man. I was a bit confused at that because I was sure she was gay. I had been around gay people enough in my life to be able to tell but didn't see any reason why she would be lying to me, so I just accepted it.

I saw Emily as witty and kind and she made me feel at ease. I felt that I could talk to her about anything, we seemed to have so much in common. She told me she was good at art at school, that she was creative, a psychic and a healer. She loved culture, food, champagne and had a taste for elegance and the finer things in life. She had this polished London accent that made me feel like I spoke quintessentially 'northern' and we laughed about that too.

After a couple of months, I started to get butterflies in

my stomach when she would come into the shop, I would flip my hair and laugh unnaturally at her jokes. I found myself thinking about her constantly, wondering if she would call into the shop that day and, if not, what she was doing when she wasn't around. I wondered what her life was like on the outside of our meetings, if she thought about me and if she found me equally pulchritudinous. I realised that I was starting to find her emotionally and sexually attractive but had no idea what she thought about me. This was one of those occasions when my psychic abilities were failing me. I started to do my hair, make-up and wear a nice dress just in case she came into the shop and when she didn't, I felt bitterly disappointed.

As time went on our friendship blossomed, we swapped phone numbers and started to send each other sweet but platonic text messages. Just things like "hi Em, how's it going today? Are you down this way or busy with other things, love B", replies like "hi my lovely girl, not going to get down there today but hope to see you soon? Emily". It was fun and I was becoming more and more obsessed with her visits, although I had to remind myself that she was straight and this was nothing more than a crush on my part, one that had become a slightly unhealthy infatuation, and truthfully, I told myself, it had to stop.

It was a Friday morning, a hot and sunny Spanish day when Emily appeared at the door. She was fresh-faced and chirpy as usual, and I was massively pleased to see her. I had this huge feeling of trepidation in my stomach that day and decided, perhaps she had feelings for me too? She seemed different somehow, excited to see me and looking back I think she was hoping we could be a bit more honest about how much we liked each other.

As we chatted and caught up about what we'd been doing the past week, I asked her if she fancied meeting up for a coffee the next day in Duquesa marina. She said yes immediately, and we made plans to meet in a little bar we both knew.

I was frantic that evening to be fair, wondering what to wear and what would unfold. I knew that if we stuck to coffee, I would be able to keep in these 'secret' feelings I had under wraps and all would be well. I knew that I wanted to meet up with her and get to know her a little more outside our current 'shop owner – customer' relationship but I was terrified that I was going to mess the whole thing up by confessing my feelings towards her.

I got to the bar early, hair and make-up done perfectly to look flawless, natural and like I had made no real effort at all. I chose a simple red dress which was casual enough to say, "I just woke up like this" and sexy enough to say, "I've got boobs, look". I ordered the necessary coffee and started to read a book; in fact, I couldn't read a single line because I was so nervous about meeting Emily. She texted to say she was running a bit late which just turned up the nerves even more.

When she finally arrived at about one o'clock, I noticed she was wearing mascara and a faint hint of lipstick. She had these amazingly long, natural dark eyelashes and the brightest green eyes, the mascara made them stand out and were nothing less than stunning (remember what I had written down as my ideal partner? Dark hair and green eyes). She was wearing cropped denims, her signature look, teamed with a baggy t-shirt and her regular flip flops. Her quick wit and gentle banter were out in full force, when she asked me what I wanted from the bar, the word "beer" involuntarily floated out of my mouth. She smiled and ordered two beers.

As we chatted, we shone and flirted with each other, lots of twirling of my long dark hair, laughter and blushing at my end, and this twinkly glint which oozed from Emily's face as we talked like we'd known each other all our lives. Two more beers arrived, then a bottle of red wine, then another. We were laughing and joking so loudly, all inhibitions went out of the window and I asked again if she was an openly gay woman (as she appeared to me). She then admitted that she was indeed gay (to everyone except me of course), she laughed and told me she had no idea why she felt silly telling me that when I asked her. She revealed that her male friend had fancied me, so she just stepped back.

Interestingly, I hadn't even noticed this male friend, he was practically invisible to me. I told her I was cool with it and had previously had lots of gay friends in Manchester, that Canal Street had been my old stomping ground and that I was even known to brush with the odd lesbian encounter.

When we realised we were drunk, having an amazing time and were both starving she asked if I wanted to go to her apartment and she would make some food. It seemed like a good idea. I had calmed down a lot since her arrival, the alcohol in my system had given me confidence and I was being my fun-loving self by this time.

Her apartment overlooked a golf course with a large terrace at the back and an open plan kitchen and living room. I sat at the breakfast bar watching her as she made some pasta dish and a bowl of sparse leaf salad. More wine was poured at this point; the night was still young; it was still light outside and we decided to eat on the terrace. She served me this dish of pasta and as I took a bite it was the most disgusting taste I had ever tasted; I didn't know it was possible for pasta to go so wrong. She saw my face, cracked up laughing and agreed that it was the worst thing she had ever tasted as well. She admitted that she was a pretty ghastly cook and we cried laughing; our sides ached long after we forgot what was so funny.

Moving into the living room to settle on the sofa with the wine we continued chatting away, talking about more personal and serious issues. Having one of those deeply profound moments you have when you are intoxicated with alcohol, when you exchange life stories, reveal things that make the other person feel special and bond over sad experiences in the past. Of course, I was still attached to 'my story' and all the bad times I'd had with men, I portrayed myself as the survivor (when in fact I was simply basking in my self-pity).

It was then that we kissed. A gentle, passionate and real kiss. It didn't feel like the experimentation of my youth or the bored sexual kicks of my twenty's, it felt to me like a deep soul connection. I had known all along that I had wanted this, and it didn't feel wrong or duplicitous. When we stopped kissing, we both admitted to each other how long we had been wanting that to happen. We told each other that we had felt this strong connection and sexual attraction for months but both too embarrassed to say anything. We talked about possible past life connections, it almost felt like soul recognition. We also admitted to each other, that meeting up that day outside my shop, we knew things would naturally progress and that the alcohol had given us the push we needed.

That night we slept with our arms around each other in her bed, kissing passionately but not taking things any further. I guessed she was a bit worried that I would wake up the next morning feeling like it was all a terrible mistake and that I'd drop her like a hot brick. I think she had insecurities which stemmed from past failed relationships and as we got on so well, I thought that maybe she didn't want to spoil our close friendship. There was also that fear that I was a straight woman and was 'experimenting' or using her to live out some twisted fantasy. It was not the case; my feelings were completely genuine and waking up in the morning I felt nothing but ecstatic love for her and myself. She told me that she was serious about having a relationship with me and asked for reassurance that I hadn't regretted the previous night. She also told me that sex would be something she was willing to wait for because she respected me.

Well, this is something I hadn't heard a man say to me, ever...........I liked what I heard; it made me feel safe and valued.

Things progressed and we became a couple, I wasn't shy about telling anyone I had a girlfriend and was at ease walking down the street holding hands, stealing a little kiss in public and making romantic gestures when we went out for dinner. I think that goes right back to that confidence I always had, even as a child. I never cared what people thought of me, as far as I was concerned unless I was ashamed or guilty myself, I was ok living my life the way I wanted. I told my mum that I was seeing Emily and she said she had known all along that I had feelings for her. She told me she only wanted me to be happy. Other friends accepted it completely and without judgement. Anyone that mattered just treated me the same as always. I guess I have always been blessed with great friends but I also think it shows the type of person I am, I would never befriend anyone who was homophobic or judgmental.

We had some great times together. I prepared a candlelit champagne picnic on the beach, bought her flowers and we talked for hours in the moonlight. We would have walks holding hands in private, secluded spots of natural beauty, we had wild drunken nights, dancing in the living room, jumping up and down on the sofa and singing loudly to cheesy tunes we both loved. We got dressed up for each other and went on dates, taking each other for romantic meals, buying each other a rose at the table and gazing into each other's eyes like we were the only two people in the room.

The no sex 'respect' thing only lasted a few weeks before one drunken night when we got back to Emily's apartment and ripped each other's clothes off for a passionate love-making session. It was not awkward at all, there were no expectations and I made love to her with my whole heart and a freedom I never had with a man. The old stigma of how I valued myself against the backlash of self-sabotage onset by the past experiences of sexual abuse, rape and aggression from men, simply wasn't there. I was finally, for the first time able to be free of self-judgment whilst engaging in sexual expression with another.

I can honestly say that throughout our relationship sex was the most intense and satiable I had ever experienced. She was five years my senior and had a lot more girlfriends than I'd had but I learned quickly and besides, sex has always been something that, with love in the mix, is spontaneous, passionate and totally in the moment. The relationship was filled with a freedom I had not experienced before but it was also much more than sexual gratification. It was a time of soul healing and letting go of fears. Everyone who comes into your life comes to teach you something and this time was right for us to meet. It was essentially a time when we would expose our insecurities and see the ridiculousness of them.

In the beginning, I felt supported in this relationship, Emily was a very kind person and was always looking out for me. She was considerate and loving, yet funny and carefree. We talked a lot and had very different perceptions of life, but they did not feel at that time too contrasting. We both loved art, theatre, culture, food and fine wine. We connected on a spiritual level and were both seeking more awareness in this field. We loved music, and as I had this affection for jazz, she had called her two dogs Ella and Dina after Ella Fitzgerald and Dina Washington. She wasn't a big reader so I would read to her with my head in her lap, while she marvelled at the spiritual wisdom the books contained.

I most definitely had the masculine energy in the relationship, she was gentle in her ways, I was the strong leadership energy. Being an Aries, I love to lead and ruled by Mars, God of War, relationships can be a challenge. As she allowed me to take the lead though, I think she started to lose herself slightly.

Approximately two months into our relationship, we had got out of bed after a great night out in the marina. We had woken up happy and in love and Em, as I now started to affectionally call her, made us scrambled eggs with toast and tea. Despite being the worst cook ever, she could cook scrambled eggs to perfection. We chatted over breakfast and decided to go into the marina for a walk. There was a bit of rubbish leftover from breakfast, a teabag, the empty bread wrapper and one or two other bits. She started carrying this rubbish in her hand to the door as we left her apartment. I asked her what she was doing with it and she said because of the problem with ants in the kitchen she was putting it in the bin outside. As we approached my car which was parked on the roadside, she threw the rubbish on the floor. I was flabbergasted and told her she couldn't leave the rubbish on the floor like that. What preceded was an unpredictable and dynamite-like fueled argument.

It just came so completely out of the blue. She was defending herself saying she would have moved it later because there was no dustbin and I was just saying how totally and utterly disgusted, I was with her actions. She stormed back into her apartment and I drove home, feeling completely heartbroken, tears streaming down my face.

I think this was the point when I realised dating a woman was different from dating a man. There was so much emotion involved in an argument and of course, it's an opportunity for every insecurity, every wrong word that was ever said to come out. We were both so vicious in our approach to each other, it was startling how a beautiful morning could have turned out so badly over something as trivial as rubbish. Later that day we texted each other declaring undying love for one another and saying we were sorry…. talk about drama.

Things continued pretty much this way for a few months after this first incident. We would start with great intentions, plans to do something wonderful and then boom… an argument would start with something simple. We would hurl insults at each other, say the most hurtful things and then feel bad and makeup. A vicious circle that we could have stopped with more maturity and less pride.

I started to criticize her over little things she did and said, I became judgmental and hard, she became increasingly insecure. There was a point when at my apartment, she found a book of my glamour modelling days, the book was filled with all the photos of models I had cut out at the time. Naked pictures of Pamela Anderson, bikini-clad cutouts of Marilyn Monroe, Playboy pictures of a young Kim Kardashian. The finding of these pictures in my possession triggered some deep insecurities for Emily. She mistakenly thought I fancied these women, which couldn't have been further from the truth. I wanted to BE these women. I copied them and looked up to the glamour I thought they portrayed. Nothing I said or did could reassure her that she was the girl I was in love with. She was neither a girly girl or a butch lesbian and I didn't know what type I was supposed to be attracted to. I had known many gay women and had lots of female friends all my life. Some of my friends were beautiful models but the attraction was with her, not just with any woman who walked by. I think the gay scene can be very promiscuous and she had a different perception of things than I did. She had grown in that environment and had girlfriends who were unfaithful in past relationships. My past relationships had not ended through infidelity, so I was not in touch with these insecurities she was feeling. Deep down I was just attracted to her, her magnetic personality and a feeling of spiritual connection, why didn't she know that?

She became jealous over men chatting me up, or so she said, I couldn't honestly say I got chatted up that much. The thing is I never looked gay, but Emily had lived around that part of Spain for a long time and most people knew she was gay. When we were out together most people (men specifically) assumed we were just friends. That meant I was available for flirtation and because I felt unavailable and none threatened by these male advances, I was able to relax and enjoy this conversation. This added to her insecurities and only fueled more arguments.

She grew her hair long, started wearing make-up, changed her clothes, painted her fingernails, lost a load of weight. She looked pretty but I was disturbed and frustrated by these changes. Her personality changed too; she was suddenly more serious, sullener. I started to lose my temper more quickly than at the beginning, my words were becoming crueller with each argument, the love I had initially was slipping away. The more she tried to look like one of the girls in my glamour portfolio, the less respect I could muster towards her. I think I felt like she was selling out, I had lost the raw authenticity I loved about her. I became the critic, at times I felt as though I would open my mouth and the mother of my childhood would be the one speaking.

I started drinking heavily every time we met just to get through the evenings, so I didn't have to confront or admit that things weren't working between us. She noticed obviously and complained that I was drinking too much. Of course, I was, I was trying to escape the reality of the pain that was all around me, I simply went back to my old habit of hiding behind alcohol. The relationship was bringing out the worse of me, a side of me I didn't like and someone who was buried deep inside like an evil twin or an alter ego.

Arguments seemed to become more regular, longer and we were nowhere near as eager to make up. It was becoming painfully obvious that the relationship wasn't working out and masked with the anger I felt a deep sadness.

Toward the end of the relationship we had one of the worst arguments we'd ever had, I told her I didn't want to be with her anymore. She took that badly, there were lots of tears, lots of violent words and I was angry to the point of sufferance. The whole thing was making me deeply unhappy, but I wasn't quite ready to let go and messaged her with an apology and a promise to make things work. It was very short-lived, a few weeks later we had our last blow out and it was her who finally said enough. I was relieved and knew it was time to let go. Almost a year had passed, and we were driving each other to despair.

Just because we both knew it was over, it didn't make the breakup any easier. I don't know how she was feeling at the time because we didn't see each other for a long while, but for me, it was a sad time of mixed emotions. I was heartbroken that something that started so happy, so deep and full of intense joy had ended with the heavyweight of aggression and arguments. Removed from it, though, I felt better than I had in ages.

Duquesa is a small place and your business is everybody else's business. The thing about expats in Spain is you must talk to everybody else just to find out what's going on in your own life. Rumours were flying around that I had slept with this guy and that guy, I am sure these made Emily feel like I had just tossed her to one side, but none of it was true. I couldn't even look at men in a sexual way for a long time afterwards, not until an old flame reappeared on the scene out of the blue.

I was very sure that I had always been gay at this time and really wanted to pursue a relationship with another female but I was raw from the drama of the relationship. I felt as though I was in no man's land, and that, I had decided was where I was going to stay. I would remain single and see what happened next. Throughout my life, I have always felt drawn to souls, rather than looks. Sex should be an expression of love, given through the body but coming from the soul. All my relationships, I believe, have been pure soul connections (possibly from past life experiences). It would be the last time I would ask the universe for specifics though, a learning curve to let go of control and trust the universe to deliver what is needed, not what I think I needed. Emily did have dark hair and green eyes, she was kind, creative and loved animals, she was interested in spirituality, but we were a far cry from being a perfect match.

A few months after we broke up, Emily and I met up for a beer at a beach bar. We confessed that we were both heartbroken about how things ended, and I told her various rumours about me sleeping with local men were not true. After that, we wouldn't see each other again.

Eleven years later, a Facebook message and a friend request, would eventually allow us to make peace with each other, laugh off some of the disastrous aspects of our relationship and form a firm friendship.

"If you prefer blindness, keep your eyes closed. If you prefer deafness keep your ears closed. But if you are wise, you will open the windows of your soul so that you can become aware of that mighty, vast power of the spirit."

~ Silver Birch

22.
Churches, Circles and Guides

Life continued in Sotogrande, the business got bigger and it was necessary to move into bigger premises. My mother and I decided to take on new, larger premises and share it between the two businesses. We combined my mind, body, spirit shop and my mother's clothing alterations business. We found a beautifully located shop next to the beach just outside Sotogrande. This gave us the space we needed to host all kinds of events. We created ladies afternoon tea parties, cheese and wine evenings and holistic workshops where we would invite various people to talk about their practices such as crystal ball readings, Ayurveda, sound therapy and aura photography. We hosted mind, body and spirit fairs and created a spiritual community where there had previously been none.

I was contacting my guides daily and the native American chief was getting closer and stronger. Samsara seemed to be stepping back a little. During meditations, I would see and converse with the legendary medium Doris Stokes who I felt had come to help me believe in myself. I had been calling my native American guide, William for over a year when one day during meditation I got the name, Red Hawk. It sounded more fitting to me, and I 'googled it' afterwards. The google search revealed that the Native American Indians which wore the red-tailed hawk feathers were the spiritual communicators in the village, the belief was that "the red-tailed hawk flew so high that it dipped in and out of the spirit world". It was fascinating! I asked Red Hawk for some confirmation, that it was his actual name. It was Halloween, mum and I decided to go shopping for costumes as we had been invited to a party at a big hotel in Gibraltar with Jo and some others from the recruitment agency.

We walked into Eroski, which is a supermarket that sells pretty much anything you could think of. Browsing the isles for Halloween paraphernalia, I was stopped in my tracks by a very large box, about a meter cubed falling off the top shelf. As it tumbled down and landed at my feet, out fell hundreds of red feather boas. I knew in my heart this was synchronicity at its best, it was a message from Red Hawk that he was indeed happy for me to refer to him by that name 'Red Hawk', and that he was guiding me.

After that, I started to immerse fully in the presence of my guide. We chatted both in meditation and in everyday life, I asked questions about spiritual matters and the development of my mediumship. He guided me and directed me in my readings. I found him often amused by my questions and sometimes would answer me in riddles, encouraging me to think things through, rather than just ask him. He told me I was to start a development circle and he would guide me. "But I don't know what I will teach!" I protested, "trust me" he answered, in his usual amused manner. His requests seemed to get more bizarre when I heard "open a spiritualist church here in Spain", "but how?" I asked again, his reply was always the same, "trust me". I got it; he was teaching me to trust in a higher spiritual power.

The first spiritualist church meeting was a huge success with over forty attendees. Since I had no experience demonstrating mediumship at that time, I hired a local medium to take the service and I chaired. I held it like a traditional service back home in the UK, with prayers, music and mediumship by the medium of the evening. It was so well received that I started to hold this every month with a variety of local mediums stepping forward to take the services. We took donations and gave them to the medium of the evening in return for their work. I was so glad I had trusted Red Hawk with his amazing ideas and knew it was helping the people who came, the healing power of spirit would touch their lives.

I was sat at my desk soon after the first few successful church services when the phone rang. It was a man's voice and he sounded English, "hi, I'm calling from Psychic News in the UK, I hear you've been running church services in Spain and we would like to run an article on you", I stammered a moment. I had been reading psychic news for years and thought of it as a true spiritualist publication. My heart was beating as I asked, "how did you hear about the church services?", his reply amused me, "we know everything here at Psychic News". The article was written and published the following month. We mentioned in the article that I needed more mediums to take services and my email address was detailed for anyone to get in touch with me. I was inundated with emails from mediums offering to fly out and take the service and do some private readings in the shop. I also received a lovely email from the author

Jacky Newcombe, who had written books about connecting with angels, books which I stocked in the shop. The email was wishing me lots of luck and success with The Book Angel and church services. I was so surprised and grateful for the email not just from Jacky but from the many other spiritualists from all over the UK.

So began my exciting journey of meeting many mediums, watching them demonstrate and bringing people together in such a wonderful loving way. The church services were proving very popular and they were always packed to the rafters. Sometimes I had to tell people to bring a chair with them because we didn't have enough.

The circle was also evolving. I had had no formal training in either psychic/mediumship unfoldment or in teaching people, but it just flowed under the direction of Red Hawk, who I listened to intently, I too was learning so much. We always started each circle evening with a meditation to connect to spirit and our guides, it would be during the meditation that Red Hawk would reveal much of what we were about to do. We tried many different activities in the circle, including ribbon readings, psychometry, past life regression, card readings, spirit communication, etc. I never knew what we were going to do from one week to the next, I trusted Red Hawk emphatically to guide me in these sessions. Everyone loved them and I had a strong core of around fifteen attendees every week.

Through this circle, I think my mediumship started to get stronger and I was extremely busy with private sittings. In my private sittings, I would see the clients past and present and would predict the future with accuracy. Loved ones from the spirit world would come through and I would give evidence from them, at this time, the information was good and natural but my ability to see detail and understand the communication thoroughly would come later. I also was learning about customers and how their reactions were sometimes difficult, that you could never quite know who was going to walk through the door.

"We need to teach people how to receive messages"
~ Gordon Higginson.

I had a lady who came to see me at the shop, called Margaret, she was in her early fifties, and was brought in by a gentleman who I had met a few weeks earlier. This gentleman was very flirtatious, a lady's man who was extremely tactile with all the females at the event. We hosted a cheese and wine party and he had attended, introducing himself as a 'great healer'. I was sceptical and kept a safe distance as he talked endlessly about his healing 'gifts'. As I watched him, I became aware that I was seeing a figure of a lady dressed in blue stood next to him, this spirit figure seemed to be holding a bowl which contained what I recognised to be a set of African fortune-telling bones. I heard the name, Mary. When I explained what I was seeing, he seemed quite alarmed but told me he had grown up in Africa where 'bone readings' were extremely common and that he'd had many of these readings himself. He also told me his mother's name was Mary and her favourite colour was blue. The spirit figured nodded and told me that he was indeed a talented healer. Well, that shut me up! It also taught me to be much less judgmental.

So, Margaret came in this day for a reading. As she sat down, she was nervy and seemed unable to sit still. She was well dressed and had a clear, well-spoken, neutral accent but, immediately I could feel she was unhappy. I told her so, I said "you have suffered bereavements you simply can't overcome", I was aware that her Mother and Father were both in the spirit world. As the reading continued, she confirmed what I was saying to be correct, I told her "you are being sent healing to move forward in your life because you have many years left on the earth plane. I can see much happiness for you in the future", at this last comment she stood up violently and shrieked "oh you horrible, cruel woman, how could you say such a thing?" I was shocked because, in my mind, this was good news. She continued, "I don't want to live, I want to die, I want to be back with my Mother and Father, I was hoping you were going to tell me I was going to die soon!", with that she fled the room without paying.

Another time when I had an unhappy customer is when a young woman came to see me, she must have been in her late twenties. As I started, very little was coming through, but I told her I was aware of a picture being shown to me, like a cartoon image of a devil. I felt that it was a gentleman who was showing me this, I also could see a red love heart, also being shown as a drawing. I know she wanted more, but with this particular communication, nothing more seemed to be coming. She told me her late husband of only one year, had a tattoo of the Tasmanian devil with a red heart by the side of it on his chest. This was the reason she had come, to speak to her late husband, as they had only been married one year before he passed away suddenly. I then told her "your father is here; he wants to say sorry". She was not happy about this at all and recoiled "please tell him to go away, I was not interested in anything he had to say when he was alive, and I am not interested in anything he has to say now!". She was in floods of tears by this time and I was unable to calm her down, she paid me but said she didn't want to go on any further. It was a learning curve for me and taught me to be stronger in my readings, to explain to people that I was simply the messenger and could not control who or why certain people came through to us.

One particularly hot August day, a lady came into the shop for a reading. She was very well to do, dressed in expensive designer clothes with a shrill, plummy voice. She wore a crucifix around her neck and told me that she was a healer and medium, but that she only worked with Jesus. To be honest, I wasn't sure if she was genuine or quite mad, but I was about to find out. As it was such a hot day, I took a cup of water from our water machine and sat opposite her. As I read for her, I drank all my water quickly, she noticed my cup was empty and offered me some coke a cola from a can she had brought in with her, I politely declined, explaining I only drank water during readings. We continued for a few moments when I looked at the cup and noticed it was now full to the brim with water. I looked at her, she looked at me, we were both gobsmacked because it was empty a few moments ago. She proclaimed it was her spirit guide

Jesus, who was with us, performing miracles. I laughed then and said "great, can he turn it into wine!", "certainly not!" She exclaimed.

As my information became clearer, so did my future predictions. One reading that I remember was when a local lady came for a reading and I could see a move overseas with her husband. I told her that she would be going to the hospital for some tests but that everything would be alright eventually, I said I saw her living in Dubai. She said there must be some mistake because her husband had got a job in Bermuda, she was travelling to the UK to see family and then, meeting him in Bermuda in a couple of weeks. I told her "I don't see you in Bermuda, I'm sure its Dubai". She left a little sceptical and confused. I didn't worry about the reading because I trusted what I was getting and felt I had done my job to the best of my ability.

Approximately one year later I received an email from this same women explaining, she had returned to the UK to see family and had received a letter from the hospital at her family home. The letter said that her last tests revealed something was wrong and would she make an appointment as soon as possible. She did so, and it turned out she had breast cancer and would have to stay in the UK for the next six to eight months for treatment. She completed her treatment and got the all-clear which was great news.

Meanwhile, her husband had started the job in Bermuda but had hated it, left and they were now both fully settled in Dubai. A lesson I learned in trust,

I never question what I am getting, even if the sitter thinks I'm barmy.

Another occasion when the information was not revealed until later was when I was doing a reading for a woman and I saw clearly an elderly gentleman falling out of bed, hitting his head and passing to spirit. I explained that the bed was a hospital bed, so this gentleman would not be well at the time of the fall, I also felt that although this was not a close relative, it would have an impact on the woman's life. I told her I could see money being left in a will. She told me she had absolutely no idea who this could be, as both her father and father-in-law had already passed and there were no other elderly gentlemen around her, certainly no one who was in the hospital, or that would leave her money in their will. She was on holiday and made a point of seeing me whenever she came to Sotogrande. The next time she visited she told me that my predication had been spot on! Her ex-husband's father who had been ill in hospital fell out of bed and hit his head on the bedside cabinet, causing him to pass to spirit on impact. She said, as he was my ex-father-in-law, I didn't think about him at all. However, her ex-husband and she had a daughter together, so the gentleman was her daughter's granddad, he had left her daughter a considerable amount of money in his will.

During the development circle on a Tuesday evening, I would experiment with all kinds of spiritual activity. One evening we explored past lives. I had read many books on past lives from a very young age, starting with Shirley MacLaine and Edgar Cayce at the age of fifteen and later reading the work of Dr Brian Weiss, my favourite being 'Only Love Is Real'. In this development class, we discussed past lives a little before doing a guided meditation by Dr Brian Weiss. I played a past life regression CD to take us into a state of regression. Afterwards, we would pair off and attempt some psychic past life readings. I was astonished when I saw myself as a jazz singer in the deep south of America. Picking cotton by day and singing by night, as some way to lighten the load of the horrific conditions we were living in. I was a young black woman who had been dragged from her home in Africa, shackled by my ankles and wrist and sold to a cotton plantation. I remembered my name was Rose. This name was a name given to me by the other slaves who lived on the plantation. I saw vividly a black male being hoisted up onto a pole, he looked half dead and was bleeding. I knew he had tried to run away, I felt as though I had loved him, my heart was breaking. The vision was so vivid to me. In my life, I not only had I always loved jazz music, but I had a deep-seated propensity towards the south of American. If I watched something on TV like Roots or North and South, it always gave me a sense of intense sadness. It felt so real to me and I would later explore past lives in a much bigger way; learning past live regression therapy and studying Buddhism.

Things were going well at this point and I had, through the practice of meditation, advanced both my mediumship and psychic awareness. I also started to invest more time in my wellbeing, I read a book by Jason Vale about juicing, in additional to The China Study by T.Colin Campbell, which inspired me to turn vegan. I indulged in a variety of smoothies, some that tasted horrific and some that tasted wonderful. My eyes started to shine brightly, I had more energy and lost weight. Since gaining the weight in Didsbury I had lost quite a lot but was now more like a size UK 12, rather than the size 8 to 10 of previous years. However, with the new vegan diet, I felt glowing and lighter. I also thought that the diet would assist my mediumship (something I now know to be completely untrue).

One evening in the late summer I was sat with my development circle; we were doing our thing. The door was locked but a tall, male figure seemed to be peering in through the window. It was Ben. I was completely floored, surprised to see him and also very happy. As always, I felt butterflies and palpations run through my torso, that familiar feeling of love that came only in his presence.

After the circle ended, we went to the bar next door for a drink and a catch-up. "How on earth did you find me?" I quizzed. Ben explained that he had broken up with his long-term girlfriend, as promised, he had come to find me. He had asked around the village and friends had said told him my mother and I were living in Sotogrande. Sotogrande is quite a big place, he had walked around all day asking if anyone knew of a dressmaker and a psychic who were mother and daughter, with no joy. He had given up and sat on a bench outside our shop before intending on heading home. As he looked up, he saw the sign 'psychic readings' in the shop window and he knew it was us.

I told him he could stay with me, as nice as it was to think he had come looking for me, I also suspected he had nowhere to stay. I had a two bedroomed apartment so offered him the spare room, because at that point, I didn't know whether it was a romantic arrangement or a friendship.

When we got home, we cracked open a bottle of wine and played Billie Holiday tunes, reminiscent of our time together almost four years earlier. We talked again, effortlessly, he told me about the breakdown of his relationship and the many arguments which finally ended things, he planned to get a job and move somewhere in Spain, he said: "if you'll have me, I'll move here". At one time it was everything I could have wished for, so I said I was happy to give it a whirl. And, just like that, I was in a new relationship, one I had given up on years ago. It was completely unexpected but, in fact, a few weeks earlier, I'd had a premonition of Ben walking through the door.

We made love then and it was a crazy feeling of years' worth of pent up passion, the release of unrequited love and a reunion of souls from a previous lifetime. I suspected that on a soul level, our love was unrequited in a past life, but in this lifetime, we were determined to find a way. There was just something between us that felt like we were supposed to meet and clear.

Ben got a job as a builder for a local company and things seemed to be going well. It was hard work in the searing heat and he often came home head to toe in mud. I felt sorry for him working these awful, long hours for crap money so tried to make his life as easy as possible by making him packed lunches, running him scented baths and preparing him a hearty meal for when he got home from work. In the evenings, we would drink red wine, listen to jazz and blues music and talk about anything and everything. His humour was infectious, he can walk into any room or any bar and have the whole place focused completely on him, having everyone laughing and engaged in his conversation. He was tall, over 6ft, with dark skin and features inherited from his English mother, and father who was born in St Kitts in the Caribbean. When he would shave and dress in white linen and Jesus sandals, he had me going weak at the knees, and every other woman within a mile radius. I did get a little jealous when other women looked at him, but I knew from experience that he wasn't the unfaithful type, so I just chilled out and enjoyed the moment. We were falling more deeply in love with every moment; however, I was very aware that the two of us were born only a few days apart. The 7th and 12th of April were both under the fiery rule of Mars. So, if there was an argument, it was like world war three had broken out. We both agreed that no-one, in our lives, had ever stirred so much passion or anger in each other.

There were about six months when things went without any problems whatsoever. Ben and I were getting on great most of the time, the shop was busy, business was booming, and the long summer days provided a backdrop of relaxation and fun. Days were filled with work, readings, church meetings and psychic development, whilst weekends were a mix of beach parties, meals out and lazing by the pool.

Ben was getting fed up of the long hours, hard work and shitty wages, he had seen an opportunity to buy a fish and chip shop in the marina where we lived.

Unfortunately, this meant borrowing some money against the house he'd built in Antequera and needed to go and speak to his ex-girlfriend about it, as her signature would be required. He set off on the Friday, saying he would be returning on Sunday to get back to work for Monday morning. Sunday night came and he didn't show. Monday morning and he still wasn't back. I was worried and called him a hundred times, eventually, he answered and said he had some things to sort and would be back soon.

He eventually arrived back on Thursday, saying his ex-girlfriend had refused to help him and he had been asking if any other friends could help him out with the money to buy the fish and chip business. He was down, I could tell but he also seemed irritated, on edge and not himself. I asked him when he was going back to work, and he told me that he'd lost his job because he didn't come back on Sunday. I wasn't massively worried because I felt he would find another job but if I tried to talk to him about things, he just snapped at me, saying "nobody tells me what to do".

For the next few weeks, he just sat around all day drinking, talking to the security guards on the complex and bumming around. He asked me for money for phone credit and cigarettes, money that I gave him begrudgingly. One night I came home, and I could smell cannabis. I confronted him and he admitted he had smoked it whilst back in Antequera. We had talked about this in the past and it was not good news. Previously, he'd had an addiction to cannabis and had told me it had an adverse effect on him, making him moody, aggressive and depressed. I think the whole 'chip shop' thing had taken him into a downward spiral of defeat and self-sabotage.

I tried everything I could to help him, but he is a strong, independent man who didn't want help. He wanted to help himself, to be in control of his own life and taking handouts from me was not making him feel any better. My mum had always liked Ben and had a major soft spot for him, you couldn't help it really, he had one of those magnetic personalities. However, she was getting increasingly cross with me for keep giving him money and all my energy. I was arguing with mum at work and then arguing with Ben when I got home. Something had to give, and it did.

I came home one day, and Ben was there waiting for me, he said he was going to Malaga to see about some work, could I lend him some money? I knew in my heart he wasn't coming back, so did he. I willed it not to be true but just as I had felt, he did not return.

This is a relationship that has been left open-ended. I have spoken to him three times, the last one was calmer in that we said, one day we will meet again. I believe that to be true, if not in this life, then the next, maybe one day we will get it right.

Just like after every heartbreak I got drunk, cried, felt down but then brushed myself off and started again. It did hit me hard though, I felt loss and grief. There was something about Ben which seemed to hit harder than any other relationship, both times. With Imran, it was a slow, gradual process which was easier in many respects. Emily had been a lost cause which needed to end for our sanity, but with Ben, I felt as though the love was there, even if the circumstances were not.

I got drunk so many times after Ben left, one night I also took a packet of paracetamol and codeine. I was happy to leave the earth plane at that moment and washed them down with four bottles of wine, I felt sure it was the end. To my disbelief, I woke up the next morning with nothing more than feeling a bit sick. I realised then that the angels were not going to let me go back. I had to sort myself out and carry on. I decided to stop drinking alcohol, get back into my health kick and join a gym. I had a vision of my grandad Joe that morning. He told me I had to stop drinking and that I had to get on with the work that spirit had planned for me.

So, I slotted back into the life I had before Ben arrived, it was like he'd never been there. I got up for work, went to the shop, did my readings, meditated, talked to Red Hawk and occasionally Samsara and taught in my development circle.

However, I started to get despondent and had little enthusiasm for anything. I told my mum I felt like I'd had enough of Spain and wanted to go back to England permanently. I had no idea how this was going to happen, but I felt I needed more. I had read online about a school in England called the Arthur Findlay College, which trained mediums and healers.

I longed to demonstrate in the spiritualist churches and wanted to gain more experience in all aspects of spiritualism. I felt it was time to find some human teachers, Red Hawk is a fine teacher and I trust him explicitly, but I felt I wanted to expand my knowledge, spread my wings and fly with a different group of angels. By this time, I had learned that the law of attraction worked a bit like this: ask, trust, wait without expectation, watch the magic happen.

One day on the treadmill at the gym, Pat Merna appeared to me, in a white dinner suit. I looked around and realised I was all alone, said "hi Pat, what brings you here?", he smiled and said, "go back to England kid", then he was gone. I knew I was going to be ok then. I had a vivid dream that night, my old school friend Adrian who had passed away from jumping of the top of a fortieth-floor hotel in Mexico, came to visit. In the dream he was driving a red Ferrari, opening the passenger door, he said "get in", which I obeyed. As I sat next to him, I couldn't help noticing how happy and vibrant Adrian looked, he told me I was going to be ok. I woke up then, but it had felt incredibly real, I knew it was a message. These visitations from spirit confirmed to me that everything would happen when it was supposed to.

One of the mediums who had taken the church service had said to remember the 19th of April, as it would become a significant date. I had no idea what to expect but kept it in mind.

I was sat at my desk in the shop and the phone rang, it was a recruitment agency who had found my C.V. on the job search site, Monster. He introduced himself as Wayne and said he was the manager of a recruitment agency in Sale, Cheshire. He was looking for someone to join his team, was I interested? "oh, no sorry, I don't live in the UK anymore" I replied, and after thanking him, I put the phone down. My mum said to me, "that call was sent to you from the angels, it's your ticket back to England", "oh, yeah!" I thought as I called him back.

I got the job, with a start date of, you guessed it, 19th of April. I rented a two-bed apartment, a tram stop away from the job and persuaded mum to shut up shop and come back with me. I honestly felt she could make a better living back in the UK. Life in Spain is hard with so many taxes to pay and we were working all the hours in the day, with very little return.

We boarded the plane from Gibraltar airport, Charlotte would follow on a plane from Malaga in a few months and the next adventure was about to begin.

"Mediumship is a diamond with many facets"

~ Glyn Edwards

24.
The Arthur Findley College

As I drove up to Stansted Hall and parked in the car park for the first time, I was so excited, I could hardly breathe. It was a sunny but chilly February afternoon and the sun shone through the large trees, creating a pattern on the roof. The building looked like it could talk, it was like Hogwarts for mediums. The gardens which surrounded it, full of huge old trees that looked like they would walk over and shake your hand. There was a beautiful ornate door which was signposted reception. I decided I would check in before getting my suitcase out of the boot.

I had saved up and waited for this moment since the plane had hit the tarmac in Manchester. I had no idea which course to pick or who any of the tutors were. I had never heard of any of the teachers there, so this course was picked at random. It was a course organised by a gentleman named Glyn Edwards, and, at that time, I had no idea how this man and this college was about to change my life forever.

I had opted to share a room with a stranger and was nervous about this experience. I trusted in the spirits to give me someone nice and I was not wrong. My roommate for the week was a Dutch girl called Monica. She was already in the room when I arrived and was shy but friendly. We were told to meet downstairs in the Sanctuary, which I was to discover was the part of Stansted Hall that is used for church services twice a week. We had a couple of hours before we had to make our way there, so I just got lost in the great walls, adorned by old paintings of people I had never heard of. Just by my room, there was a glass-encased museum that seemed to house all kinds of things; old books, photographs and inanimate objects that I had no idea about. There was a beautiful sweeping staircase, with a thick banister, oak panels were everywhere you looked, long glass windows which were framed by heavy velvet curtains of different colours around the building, windows looked out onto expertly tended gardens and there were various shapes, sizes and colours of chairs and tables scattered randomly in every nook and cranny. As I looked around, I saw antiques of all different objects on shelves, attached to the walls and stood at doors that were as big as oak trees. It's distinctly Victorian in its splendour but is also steeped in much more history than just the Victorian era.

As I strolled down the grand staircase, there seemed to be hundreds of people milling around. There was a young male, with long dark hair and twinkly brown eyes sat in an armchair. His dress was unkempt, he was wearing a thick jumper and his hair needed a wash. He grabbed my attention immediately and I made a beeline to speak to him. Unfortunately, I got collared by a loud American guy, and someone sat in the empty chair next to the boy with the twinkly eyes.

When we did eventually get to sit next to each other, I looked at him and thought, *hmmmm, he looks like a homeless person.* I asked him, "so what's your day job?", he replied in a very London accent "well, I know I look like a homeless person, but I'm an actor", my jaw dropped, and I told him I had just thought that very *thing* about him. We laughed and chatted away like old friends. I knew he was gay immediately, so there was no sexual attraction, (by now my inbuilt gaydar was well and truly in place) but I knew one of the reasons I had chosen this course out of over sixty was to meet Kyle.

We made our way to the Sanctuary together and sat right at the very front. I had no idea what to expect from the week and had no direction about spirit from anyone other than Red Hawk. When Glyn Edwards took the platform to speak, there was a spiritual presence with this man I had never seen before. He introduced himself and spoke so beautifully, lovingly and wholeheartedly about spirit, I was completely taken in by him. The other tutors spoke one by one after him, there was Matthew Smith, Sandie Baker, Eileen Davies, Maureen Mernan and Kitty Woud. We were instructed to listen to each tutor and write down on our sheets who we felt drawn to. The next morning, we would find out which group we would be joining. I wanted Glyn but so did everyone in the room (over a hundred people), but if I was being really honest with myself I felt most drawn to Kitty. So, I guess it was no coincidence that I was placed in Kitty's group.

At mealtimes, you are instructed to sit in the same seat for the whole week. Kyle and I chose a table which had five visitors all from the states. Four girls who had travelled together from Salem and Kevin from Philadelphia. Mealtimes were extremely funny, loud and memorable.

There is a bar where you can buy alcoholic drink after 9 pm, I had decided not to drink this week and to concentrate fully in my mediumship. Kyle said he agreed and so we socialised in the bar after hours but decided to abstain from drinking that week.

The first morning, after breakfast, we were told to join our groups for the first session. I was nervous and excited; I didn't expect so many different ages or nationalities to be there and marvelled around the room as everyone sat in a semi-circle facing Kitty. We were in a room called The Blue Room, which was decorated in traditional stately manor house attire, with ornate chairs and beautiful paintings of interesting but unknown characters on the walls. Kitty was elegant, attractive and direct but gentle with her teaching.

During the week, we all stood in the middle of the semi-circle to demonstrate mediumship and give messages from spirit. There were blindfolded messages, messages where you had to form a double link with another medium, and messages where you had to get two links on your own. I had no idea that there were so many amazing things you could do in a demonstration. When it was my turn, I was super nervous, but at the same time, I had been waiting for this moment all my life. To my astonishment and excitement, it flowed, and the information understood.

When we weren't in our groups there were so many different activities, it made my head spin. Glyn taught us a wonderful meditation called Sitting in the Power, a meditation which we all did together in the morning ready to start the day, he also had sessions where he would simply talk about spirit and the 'unlimited potential of mediumship'. There were workshops about private sittings, shamanism, healing and trance mediumship. We learned about the phenomena of physical mediumship and sat in a physical séance with Scott Milligan.

There was also an opportunity to have a private 'spiritual assessment' with one of the tutors, this is where the spirit world gave communication regarding your development and mediumship. When I went to reception to book, there were only a few slots left with Maureen, so I booked, feeling like she was the right person to do the reading. Interestingly it was Maureen who took the shamanic workshop. When I sat down in front of her, she said to me "you have a powerful Native American Indian guide with a beautiful red feathered headdress, he tells me his name is Red Hawk", well, I nearly fell off my chair. She told me that Red Hawk had been waiting for this moment for all my life and was eager to get going with my mediumship. It was just the confirmation I needed to follow my path of mediumship. Since my return to Manchester things had not been easy, getting back into recruitment had been a disaster and I had resigned myself to full-time readings once again. It was a powerful reading and one that I will not forget, I needed to hear that Red Hawk was pleased I was finally getting some training in the physical world. He must have been worn out with me! Thinking *thank goodness I can have a bit of a rest while she's at the college.*

The week opened up my eyes to a completely new facet of spiritualism, the history of mediumship in the UK and the pioneers who worked so hard to gain its acceptance. Demonstrating mediumship opened new doors for me and Kitty read some wonderful philosophy at the start of each session. I was a changed person as I learned how to *sit in the power* of spirit and build up my power for the purpose of mediumship. Sitting in the power is a form of meditation that was given to the world by spirit through the mediumship of Mark Webb. Mark Webb then asked Glyn to explore the possibilities of the power and it became his baby. It would change my mediumship, my connection with my own spirit and in turn, my life. Glyn told us that spirituality *was developing a relationship with your own spirit* (something I had never heard before) and Eileen Davies said that the best mediums worked on their spiritual self as well as their mediumship.

At Stansted Hall, there are two church services held on Wednesday's and Sunday's, these are traditional church services that are open to the public and attendees of the college. The tutors took turns demonstrating and I was ill-prepared for the standard of mediumship that I would witness there. I was dumbfounded as I watched Eileen Davies give fast, accurate, specific evidential messages to members of the congregation. I observed trance mediumship by Glyn Edwards which was both empowering and entertaining, and some of the most accurate messages I had ever heard from the other tutors. Having encountered mediumship often during my life, this standard, inspired me to push my communication to new heights. I remembered Mrs Alexander and her incredible message she had given me at just thirteen years old. I had not seen or heard mediumship as accurate until I had attended the Arthur Findley College.

This was one of the best weeks of my entire life, your first visit to The Arthur Findley College can never be repeated, it's a special time when doors open and pull you into new realms of awareness. I have since been back to the Arthur Findley College, each time is unique and magical but the first time and meeting Glyn, who made is transition soon after, holds a special place in my heart. I had always known that spirit was real, that they had been teaching me, guiding me and calling my name for many years, but I had not known how much time I had misspent drinking, feeling sad and squandering my time on relationships that would never serve me. I realised there was valuable spirit work to be done, healing and being of service to the world. I was finally ready to step into those big shoes and serve spirit.

On the last night, Kyle and I decided we had worked hard and would join the others for an alcoholic drink. We danced to the 'Grease Megamix', partied to cheesy tunes and got drunk in a happiness that was mixed with sadness as we realised the week had ended far too quickly. We all swapped numbers took photographs and hooked up on social media. Kyle and I hugged as we parted, he was going back to London and I had a long drive back to Cheshire, we promised to keep in touch and made good of that promise, speaking to each other almost every day for the next seven years.

"Spirit communication would roll like a mighty flood across the world; it would be a period of steady growth and development"

~ Emma Hardinge Britten

25.
Stepping Into Service

On my arrival back from the Arthur Findley College, I was so excited to get going, having been motivated to work for spirit and had so much confirmation of all those who were guiding me. I had messages from Pat and my grandad almost every day whilst I was there. I even got the most amazing communication from my mothers' great grandfather who invented the bobbin for the cotton mills.

I got to work immediately contacting the spiritualist churches and letting them know I was available for bookings and was booked by several churches in the North of England, I figured that if spirit wanted me to work the opportunities would come and I would be supported. I was approached to do readings at a local mind, body, spirit fair and set up a weekly development circle again, but this time I felt I had more to teach.

My first time taking a church service was a daunting prospect. It was in Nottingham, quite a drive but I figured if I flunked, no one would know me anyway. Most people sit in a circle in a local spiritualist church and then get up on the platform for the first time with a more experienced medium, however, I had never done anything traditionally before in my life, and I wasn't about to start now. The booking secretary had told me that it was a divine service so I would do the opening prayer and then give some philosophy, then forty minutes of mediumship, followed by a closing prayer. *Right,* I thought, *this can't be difficult after all I had chaired enough church services in Spain.*

My mum had come with me and was waiting in the main hall while I was ushered into a small meditation room. As I sat there, *I thought shit, what on earth was I doing? Was I completely insane?* I called upon Mrs Alexander then, I said to her in my mind "come on Mrs Alexander, you got me into this mess, making that prediction all those years ago", just at that moment, the radio started playing 'Lean On Me' by Bill Withers. I knew it was a message from Mrs Alexander, not just to lean on her for support but the memory of her leaning on her Zimmer frame in that church demonstration all those years ago. I felt a sense of calm come over me. As I went out for my first ever church demonstration, I felt confident and unflappable. The information came easily with names, descriptions and messages that were understood. Spirit was kind and held my hand.

After this, I got booked for more services in and around Manchester, Bolton, Stockport and Blackpool. I always got a bit nervous before I went on and prayed that the spirits would be with me, which they always were, but it took a little time to step into the energy and enjoy it, in those early days.

The stock from my shop in Spain had arrived in the UK, as had the cat, and I opened a small room in my mother's sewing business on the main road in Altrincham, Cheshire. It was tiny but adequate, I had shelves full of lovely books and a few gift sets which surrounded a table and two chairs where I would do my readings. The development circle would be held in the main sewing room. I put two cards in the window of the local post office, one said 'Psychic and mediumship readings' and the other said 'Psychic development circle, every Tuesday 7-9 pm'. People called, people came, and word spread. I worked around the clock doing private readings, teaching and demonstrating in churches and at mind, body, spirit fairs. Most of the fairs had their regular readers so I was unable to get a table doing readings. In the end, I just had a stall selling books and did a demonstration of mediumship instead. These dem's were always packed to the rafters and I felt they were more beneficial and used up less energy anyway. After the demonstration people always wanted to book in for a private sitting.

I had invited Kyle to come down and take my development circle as a guest teacher and he agreed to come and stay for a whole week. I was sharing a tiny house with my Mum at this time, but she had taken a trip to Australia to see a friend which meant Kyle could have her room. He travelled down on the mega bus from London and was arriving at Manchester City Centre bus station, I was to pick him up in the car from there. When he arrived, as we passed Manchester Arndale Centre, I turned to Kyle and stated, "this is Manchester's famous fish market". I had no idea what had made me say that because it was not famous at all! Kyle laughed then and told me he had asked his spirit guide on the way up, "can you give me a sign as to whether this is right for me?", he said he was shown a vision of Billingsgate Fish Market in London, a place he knew well. It was an ambiguous message and one that he didn't understand until that strange statement about Manchester's famous fish market rolled off my tongue.

He was intelligent, witty and charismatic during the development class and they all loved him. He not only offered them some wisdom I had not but also demonstrated his mediumship to a high standard. The rest of the week was work free and I took him out to see Manchester's gay scene on Canal Street, to a local a jazz bar in Altrincham and a country pub in Hale. We stayed in watching Julia Davies' comic genius Nighty Night and laughed until our side's aches. He was my spiritual 'go-to' person at this time and we discussed all different elements of spirit till the early hours, both on his visit and when he returned to London.

My mediumship was getting stronger and I was aware that spirit was teaching me new methods of communication. I was sitting in the power every day and reading about the pioneers like Gordon Higginson, Estelle Roberts, Helen Duncan and Harry Edwards, I was also studying work from the communication of Silver Birch and books by Arthur Conan Doyle and Sir Arthur Findley. It was a magical time of self-discovery and spirit brought such love and peace into my life. I was asked to do a radio show broadcasted across the USA, and Skype readings in American, Australia and Ireland. I was learning that spirit was not limited by time and space but transcendent throughout our physical world.

One Irish client had asked me to do Skype development training with her, I wasn't sure how this was going to work but as always, I decided that if spirit brought it to me, they would take me through it. So, I agreed and started the Skype training sessions.

A few weeks earlier I had done a reading for a young married woman who wanted to know if she would leave her husband and be with her lover. I told her I couldn't see this happening and felt that she would stay with her husband and have a child. She seemed disappointed and sad at what I told her, but I could only give it to her the way I saw it happening.

Midway through the Skype session the internet completely lost connection and I couldn't seem to get it back. This was followed by a frantic banging on the door, when I opened it, I recognised the young woman who had been the previous week. She was in tears and I asked her to sit down. The communication came in thick and fast from a young man who had taken his own life, just days before. He gave her evidence of survival and a message of love. It was sadly, the lover who she had expected to be leaving her husband for. Not only had he interrupted my internet connection, but he communicated days after his passing. I saw both, as a miracle that had occurred due to their true love connection.

I was aware that spirit was experimenting with me. A lady came to see me for a reading and I started to feel bigger in my body, not literally but my arms and legs felt longer and heavier, my feet and hands bigger. I was aware of a male presence blending with me and all of a sudden, involuntarily started to speak to her, "Hi Rebecca, its Dad here" I heard myself say. This wasn't in a trance state, it was in my voice, it felt more like I was channelling her father's message. He went on to talk about various family members and business affairs. I just sat back and allowed this to happen, I had not experienced anything like this before but trusted spirit completely. I knew they were experimenting, guiding and teaching me. I don't know who was more shocked me or my client, but it was a wonderful communication with lots of evidence. Afterwards, I asked her if her father was the type of person who likes a challenge and to try new things (this was certainly new to me). She told me her father was a powerful businessman who thrived on taking chances and loved a challenge.

Around this time, I gave a reading from a grandfather to his granddaughter, I became distinctly aware of a taste in my mouth which I recognised to be a humbug. When I conveyed this to the girl, she told me that they bought her grandfather a jar of humbugs every year for Christmas, for as long as she could remember. Had I not known what a humbug tasted like I couldn't have told her what it was. Spirit are so intelligent; they know exactly what the medium will understand, and they were showing me various ways of communicating. Not a day goes by when spirit does not amaze, inspire or intrigue me to move forward and be better.

When I arrived back in the UK I went to the doctors to get checked out because my energy levels were low and had gained some weight. I was still following a vegan diet but had started to drink alcohol. It was different though; I had made my peace with alcohol. I had let go of using alcohol as a self-sabotage tool. In the past I had felt like I couldn't let go of alcohol because it was my friend, (my false friend of course), when I abstained completely I felt like it still had a hold on my life, laughing in my face, telling me it would always be the temptation I'd dread. So, I just let go, I trusted in a higher power to support me and it took the pressure of alcohol away. I was able to drink in a social environment and then stop, go home, go to bed. I didn't drink alone or when I was sad, now I don't have sad days, as I have done the healing work I needed to do, alcohol has become a social, fun activity where I rarely get drunk or have a hangover.

These days my go-to practice is meditation when I need clarification, cleansing or confirmation. Alcohol is nothing more than something I can take or leave. This has been a very powerful learning experience for me. Recovering alcoholics abstain completely and that is fine for whoever needs it, but I needed to make peace with it and its illusionary power.

The doctor told me my thyroid hormone levels were so low, I should be seriously ill, and he accounted it to my vegan diet. I'm not sure if it was the vegan diet or not but I didn't feel as ill as he told me I should be and recommended I take Thyroxine, a man-made drug which replaces the hormone your body is not producing enough of. I felt uneasy about this and decided that I would try to find an alternative method of healing. It was during this quest for seeking out alternative treatment that I stumbled upon Brandon Bay's, 'The Journey', a book, CD and workshop which has helped thousands of people heal physical ailments with the power of self-love and forgiveness, as well as the forgiveness of others. I worked through the book as directed, forgiving and letting go and immersed myself completely in the process. The Journey process is a light meditation where you invite anyone who has ever hurt you to come and sit with you at a campfire. You then tell each person how they hurt you, wait for them to respond and forgive them. When you have completed this part of the process you work at loving your inner child, before moving on to physical illness. The idea is that negative emotions which you are harbouring are creating unhealthy cells in your body. Since these cells regenerate regularly, by removing the negative patterns, you can regenerate healthy cells, thus eliminating physical illness. It was worth a shot.

I did the meditation and invited those people who had caused me pain to show up. First was Tom, who I forgave and through into the fire with ease. Next came Imran, I told him he'd let me down badly but that I'd let him down too. I said I forgave him and asked that he forgive me. The last person who showed up in my Journey work was Paul. This was tough because, although I went through the motions of the forgiveness, it didn't feel authentic. I had to do the Journey a few more times to rid myself of that completely. I decided not to take the medication at this point, wanting to see what my next blood tests would reveal. To my delight after just four weeks of journey work, my thyroid levels went up from an alarming 3 to a more respectable 11. However, it would fluctuate as my belief system would fluctuate and I did eventually give in to taking a small amount of Thyroxin. I have since learned how to handle underactive thyroid and feel in control of this part of my physical experience.

"In this world you can become a spotless mirror, in which the holiness of your creator shines forth from you to all around you."

~ A Course in Miracles

26.
Daniel

Lucy had asked me if I wanted a night out in Bolton Town Centre. Since returning from Spain we had reconnected and were getting along like the old friends we are. She had invited me to her house for William and Kate's royal wedding, we had a party and rekindled our friendship. There had been a few good nights out and I was seeing her about once every month. On the day we were due to go out, nearing Christmas, it was freezing, the plan was to go for some drinks in her local pub before moving on to a small night club in an old bleach making factory, aptly named, The Bleachworks.

In the morning I had been doing readings in my little shop and had thought, it was cold, Bolton was far away, and I'd just rather curl up on the sofa with my cat, Charlotte. I absentmindedly laid out a few of my fortune cards on my reading table, thinking to myself *should I go out tonight?* In hindsight, I definitely should have stayed in, but then I would not be where I am today, and today I am blessed. The cards fell out in the order they were supposed to and as usual, I knew what they were saying. We have a language which is all ours, they show me, and I hear them. They said, *go out, you're supposed to meet a soulmate tonight.*

Being back in the UK had felt like peace had floated over me, I was in the right place and for the first time in my life, I felt healed of many of the past traumatic and unhealthy patterns of my youth. I was in a good place and had decided, that, although I wouldn't just give myself to anyone, I was ready to pursue a relationship. I was open to marriage and a baby if that was going to happen for me. I had not pursued relationships relentlessly, but I had my eyes open in case a soul match arrived. I was looking for a female but the universe was ready to show me more pain with men before allowing me to find my princess charming.

So, following the cards advice, I got dressed up and showed up as planned. Lucy and I had arranged to meet at her local, I would drive down, park my car outside her house and walk to the pub. It seemed that my seven-inch studded boots were not the best choice of footwear for the snow and I slid all the way to the Brewhouse. We had drinks and giggled like we were fifteen again, Lucy had recently broken up with her husband, so we were both single and out on the rampage, just like old times. There were lots of other girls out with us that night, they were all lovely and I had managed to slither right in with the friends Lucy introduced me to. After last orders, Lucy and I parted company with everyone and took a taxi up to The Bleach Works.

When we arrived at the nightclub, there had been a private Christmas party on earlier in the evening, the remnants still visible by way of discarded party poppers, shells from Christmas crackers and empty champagne flutes. As I scanned the room Lucy hot-footed it to the toilets and I was left to wander while the club filled up quickly. I remembered the cards and said to Red Hawk, "so where is she then? This girl I am supposed to meet?", Red Hawk responded immediately, "he's there". I looked over to see a tall, slim male stood on his own, looking slightly awkward and a bit lost. I walked straight over to him, if he was my destiny, I wasn't going to waste any time. I trusted Red Hawk and thought he was guiding me to love, what I know now, is that life doesn't give you what you think you want, it gives you what you need to heal and grow.

He told me his name was Daniel, that he was a chef and had been responsible for cooking the Christmas meal earlier in the evening. He explained that his car had broken down, so he had to wait for his boss to give him a lift home. Had his car been working, he would have been long gone by now. We chatted away about food, music, and travel, he had told me he was born of English parents but was raised in South Africa. The chat was brief, but we swapped numbers before he left.

The next day I received several flirty texts from him, one expressing how easily his car had started that morning (coincidence, I think not!). We arranged to go on a date the following Wednesday. Since he lived in Wigan and I lived in Altrincham, which was some twenty-five miles apart, we plumped for Manchester as a midway point. A Spanish tapas bar called La Tasca on Deansgate before moving on to dinner.

I chose a slimming, low cut black dress, black stilettos and a long wool coat with hat, gloves and scarf, as it was freezing in the crisp December evening. I took the tram into Manchester so I could have a drink, which I felt I needed for Dutch courage.

I chatted to Kyle on the phone all the way there and he made me promise to text him mid-way through the date to let him know I was ok (not spiked or murdered). I promised I would and entering the bar, realising he hadn't arrived yet, took a seat and ordered myself a San Miguel.

As he arrived, I notice then he was quite tall, he had dark blond hair and blue eyes. He was just about passible to me as attractive; his South African accent was not pleasing to my ear and his clothes needed an iron. He'd told me he was a Scorpio and I was aware of the possible chemistry and the clash which could exist between an Aries and Scorpio love combination. Put it this way, if Emily had been the list of perfect qualities, this was the exact opposite. I had said that I trusted the universe to deliver, so, something in me just said, *give it a chance*.

He sat on the stool next to me and asked me if I smoked, to which I replied that I didn't. I told him I hated smoking and drugs and he agreed that he felt the same. He went on to tell me about himself and his life. It was a bit of a sob story, but he didn't come across as depressed or sad, more of regret from the past and excited to move forward. He told me he had returned from South Africa with his Mum as the trouble there was getting dangerous, his Mum and Dad were divorced, and his Dad decided to stay with his new wife. He was eighteen when he had arrived back and quickly hooked up with a girl who had got pregnant after three dates. The girl had insisted on having the baby and unfortunately had died in childbirth, leaving him with a son called George. At first, the baby had lived with her parents but after meeting Carol, they had decided to move in together and adopt George who was two years old at the time. As he drank his beer, he told me that around this time, his father had also taken his own life. Explaining how this created a sad and lost young man and that had immersed himself completely in a relationship which he realised was very wrong for him. A few years down the line, he and Carol would have another little boy called Arthur. He went on to tell me that she had been unfaithful to him and so the relationship had completely broken down. He was currently living with his sister and a lodger in Wigan and worked as a chef for a high-end outdoor catering company. I just sat and listened as he told his 'story'. Later I would discover there were many inconsistencies in this 'story', but at that time I drank it in. The inner healer in me probably felt crazed with excitement that I was being presented with someone who needed 'fixing'. *Maybe I am meant to save him*, I (stupidly) thought to myself. I told him about my adventures in Spain and what I did for a living, mentioning that I could give him a reading to see if his father made contact.

After the initial introduction and beers, we headed to a restaurant for food. He had pre-booked the restaurant and had somehow managed to choose my favourite restaurant in Manchester, somewhere I had been eating in for years, The Restaurant Bar and Grill. To my amazement, we ordered the same meal and we agreed on the same bottle of full-bodied red wine to accompany it. Being a chef and me being a complete foody, we talked about food and cooking. I was impressed with his culinary knowledge and he was impressed that I had dined at the Ritz in Paris, and various other eateries. We were getting on well, in that first date, best behaviour kind of way. He looked way older than his thirty years of age, he was seven years my junior, but I looked much younger than him. He told me it was due to lack of sleep because of the long hours he worked in the kitchens and at these huge events. I watched his pale blue eyes, slim face and sharp jaw as he talked easily about himself. He was not particularly good looking and I noticed his teeth were a bit brown, but he was tall and wore his clothes well, he had a sense of humour and seemed warm and amiable. We moved to another bar for a nightcap and more conversation.

At the end of the night, he walked me to the tram stop and kissed me. The kiss nearly made me fall over. It was as if I was lifted out of myself and into a floating sea of magic. The kiss told me chemistry was most certainly present, and that was half the battle in finding a new partner. As I boarded the tram, he asked me if I wanted to see him again, "of course I do!", I shouted as the doors closed and the tram peeled away slowly from the station.

Over the next few weeks, it was the run-up to Christmas and he would be very busy catering at various parties around the northwest. He arranged to come to my shop for a reading just before Christmas. I had known that his father had passed away in South Africa, that he lived with his sister and about his two sons, but he hadn't told me anything else about his family. He sat opposite me and I told him I was aware of a very small lady and an extremely tall man, but that the man was not his father as he was much older. I told him this gentleman had been afflicted with a lung problem and I was aware that he found it difficult to breathe when he was alive. He said that this was his little nana and grandad who was nearly seven-foot-tall and had passed with lung cancer, even after a lung replacement operation. Next, I told him I felt the presence of his Dad who was giving me a funny metallic taste in my mouth and that he had drifted off to sleep before he passed, feeling no pain. He revealed then that his father had killed himself by feeding a hose pipe from his exhaust through his car window. He was pretty shocked but very pleased with the reading. During the relationship, there would be many times when I would give him messages from his father, grandfather and nana. It was not your everyday date, but he said it gave him peace.

We continued to see each other and the following May 2013, he moved into the house with me. Mum had found a house of her own, we both felt we needed our own space, living together was only ever going to be temporary until we established ourselves back in the UK. It wasn't ideal for him in terms of location because he worked in Blackburn and his children lived in Wigan. My house was on the other side of Manchester in Cheshire, so the long drive would add to his already, arduous working day.

At first, it was ok, but I realised that he had no idea how to have a relationship or talk about his feelings. I also became aware that we had very different ideas about life. I had been used to getting dressed up and being taken for dinner by my partner or staying in cooking meals, listening to music and drinking wine.

Romance was always fully present in my long-term relationships and was used to being shown love and affection.

I discovered that he had never done any of these things with his previous partner, instead sitting in watching TV most nights. On the weekends he had gone to nightclubs where they had played dance music and taken drugs, spending Sunday's smoking weed to come down from the previous night, binging on chocolates and sweets. This was not my idea of fun at all. I was someone who preferred to drink red wine or champagne and listen to Jazz music, nibbling on savoury snacks and putting the world to rights in deep conversations about life and the universe. I would be happy never to switch on a television, and today I don't even own one. We had a wake up call when we realised that we lived together, yet, seemed to have opposing ideals.

He was always tired which he put down to the horrendous hours at work, sometimes working a sixteen-hour shift followed by a thirty-mile drive home.

His ex-girlfriend appeared overly demanding and he didn't seem to talk to her about arrangements with the children or maintenance. I found out they had a mountain of debt, debts which *he said* she had run-up in both joint names and his name. There was an agreement that he would pay her six hundred pounds out of his one thousand-six-hundred-pound monthly wage. This seemed unmanageable; after he had paid me half of the rent and the bills and covered his petrol expenses there was very little leftover. The arrangements over the children were also causing problems. They were used to being at his old house a few nights per week and had treated it like a second home. Carol didn't want the boys staying at my house because she said it would be too distressing for them to see their Dad with another woman.

The situation felt impossible because I would try to help him but whenever he spoke to Carol, everything we agreed went out of the window. This infuriated me as I couldn't see how we could be a couple and move forward when we weren't stood together as a team. If we argued he would shout and throw things and then zoom off in his car, disappearing for hours or sometimes overnight, preferring to sleep in the car outside, rather than come in the house and face me. This was completely alien to me and I was dumbfounded as to this behaviour which I deemed both wacky and immature. I realised that not only did he not understand what I needed, but he simply didn't have the tools to give it to me. No-one had ever shown him how to express himself or demonstrated that when he did express himself, that anyone was even listening.

After a few months of this, we did manage to sit down and talk it through. We decided that he would get a job closer to home so he wasn't as tired, and he would talk to Carol about reducing the maintenance payments to something much more manageable and discuss proper access to the boys. This took a long time to sort out, I soon fathomed that his previous relationship was consumed with drama; drama that was still playing out well after the relationship was over. On and on it went, backwards and forth, arguments, silence and then emails, letters, more arguments, more hurt. His relationship with his children suffered through this and I had no chance of ever building any kind of real relationship with them.

Carol allowed them to come and stay at the weekend eventually, but it was stilted and awkward. They would tiptoe around me and move rooms if I entered, I would buy them cereal, chocolate bars and cakes, but whatever I bought them, it was always wrong. They were protecting their mother and I had no experience with children and very little motivation since it was always a strain when they were at the house. Dan would disappear for an hour or more when they were visiting, he said to the shop, but the corner shop was a two-minute walk away. He would come back and sit in bed with the boys watching a movie in the dark. I felt ostracized and suspicious of where he'd been but didn't want to cause a scene while the boys were there. Something I am pretty sure he was counting on.

Six months into the relationship Dan admitted he smoked cigarettes but said that he wanted to stop, and I agreed to help him. For a whole six months, he had gone through this painful routine of hiding the fact that he smoked from me. Smoking cigarettes in secret, spraying himself with deodorant and aftershave and brushing his teeth before kissing me an hello. This was the start of a whole barrage of lies that he would tell me. In all the years we lived together, I never saw any evidence that he wanted to stop smoking. I hated the smell and the taste on his breath.

I made him smoke outside, take a shower and brush his teeth before bed because it made me feel physically sick. Looking back, I should have just ended things here, because it was obvious we were too different, but forever the fixer, I was determined to make it work.

I was asked to go to Switzerland by a lovely client called Sandra. She had been to see me in my little shop and had said I could stay in her house with her and she would organise private sittings for me. I jumped at the chance, Switzerland was a place I had always wanted to visit, Sandra and I had hit it off immediately. Switzerland is beautiful and Sandra and her husband were two of the warmest people I'd ever met. I had two full days of readings and we went sightseeing in the beautiful Swiss mountains and into the city of Zurich on the days I wasn't working.

Daniel was not happy at me leaving and I couldn't understand why. With Imran, we had always taken holidays with our friends separately, as well as together. However, for me this was work, surely, he could understand it was a great opportunity for me. He was supposed to take me to the airport but the night before I was due to leave, he caused a stupid argument over absolutely nothing and stormed out of the house, sleeping in the car again. Leaving for the airport he didn't answer his phone or reply to my texts, I had no idea where he was, if he was ok, or if he was even going to feed the cat. He didn't answer the phone the whole time I was away, and it created stress that could have ruined the whole experience for me. Luckily, I didn't let it stop me from enjoying Switzerland and the wonderful people I met on the trip, but had things been peaceful at home, it would have been dam sight more enjoyable.

This emotional bullying tactic was something he would use time and time again. It does two things; makes you question whether doing something they don't want you to do is even worth the hassle, and it makes you worry so much that by the time they do pick up the phone, your just so relieved they are ok, you simply forgive them and move on. If anyone is in a relationship with a person who behaves in this manner, my advice is leave, now. The behaviour is manipulating and debilitating. It's lucky that most of the time, I never let it stop me from doing what I wanted but it made each event very stressful. If I was going away with my mother on holiday or had an important event planned, that didn't include him, he would cause a huge argument before I would go. He would sabotage every event and at every opportunity. If he could make a day about his drama, he would do.

On the other hand, he could be funny, charming and romantic in his own way. He would cook me lovely dinners and buy me flowers. He always held the car door open for me and pulled out a chair if we went out to a restaurant. We had sexual chemistry too, (if he wasn't too tired) and I learned to compromise and stay in a bit more often to watch a film with him.

When I met him, his wardrobe was an horrific array of rags, reminiscent of the rag'n'bone man of my youth. I revamped his wardrobe and because he was tall and slim, he looked good in the suits and designer jeans I picked out for him. If he shaved, he looked pretty decent. There were times when we would giggle and act silly and I liked the fact that I could be carefree and daft around him. We would dance in the living room to Vanilla Ice and Queen, dress up for The Rocky Horror Show and he would show his camp side without inhibition.

He landed a fantastic job as the manager of a staff canteen in a global company which was better pay than at the outdoor catering, and only 7 am to 3 pm Monday to Friday. The job was much closer to home and halfway to his children's house, which meant he could take them swimming once a week. You would have thought he'd have been grateful, all he had to do was turn up, cook the food and smile a bit, but this job was the start of a decline in his mental health.

A few months into this job Mum had decided she would work from home and leave the commercial premises we were renting between us. I looked at a small shop on the internet and arranged a viewing with the estate agent. The shop was situated on a busy main road, close to a set of traffic lights and five minutes from where we lived. It looked much bigger empty than it did when it was full of stuff, but it had a good size kitchen and two toilets with a washing area downstairs. It was badly in need of a coat of paint and the stairs and basement were in an awful mess, but I thought we could fix it up. On the day of the viewing, I didn't have all the money I needed to sign the lease, but I was confident it would come. I had started to get a good reputation for private readings, demonstrating at the local churches and was asked to speak at various events. So, I signed a twelve-month contract on the shop and called it The Psychic School and Healing Centre.

Dan was struggling at work, he said there was so much pressure and paperwork to do, he became withdrawn at home, stayed much longer than he was supposed to at work and was moody most of the time. I tried to help him by planning his menus, making prep lists and order lists for each week and he was grateful, but his moods were unpredictable. He wasn't so much angry as sad and depressed but also, he seemed to disconnect from me and started going out with the staff from work more and more. His boss had noticed the decline in his personality and suggested he take a week off. This coincided with signing the contract and getting the keys to the new shop and we agreed to decorate together. He did give me all his wages that month too, which would pay for the remaining money I needed to sign the contract. That was the thing with this relationship, he would drive me nuts most of the time but would come up trumps when it really mattered. There were many times when he put me first and made me feel valued and those times when I was decidedly, last.

I had chosen a pale green paint for the walls in the main room with a feature wall of bright floral green and silver wallpaper, white woodwork and a brighter green paint in the kitchen. Daniel would concentrate on getting the basement, staircase and toilets into some kind of reasonable state for opening and I cracked on with the paintwork. He was enthusiastic in the morning and made good headway, cleaning out the basement, carpeting the stairs and fixing up the toilets. I noticed that periodically he would keep going outside and disappearing. When I questioned him as to where he was, he became irascible and stroppy. Since he was having time off work, because he was stressed, I didn't push it but was wondering what he was up to. His phone would be left on the stairs, so he wasn't calling anyone. His behaviour was often ambiguous and cabalistic to me.

At the end of a long day of painting and decorating we left for home, the shop was looking good and I was excited. As soon as we got home Dan flaked out on the sofa and fell into a deep sleep. I realised I left some things in the boot of his car so went outside to have a look. I rarely went into Dan's car because it was always a mess with cigarette ends and ash everywhere. When I opened the boot, I saw a small packet of what I recognised to be cannabis. Even though I had never taken drugs, I had been around them enough to know one from another. There was also a cigarette packet filled with cigarette papers and a lighter. I took the whole thing and threw it down a grid. I was shaking, disgusted and angry with him. He had known right from the first date my feelings towards drugs. I was angry at myself for being so stupid and not realising this was the reason for his mood swings and lethargy. That all the disappearing acts were related to smoking this vile stuff.

A few hours later he was pacing around like a bear with a sore head, outside to his car, back inside the house, checking pockets, drawers, he was erratic and confused. I asked him what he was looking for, he said he was searching for a packet of cigarettes, to which I pointed to his packet on the side of the kitchen worktop. I was enjoying watching him squirm for a minute before confronting him about the drugs. He broke down in tears then, saying yes, he'd been smoking weed for years and felt that he couldn't function without it. It all came out then about how he was struggling at work and felt that he couldn't cope, a stream of thick wet tears running down his face. He said that all the arguing over money and the boys with Carol was taking its toll, he had been hiding a mass of debt collection letters from me. It seemed they had a forty-thousand-pound debt to pay off that was attached to the house where Carol and the boys lived. I had compassion for him and told him I would help him if he promised to help himself. I was angry though; the drugs were in my house and I was not happy about that. It was also the lies, if he had been honest about who he was I could have chosen whether I wanted to get involved. I had been on a date with someone a few weeks before I had met Daniel and he told me he was a weed smoker, so I didn't call him again. I just didn't want drugs in my life on any level.

We felt a little closer after he came clean and I think he had been bottling up so much, the lies were adding to the stress. I started to sort through his debt letters, arranged an appointment with a debt management company and to see a solicitor over access to the boys and selling the house to pay off the joint debts. I also applied to the CSA (child support agency) on his behalf, to decide about how much money was a fair amount to be paid for the boys each month. All negotiations between the two of them seemed to fail, ending in arguments, it wasn't all Carol's demands either, it was his inability to behave like an adult that probably drove her nuts. He promised that he would get some help to stop smoking cannabis. It was obvious that it made him depressed and anxious, I felt that he needed a clear mind to do his job properly.

How he felt or what was going through his mind, I have no idea. He always told me exactly what I wanted to hear, and I never knew how he *really* felt about anything. I realised later that he had spent so much of his life, from early childhood, disguising his emotions, it had become second nature. He told me he had been a sensitive child, his father had told him to 'man up' and 'not be stupid'. It seemed that his father was very much a man's man, charismatic, charming but direct and selfish. He had looked up to his father and wanted to be like him, however, his early departure from the physical made this impossible. He had wanted his father to be proud of him, but he was never going to get that now. Remember Imran? This was my pattern. It's easy to identify your patterns when you're out of a situation but when you're in the mists of it, your blinded by your own story, and at this time I projected it all on to Daniel. I did not realise he was my manifestation, my vibrational match and my mirror. Things had to get an awful lot worse before I would gain any clarity.

"But it's no use now," thought poor Alice,
"To pretend to be two people! Why, there's
hardly enough of me left to
make one respectable person!"

~Alice In Wonderland, Lewis Carroll

27.
Adventures In Wonderland

The shop was ready for opening in October 2015, it looked lovely and I was so excited to be presenting myself on the high street. My idea was that people who were interested in spiritualism could come in and find out more. I was aware that spiritualist churches were not for everyone, but that more and more people were looking for something non-physical to trust and believe in. I wanted to develop an outlet for those people who had no idea where to go.

I had a desk with two chairs and a healing bed with a huge curtain I could pull over to create privacy. The front of the shop was full of mind, body and spirit related books, card decks, gift sets, crystals and various other items to promote love and harmony. I had a sign fitted at the front which said, 'Beverley Anne Freeman's Psychic School and Healing Centre' and vinyl lettering on the windows which spelt 'psychic readings', 'healing' and 'workshops'. I had leaflets and price lists printed out and were ready to help the general public find their version of spirit.

As soon as the doors opened people flooded in, all different people, from all walks of life. One thing I hadn't counted on was, that the shop was situated in front of a builder's merchants. Large trucks and vans would pull up and big burly men would pour out to collect their products from the builders' yard. On their way back to their van they would call in the shop and book a reading or healing session, buy a crystal for luck or ask questions about spiritualism. It was a surprise, but I realised that all kinds of people were interested in spiritualism. These men were very unlikely to chat about spirituality down the pub or on a job, but the interest was there. Presenting myself on the high street had created a point of contact without the embarrassment of having to ask anyone. I had little old ladies, young men and women, different cultures and languages coming in, it was wonderful to see such an array of interest. I continued my weekly development circle and again, it was very successful, with a core group of between ten to fifteen people attending each week. Healing became more popular and I worked with my guides to provide healing for whatever people needed.

Healing was relatively new to me. I had always thought of my mother as being the healer in the family, but after a few lessons at the Arthur Findley College and some direction from Red Hawk, I developed my own style. I asked my clients to lie on the healing bed, turning down the lights and lighting a candle. Then I would say the 'Prayer of St Francis', "make me a channel for your peace…", before taking my client into a form of meditation, akin to 'Sitting in The Power', that Glyn Edwards had taught us. I would place my hands on the head or shoulders of the client and then go into a deep trance, allowing Red Hawk or whichever guide came to work with me to put healing in the recipient's soul. I learned this method pretty much alone, I later learned that this is very similar to shamanic healing. It was just as Red Hawk had instructed me and I trust him unquestionably. I had some good results.

One young lady had come in because she said she felt stuck, depressed and lost. She had dishwater blonde hair, was thin and fragile and her eyes were lacklustre. I told her we could have a go at the healing but couldn't say what the results might be. I gave her about forty minutes of healing and felt my guides coming in strongly. When she left, I prayed for a miracle to happen as she didn't say anything about feeling better, and I wasn't sure if anything had happened.

One year later a gorgeous blonde girl came bouncing into the shop, smiling and happy. She was dressed in a fitted outfit and looked vivacious and gleeful. It was the same young girl I had done the healing on! She told me that after the healing session, a fog cleared in her mind. She had ended her dysfunctional relationship, got a new job which she loved, highlights in her hair, a better diet and was feeling on top of the world.

There was a lady who approached me because she had been diagnosed with stage four cancer in her breast, lymph glands and lungs. She had had a double mastectomy, but the cancer had spread, and they told her she would only have months to live. Someone had given her my name as a last resort, she didn't feel ready to go home to the spirit world and wanted me to help. I told her I couldn't promise anything but would try. I did the healing as directed by Red Hawk and felt new energies coming in as I went into a trance state. I thought I saw some images of people reminiscent of Jesus and Mother Teresa.

I told her that she should come once a week until her

next check-up and we did six sessions altogether. I was as anxious as she was on the day of the appointment to see if there would be any improvement. Her text came through and I burst into tears as I read "I can't believe it they said they cannot see cancer anywhere on the scan". We both rejoiced in her recovery and she continued to come for sessions to heal her mind and the worry of cancer returning.

I did a lot of healing treatments whilst working at the Psychic School and Healing Centre and I felt that, together with the spirit world, we did some good work. I know that when you trust in spirit, miracles happen. When I did the healing, I saw a man that I often thought was Jesus coming to help. One day I asked him, "are you Jesus?", he smiled then and replied, "no, I'm John The Baptist". I don't question what I get, I just feel a bit like Alice in wonderland sometimes. This gentleman has appeared to me many times whilst in meditations and deep healing trance states and if he tells me, he is John The Baptist, then I am not going to argue.

Readings became clearer, more information was coming through and all my psychic senses were being used during communication. I was getting direct information through clairaudience and clairvoyance but also taste, smell and feel. I was aware that often if the conditions were favourable, I was able to take on the mannerisms of the spirit communicators. I could stand like them, use their hand gestures and sometimes say things in a way that felt it was coming directly through me rather than being passed on. I was enjoying everything spirit were teaching me, embracing it all as my unique journey.

The shop was getting busier and busier, I was making good profits and invested it in more stock. I was selling all kinds of crystal jewellery, gift sets, candles and more and more books. Of course, I was also reading these books myself and expanding my knowledge on many different subjects. I started to do some courses in crystal healing, reiki and hypnotherapy. The more readings I did the more I became aware that people needed healing as they felt lost in their lives. I took courses in life coaching, counselling, EFT, NLP, mindfulness, nutrition and even completed my Personal Trainer level 3 certificate. I studied A Course in Miracles (an ongoing journey), the Tao Te Ching, work by Wayne Dyer and Marianne Williamson. This enabled me to develop my style of spiritual life coaching. The spiritual life coaching and one to one psychic development gave me a break from the readings. I felt the readings consumed most of my energy and I was aware that if I did too many readings in one day, my energy would deplete, and the quality of the readings would suffer. I was getting booked to go to parties in people's houses and was invited to hold psychic nights in bars and pubs. It was great to be busy and I figured that if spirit wanted to use me as a channel then I would do the work without complaining.

My old friend Sonia from Bergerac's was recently back from Australia where she had lived for some years and asked me if I wanted to go with her to London to train with Dr Brian Weiss on past life regression therapy. I jumped at the chance to go, of course, Dan created loads of drama about this, but I didn't care. I wanted to go and so packed up for London.

We stayed at a gorgeous boutique hotel at Kings Cross, close to where the workshop was being held. On our first day, Dr Weiss took us into a group regression. As we were guided into a hypnotic state, I became aware that I was being transported back in time. I was a child and had brown feet with no shoes on, I could see and feel these little brown feet and hands. I didn't get a date, but I knew it was a time long ago, I was alone and felt anxious and distressed. I must have been about four or five years old and was in a hot, dusty country. It was noisy and there was something serious going on because people were shouting and screaming, I was hiding and watching from a safe distance. I climbed up a tree to get a better view and could see a huge wooden frame being dragged along the dusty path, people throwing stones and shouting in a language which sounded alien to me now. There were two men covered in blood being dragged along with this wooden frame, chained and near dead. I was scared then and ran home. When I arrived, my mother was sobbing uncontrollably and I went to console her, asking her what was wrong. She just kept saying, "Jesus, Jesus, my precious son". Dr Weiss then took us further forward in this life to an important event. I was older now but still only a teenage boy. I was sat in a dark room with one window and there was a large table, where a group of us were sat, I knew these were my family. We were remembering our brother that had been brutally murdered years before. I would say that there were about twelve people sat around the table, mainly men. When we came back into our normal awareness, I was shocked at what I had seen. It seemed clear to me that I had witnessed the crucifixion of Jesus, that he had been my brother and Mary my mother. If someone would have told me that, whether, about me or them, I would have thought them deluded. All I can say is that the experience felt completely real to me. I had often joked to Kyle that he had been Jesus in a past life because of his deep knowledge at such a young age, his dark eyes and his fear of fame. Who knows, maybe it was true?

The days with Dr Brian Weiss continued and I experienced many other past lives, noticeably one of French royalty in The Palace of Versailles, a poor, young flower seller in London and a German lady in Hollywood who seemed to be friends with the icon Marilyn Monroe.

Emily and I had often thought we were in Hollywood together in a past life (there was certainly a fine amount of drama). Once we had been messing around with past life charts and a pendulum and her past life came out as female, actress, initials NJ, which could have been Norma Jean, aka, Marilyn Monroe. Marilyn Monroe's acting coach was Natasha Lytess, a German woman who had escaped as world war II had broken out and fled to America to become an actress. Whether these past lives were true or not, it was certainly a lot of fun discovering them and explaining the different facets of one's personality. The propensity I had to acting, singing, jazz music and glamour could have come from one of these lives. I have learned that anything is possible but not to take anything too seriously, after all, it's the present moment which is precious.

I took all the knowledge and wisdom from my week back to my development circle, teaching them all I'd learned during my time with Dr Brian Weiss.

The business was a triumph and I was helping people, making a good living and serving spirit as a messenger, teacher and healer. Back at home things weren't going so well.

We had managed to take legal action to resolve the debts Dan had accumulated with Carol by forcing the sale of the house. The CSA had ordered Dan to pay much less in maintenance based on his income and his debts were now in the hands of a debt management company, seemingly more affordable and less pressure. So, things that he had said were stressing him out, were being resolved.

However, the drama in his mind continued. He was paranoid about the male customers I had at the shop and was always accusing me of having affairs, a ridiculous notion, I didn't have the time, energy or inclination for an affair. He was jealous of Kyle, of my mum, of anyone I was friendly with, anyone male or female who I liked. I felt this could be reverse psychology and with finding the drugs in his car, I started to disbelieve what he was saying to me.

He would fall asleep often on the sofa and I would take the opportunity to check his phone, pockets and his car. I never found any more drugs, but I did find numerous flirty text messages between him and his old female friend from way back. There were messages from people at work also asking him if he was going out to a rave with them on the weekend. I didn't trust him and told him so, this pushed him away even further and he spiralled into a manic chaos of partying with people I didn't know, we became more and more distant with each other. I was also becoming paranoid and it was deeply unhealthy. I hadn't been jealous in any of my previous relationships, but then I hadn't been suspicious of lies either.

Money was going missing out of my purse. I often brought the takings home with me in my handbag and went to the bank first thing. I was sure it was Dan but I couldn't prove it, so I had a safe fitted in the shop and left my money in there instead, preferring to take the money to the bank at lunch time. This news made it obvious that it was him, the look on his face when I told him of my new safe, was a picture.

It wasn't long before I became aware of some sort of infection down below and when I got this checked out was told that it was syphilis. The only person I had slept with in years was Dan (and not very often due to his depression and my attraction to females). The atmosphere at home had become heated and you could cut the air with an axe, I confronted him about the infection and said I knew he had been unfaithful. He confessed that he had gone to a type of rave with a friend and taken ecstasy, slept with a girl in a toilet cubical and realised later that he also had contracted syphilis, he had it treated in secret, hoping I hadn't contracted it.

As he talked about the evening in question, he started to open another can of worms. He revealed that he was wrestling with a much bigger drug problem than smoking weed. Members of staff in the canteen at work were giving him cannabis, cocaine and ecstasy tablets in exchange for meals at lunchtime. He was taking coke in the morning and then smoking weed in the afternoon to help with the comedown, coming home and sleeping it off and taking ecstasy at the weekends. He said he was completely exhausted, the lies he was telling me and his bosses at work was incapacitating. I was stupefied then, because I thought he had outgrown the drug taking of his youth, but it explained much of his behavior. I told him he needed to sort himself out or pack his bags and leave. During our relationships he had cut himself off from his family completely. He wouldn't speak to his mother or sisters, nor did he have any good friends. His family thought I was the one who was taking him away from them, but he was convinced he didn't need them. He leaned on me all the heavier. He made it so that I was the only one he could turn to, this is another form of manipulation. One of the reasons I didn't just pack his bags for him is because I was aware, he had nowhere to go. What I didn't realise at the time though, was that it wasn't my problem. I didn't know I wasn't responsible for him.

During the week that followed, we didn't speak. He went into his usual routine of silence and sleeping in the car and I used this time to think things through, deciding if I wanted to continue helping him or walk away. I knew that the infidelity was nothing to do with me or the relationship but a symptom of his drug-taking. I also knew that if he could get clean, underneath everything there was a kind, decent human being. He, on the other hand, was sending me a string of text messages telling me he was going to kill himself and that he had hit rock bottom.

When we talked, (something he was learning slowly) I told him that he must get help with his drug addiction otherwise I was out. He agreed and made an appointment at the doctors. He told me the doctor offered him no help, other than advising him to join a gym. I can't be sure of anything he ever said to me because he told so many lies, but he assured me he felt confident he could get off the drugs himself. He said he felt that he needed to leave his job and do something else for this to happen. So, I agreed that if he was serious, I would stand by him.

Christmas was coming up and it was probably the worst Christmas we ever had. It was a strain, I wanted to celebrate it because of my Mum, I wanted it to be happy for her sake. Mum and Dan did not like each other. Mum could see he was causing me anxiety and stress and was protective and Dan was jealous of anyone I cared about. Mum was also a little jealous of him because previously we had done everything together and now, I had to divide myself between him, her and the business. I was also booked to do churches services once a week and was demonstrating mediumship at mind, body, spirit fairs around the country.

In June the following year, Dan got a new job working for an outdoor catering company and there was a big event coming up. I was taking my mother to the Ritz in London for four days for her 70th birthday. It was a sumptuous stay in a fabulous hotel. We packed all our best clothes, drank champagne in the Rivoli Bar and had afternoon tea in the Palm Court. We went out on the evening of her birthday to experience a tasting menu prepared by Michelle Roux Jr. We had a marvellous time and for four days I was able to forget about Dan's antics.

On my return, I learned that Dan had been sacked from the outdoor catering company, he told me that the chefs were all on drugs and were not functioning properly (more lies). I was at a complete loss as to what to do with him. I had such a busy schedule and was starting to feel completely burnt out with it all.

There were a few occasions when I couldn't face customers and just locked the doors at the shop and sat down and cried. I cancelled bookings for parties and church services and started to feel like a complete fraud. On the outside, I was this confident spiritual teacher, but in the background, I was crumbling under the weight of Dan's total dysfunction. It was good to know that I was no longer the dysfunctional one in the relationship, but it was still a mess. Simultaneously, the basement in the shop started to flood and burst pipes would release human excrement from the toilets. It was a direct manifestation of the shit I was drowning in, my relationship being the root cause.

I would spend hours on the phone to Kyle but even he was getting impatient and frustrated with me, not understanding why I didn't just throw the towel in and call it quits on the relationship. My eternal optimism and tenacious outlook on life, simply wouldn't let me give up. I had a reading from one of my favourite psychic authors, Sonia Choquette, hoping to gain some clarity on the situation. All she told me was that I should ask myself, "why had I manifested this situation and what was it showing me?". At the time I felt like I had wasted the three hundred dollars I had spent on the reading, but later I realised that was the exact solution to the relationship problems.

Dan and I had many talks about moving forward and he promised me he could do better in all aspects of his life. He said he loved me and wanted to make things work, so I said I would give him one last chance. It was all I had left in me, to be honest. I suggested that we opened our own catering business. I would do the administration and the marketing, and he would cook the food and run the events. It was a fresh start and we were both excited.

Inspired Dining was born in September 2016 and I acquired a large three-bedroom semi with a big garage to accommodate the new business venture. Dan was great at all things DIY so he kitted out the garage with large fridges and workbenches where he could prep the food before taking it to the venues. Things took off and we won contracts with companies in Salford Quays and Warrington. Dan was clearly off the drugs and seemed to be getting happier every day. I was pleased that we were finally making progress and there was light, seemingly, at the end of the tunnel.

My shop was getting busier and busier and I was in demand as a medium, psychic and teacher. It was still a little draining, but I managed my diary, so I had more free time to enjoy my success. My mother and I would enjoy days out shopping in Manchester and Wilmslow and nights dining out and to the theatre. We went on holiday to Dubrovnik and Brussels and I went to the Arthur Findley College again, this time sharing a room with Kyle.

Dan became the perfect boyfriend, buying me flowers, cooking me delicious meals taking me for weekend's away in the Lake District. We went on holiday to Marbella and Mallorca and we agreed to get married. On the exterior it was going well, he still had his down days and motivating Dan was always going to be an uphill struggle, but he thrived on the praise he received from his customers. His cooking ability seemed natural, almost pre-birth, he made things look beautiful and breezed through most recipes with delicious results.

I was asked to film some scenes on the popular TV show, The Real Housewives of Cheshire, due to my friendship with cast member Ampika Pickston. In the first scene, we were filmed participating in 'Sitting in the Power' meditation. It took hours to film and only lasted thirty seconds on air. After this, the producers wanted to film some more scenes, but we were unsure what exactly these would entail. They asked me if they could film me giving Amipka a private sitting, but I felt uneasy doing this as I thought I was too personal for a TV show. In the end, we agreed they would film Ampika and some of the other cast members in a development circle type situation. They asked me to organise twelve to fourteen people to film the scene. We did real mediumship and ran it exactly as I would have any normal night. The only difference was the cameras, but everyone was brilliant, and I was pleased with the outcome.

The showing of this episode, unfortunately, was on the same night as the horrific terrorist attack at the Arianna Grande concert in Manchester. No one was watching the Real Housewives of Cheshire, as everyone was shocked and devastated about what had happened in our beautiful city and the lives of the innocent children lost. Not long afterwards though, people would catch up with the show and I was overwhelmed with messages and requests from all kinds of people to do this and that, and acquaintances I hadn't heard from in years got in contact.

I was devastated however when I saw the footage and found that I looked huge on the TV. The weight had crept on and without me realising just how much. This was mainly due to living with a chef and my sedentary lifestyle. To add to this, Dan was a 'feeder', he'd laughed many times about how Carol had been quite slim when they met but had gained at least four stone in weight due to his cooking. He liked the fact that I had gained weight because he thought this made other men (and women) less likely to be attracted to me. My cortisol levels were through the roof with all the stress, Dan and I frequently ate three-course dinners, resulting in my dress size going up from a UK 12 to a 16.

This gave me the push I needed to lose weight and so my love affair with weight training began. I joined Hale Country Club and commenced an intensive weight training programme. I didn't lose an awful lot of weight on the scales, but I became firm, strong and had tonnes more energy. I started slowly with light weights and watched videos to copy the posture. As time went on I increased the weight and intensity and before I knew it was training at 7 am every morning and doing 100kg deadlifts. Of course, this made Dan super insecure, but I was way past his manipulation and there was no way I was going to give it up to satisfy his psychological issues.

I had an amazing time at the Arthur Findley College, Glyn Edwards had passed away, so Kyle and I decided to go on a course with Eileen Davies. The brilliant and legendary Jose Medrado would be attending the college that week to do a demonstration of trance art. Jose Medrado is an incredible trance medium and healer, who goes into trance and is said to channel famous artists like Renoir, Monet and Van Gogh. It was an unforgettable experience and I came home with a trance painting channelled by the pint-sized Moulin Rouge painter, Toulouse Lautrec. The painting hangs proudly on my wall as I write this. On this week I fell completely in love with the mediums, Eileen Davies who introduced us to becoming a 'spiritual medium' and the beautiful Colin Bates who would be my tutor for the week. It's amazing that each time you visit the Arthur Findley College, you become so much more when you come out the other side.

Kyle and I organised a joint demonstration of mediumship in my shop a few weeks after our return. We did individual messages and double links, giving evidence of spirit and beautiful messages. Kyle stole the show with wit and charm and rather than being jealous, I celebrated his success as the fine medium he was becoming. He stayed at the house but Daniel skulled about avoiding us, making sure he didn't see Kyle the whole time. It was both embarrassing and painfully obvious that he was jealous and immature. He was incapable of supporting me unless he was involved on some level. If I did an event in the shop and he was doing the catering, he bathed in the success of it all, otherwise, he was completely nonchalant. Even though Kyle was the person who knew me best at this time, I still didn't reveal to him the depths of despair I was feeling. I was too embarrassed to admit my personal life was a mess.

One evening not long after my return from the Arthur Findley College, I had been booked to take the service at Preston Spiritualist Church. I was running late and was a bit nervous because I'd been busy at work with private sittings, I was tired and could do without it but having cancelled a few services the previous year, I had decided I would fully commit to all my appointments. I had been reading a book I had purchased at the college by spiritual genius Gordon Higginson. I had watched to Gordon Higginson on YouTube and listened to a collection of his teaching on CD's I'd purchased from the Barnabell Centre whilst working there at a mind, body & spirit fair, (the Barnabell Centre is part of the SNU and runs courses like the Arthur Findley College but is located in Stafford, much closer for me then). To me, Gordon is the most incredibly accurate medium, giving full names and addresses of communicators, as well at other remarkable evidence of survival after passing. I called upon him for assistance as I drove to the church as fast as the speed limit would allow. "Gordon please come and help me this evening!", I asked aloud in the car. I arrived with minutes to spare. The demonstration was going well, and I was aware of a communicator who was blending with me, an older lady by the name of Elizabeth who was telling me she was the grandmother of the lady in the audience, that she had passed with pneumonia. All was going great until she completely disappeared, I felt no communication at all. Unsure of what to do I, I stopped, turned around and took a sip of water, a little trick I learned if you need a minute whilst on the platform. As I took a sip of the water, I saw, standing in the aisle of the church, very clearly, Gordon Higginson smiling at me as if to say, "you called". It was a split second before Elizabeth returned and I said, "would you understand number 9 Green Street?", the lady who was receiving the message, replied, "yes that was where she lived", of course, it was! Silently, I said, "thank you, Gordon".

I have learned over the years you can call upon any energy of any spirit person and they will come. I have called upon Mrs Beaton to help me make a cake, which rose beyond all expectation. When invited to be the guest speaker at the International Psychic Society I called upon Martin Luther King Jr and whilst writing this book I have at many times called upon, the inspiring Wayne Dyer to help me. They always come and I have leaned upon those in the other world many times.

Money was coming in from both businesses and as Christmas was approaching, myself, Mum and Dan decided to spend Christmas at The Ritz in London. Things were often strained between my Mum and Dan, but they managed to keep up appearances, so to speak. On the train to London, we cracked open the champagne and were excited about this new experience. Ever since going to The Ritz in London for my 31st birthday my mother and I had begun a love affair with the place. The elegance, food, service and decadence of The Ritz was glamour and sophistication for us. Dan just about managed to keep it together but not without drama and a few stroppy moods. It would have been unquestionably more enjoyable without him.

As we moved into January 2017 Dan fell into a depression, Inspired Dining work declined, and he started to spend hours in bed. Another revelation was that the garage didn't pass hygiene standards for the catering business and they needed us to make major modifications for it to get certified. I found suicide notes he had written to me and his children and was getting increasingly worried about his mental health. He lost loads of weight, his skin became sallow and his cheeks hollow. Dan was sleeping in the spare room by this time and we ceased intimacy almost completely. Dan's depression overshadowed everything. It was always about his drama. He point-blank refused to see a doctor, wouldn't speak to his mother or family, so I invited him to come into the shop for some healing and something must have shifted.

One morning he got out of bed and went to my Mum's house and started to build her a Zen garden on the back of the house, something they discussed at The Ritz. He collected organic wood from parks and bits and pieces from skips and Mum gave him some money for extra building materials. He said he just felt guided to do this and it came together like he'd been doing it all his life. He told me he didn't want to do the catering anymore and instead fancied himself as a builder and gardener. I just wanted him to be happy so supported him in his decision. I designed a leaflet for him, it was a picture of the Leaning Tower of Pisa with a strapline "You should have gone to Homes and Gardens Cheshire". I built him a website and sent him out leafleting in the local area. We still had a contract with a company in Salford Quays so until notice was given, I said I would make and deliver the food.

Dan got phone calls for painting, fencing, fixing and wall papering. I was making buffets at 6 am and dropping them off at Salford Quays before arriving in work to see clients, doing church services and mind, body and spirit fairs at the weekend. I was exhausted and although Dan was busy again, he started to have melt downs because, to be honest, he had no idea what he was doing. He was good at learning and copying videos off YouTube and he was surprisingly resourceful with materials, however, he lacked confidence and knew he wasn't a professional. To be fair he did a good job and most of his customers were pleased and gave him repeat business. He should have been happy but started to doubt himself and his abilities again and again; no amount of reassurance could persuade him otherwise.

Things started to get bad again and we put the wedding on hold because he was in no fit state to get married and I didn't want to be tied to him for the rest of my life (the way he was). It would have been a mistake. His behaviour became erratic and it was obvious he was back on the drugs. I was at my wit's end. I had no fight left in me and my support for him had seemingly left the building. He started bringing loads of crap home from the tip and various skips which he had gone through during the day. He made an irrigation system in the back garden out of a buried wheelie bin which brought water up and over a mound of stones and he then placed garden gnomes all around it. It was bizarre and I felt that he was having a serious breakdown. His son, George, sent him a text message saying that he wanted nothing else to do with him and this was the straw that broke the camel's back. He brought home loads of this 'recycling' (as he named it) and the garage, back garden and front garden were loaded up like the Wombles back yard. I lost my temper with him and told him to move it all. He started throwing things all over the garden and in the road, screaming like a five-year-old having a tantrum. I told him it was over, and he needed to leave. He got in his car and sped off, not returning for three days. When he did eventually return, he took to the usual spare room, was pacing up and down all night long, sitting in the back garden and taking photographs of the moon.

It was Monday morning, after a difficult weekend. I was alone in my shop and I just sat there in the dark behind the curtain, feeling so lost and morose. How had I got myself into this mess? A customer who had an appointment for a reading was knocking on the door, but I couldn't answer, I just sat there sobbing, until she stopped, my head held despairingly in my hands. I was disturbed by a voice message notification on my phone. It was from Dan, saying he'd taken loads of pills and he was calling to say goodbye. Part of me wanted him to die then, feeling like it was the only way I was ever going to be free of him. It had been the tenth message to this effect in the past year and I just wanted it to be over. I sat there in the dark, contemplating, whilst another customer started banging on the door, mascara dripping down my face, I couldn't answer. I took a deep breath and exited via the back entrance, driving home, figuring I'd better check up on Dan. Not because I cared, I no longer cared, but because I am a decent human being and needed to see if he had gone through with it. My heart was beating wondering if I would find a dead body or a whimpering mess of a man waiting for me.

On my arrival, I found the front door ajar and Dan lying, seemingly unconscious in the hall. I called an ambulance and the lady on the phone talked me through the recovery position. When the paramedics arrived, the female went through his car and found empty paracetamol and ibuprofen bottles all over the seat. She then searched through the glovebox and found plastic bags full of the tablets. He hadn't taken anything, he was just acting and wasting everyone's time. I was relieved though, part of me still cared for him and I did have love for him, the other part of me just wanted out.

They took him to the hospital to check him over and the mental health team had talks with him about getting some help. He told them that he had only pretended to take the tablets because I had ended things with him. He wouldn't see the psychiatrist or go to counselling, so they just sent him home.

I took him home and gave him some love and TLC, it was all I could think to do. We sat down a few days later and had a serious talk. He told me he just wanted to die because he saw no purpose for being in the world. He had no idea what he wanted to do for a job, he had lost his sons and all he wanted was to be with his father in the spirit world. I suggested that he needed to get away. I pointed out that he was young, only thirty-four, in good health and the suicide attempts he had tried previously, had all failed. He had stood on bridges, sat in the car with the exhaust fumes funnelled through the window and had tried to hang himself in the garage, but he never had the guts to follow any of it through. I told him the spirit world weren't going to take him back and he needed a new plan. I had often thought I would like to live in the Algarve in Portugal and wondered if a change of scenery and some sunshine might give him a new perspective. He figured he had nothing to lose.

August bank holiday weekend we loaded up the car with all his things and drove to Portugal. I gave him every penny I had to rent some accommodation and spending money until he found a job. It was a sad time, the relationship which had lasted six years was coming to an end and I worried that his mental health was not stable enough for this new start. The apartment in Villamoura was beautiful and I had typed him a CV and left him with numerous copies. I sorted him out with a Portuguese mobile, bank account and national insurance number and left him to start his new life. I as boarded the plane home I was filled with anxiety and prayed to God to keep him safe.

On my return home I realised I didn't have enough money to pay the rent on the house and the shop. There was a mound of bills waiting for me behind the door and I realised I was on my own with it all. Dan had been a heavy weight, but he had always helped me with money and paying for the upkeep of the house. I was struggling. I decided to have a chat with the owners of my shop, if I was hoping for sympathy, there wasn't any. I decided that the house was large enough to work from home so I moved my whole business into my dining room and would run the development circle from the living room. It seemed like a sensible option to save some money and I advertised the shop for rent on behalf of the owners in an attempt to resolve the problem of the remaining time left on the tenancy.

People still came, and regardless of the stress I was under spirit didn't usually let me down. There was an awful night at Sale Spiritualist church when I was so tired and stressed out that I simply couldn't connect. Brian, who ran the church, thankfully stopped the service and created an open circle. I understood that you needed to be in the right place to serve spirit but didn't want to let people down. If it was advertised that I was taking a service, people would come to watch. I had a small collection of followers that would turn up wherever I demonstrated and that made me feel responsible to attend. However, I now know that being of clear mind is more important.

Dan was on the phone every five minutes saying that he needed me and couldn't live without me. It was heart breaking to hear him on the other end of the phone and wrongly, I felt responsible for him. He had managed to get a job as the head chef of a beach bar in Praia de Luz and a new apartment in Portimao. Things were looking positive and I agreed to visit him regularly until he got more settled. He begged me not to tell any of his family where he was, but other than a distance uncle, no one even attempted to get in contact.

I had gained weight and looked horrendous, the adult acne came back and when I went to the doctors for a check up on my bloods, it shown early stages of diabetes type II. I was horrified, because, wrongly or rightly, I'd always seen diabetes type II as an 'over-weight' disorder. I was determined to lose weight and sort it out without medication. It took over twelve months for me to achieve this, but, thankfully, it did heal. It was just a symptom of the strain I was under with Daniel. Daniel was making me physically ill. All emotional trauma comes out in illness, which is why working on your emotional well-being is so important. I was carrying Daniel's pounds of pain.

I went over to see him in October and he seemed well. He introduced me to the staff at the beach café and to the new friends he had made there. They were a nice bunch and I loved the place. Luz was seductive and I thought that maybe I could open a shop there, doing readings. Maybe Portugal was calling and in need of spirituality. Dan said he loved me and didn't want us to break up, that he wanted me to move to Portugal and make a fresh start. It was appealing to move to this beautiful part of the world, so in a moment of utter madness, I agreed.

The plan was to send Charlotte over a week ahead of me, Dan would collect her at the airport and then my mother and I would arrive in time for Christmas. Mum would return home in the new year.

It was hard work packing up a three-bedroom house and a business. Wrapping everything up and paying for things before leaving, but as if by magic I did, it all fell into place. My mother and I drove over to Portugal in my car from Plymouth, via the ferry, stopping off in Salamanca along the way.

When I arrived in Portugal with Mum, something was off. I recognised the signs immediately; he was back on the drugs and in a bad place. I was so angry, not only was Christmas here again, (I wanted mum to have a nice time), but I had closed down my business and handed my house back to the estate agent. I had absolutely nothing in the UK and had fully relocated to Portugal.

After my mother left, things went from bad to worse and he started staying out all night with a girl he'd met at work. He said that he was in love with her and was moving in with her. I didn't argue. I didn't fight for him. I'd had enough, it was time to let go.

Growing up, whenever someone was sick at school or fell over and bled all over the floor, the caretaker would come and poor this white antibacterial powder called 'Vim' all over it. That what this relationship represented, it was the Vim, being poured over my life, cleaning up that last residue of hurt, pain and self-pity. I needed this relationship to show me that I had a higher purpose in life and that I was ready to let go of the past and step into the fullness of the present.

Even though I'd moved to Portugal at his request I felt that Portugal represented a healing time in my life. Sonia Choquette had, in my reading, asked me, "Why did you manifest this situation?". It strikes me that Daniel was my mirror, showing me the complete lack of self-love, I had for myself. To heal diabetes, I made myself a hypnosis recording of 'self-love'. I listened to this every night in the months leading up to my move to Portugal. As my mindset started to shift into a place of self-love, so Daniel started to leave my life. I had grown a successful business but deep down I don't think I ever really thought I deserved that success. One of my many inspirers is Iyanla Vanzant, the life coach who began her career on the Oprah Winfrey Show. I remembered her saying in one of her books, that she had "a million-dollar contract, with a welfare mentality". Well, this was very similar. You have to know deep in your bones that your worthy enough to deserve that success. The way men had treated me, or more to the point, the way I had allowed them to treat me, had created that lack of love in my own heart. I was starting to learn to love me and that meant men had to go. All men, I was ready to step into the realisation of who I am. Self-love was followed by self-realisation. My truth was that I had been and always should have been a gay woman and that it was the 7 year old child that was still sleeping with men.

"All shallow roots must be uprooted, because they are not deep enough to sustain you"

~ A Course in Miracles

28.
Portugal

2018 was spent strolling endless sunny days in Portugal, walking the beautiful Algarve beaches and around four hours of meditation per day. During these self-indulgent, reflective and healing twelve months of my life I embarked on a deep spiritual peregrination. Through prayer, meditation, reading thought-provoking books and watching inspirational talks I pieced together the layers of my life. I started to form a deeper understanding of Self and in turn, a peace that only love can deliver. A love experienced through a deep awareness of that which already Is.

I no longer went to the self-destructive mode of drinking alcohol. I had healed that part of myself. The relationship with Daniel had shown me what self-sabotage looked like, it was grotesque, and I now had an inclination of what I had put Imran through. I know my soul needed me to heal the last residue of pain so that I could fulfil my life purpose as a healer, author and spiritual inspirer. I was aware that Dan was my mirror and my greatest teacher.

All days rolled into one and time became irrelevant, knowing only light and dark; day and night. Initially, I went to a familiar spiritual practice for me, meditation; spending many hours on the beach, listening to the rolling waves, lifting myself higher to become the glorious, solid rock formations that surrounded me. I became lighter and lighter as my consciousness floated up into the clouds. During these meditations, I started to feel a deep connection to my soul. I saw myself as a huge reflective being that could create as nature creates. I understood that all in the physical existence can create, reflect and perceive whilst being completely connected.

As hours, days and months unravelled so did the conditioning of my mind. Once I had felt the warmth and love of my soul I started to move into the expanded awareness of collective consciousness and the oneness of all. Meditation allowed me to hear the heartbeat of all humans, all trees, plants, animals and birds. To transcend beyond the veil of the illusion into the reality of all that there is. I understood completely that the physical reality is filled with illusions that cause so much sadness and yet can equally give us a perception of joy. I understood that only love is real. All is pure love energy expressing itself in different forms to 'experience' at various levels of consciousness.

Meandering the streets of Portimao I started to see myself in all that surrounded me, every face I met, every voice I heard and every landscape and building. Looking at the outside world to understand your inner world gives a lighter look at situations, knowing that the creative life force energy within you, the true essence of who you are and the 'God mind' is experiencing as you experience.

Meditation led me to a deep love for God and all that was around me. This led me to prayer and prayer led me to gratitude. Daily spiritual practices enhanced my understanding without saying a single word. All the knowledge I had gained of some thirty years of reading spiritual books could not have given what a year of deep, extended periods of inner work had (and continue to do so).

You maybe be wondering how I afforded to pay my bills and do all this inner work. Well, once I felt the pure unconditional love that was me, my creative juices flowed beyond anything I had experienced before. I started to transform my business from the UK high street to a global online business through creative marketing and new concepts. Once I walked into a place where fear did not and could not exist, I began to 'download' ideas at a rate so rapid that I could barely keep up.

Online projects that in previous years had only drifted in like shadows. Books that needed writing, courses, new teaching methods and other products and services that felt perfectly in alignment with my soul. When working with clients online, I was downloading information and involuntarily using 'inspired speaking' to nurture, inspire and coach. I sat for trance and gave distance healing to people thousands of miles away in far off countries such as Africa, Australia and America with reports of extraordinary results. I met amazing people, made some lifelong friends and felt only beauty and joy in interactions with others.

When I moved into my apartment in Portimao it was a relatively new build with open spaces of overgrowth and wild, unruly flowers and trees, entwined with recalcitrant weeds. This was not only a reflection of my relationship but of the torrid state of mind, I had been convincingly (to most) holding together for many months. The cluttered, unorganised, oppressive and unattractive view was a reflection of my self-worth. It was showing me how chaotic my life had become, and the relationship with Dan was toxic like the weeds, taking my breath and binding me from physical and spiritual progression. During my remembering process that I was indeed unconditional love, a miracle occurred. In spring bulldozers came and started to clear the wild plants which surrounded my apartment. A direct reflection of the healing and inner cleansing I was doing. Within weeks the landscape changed from unkempt foliage to flat, smooth, clay coloured open views.

By summer 2018 a new apartment block was erected, showing me how I had started to rebuild the parts of me which required it and mirroring the creative life force which now flowed effortlessly through me. As the summer started to end and September dawned, new paths were built, small plants which would become great, beautiful trees formed gardens which represented it was time to move forward. I have successfully moved from a perceived shadow to a realisation that all life is an expression of God's love in a physical form.

I was finally free of the confines of my mind. I was able to move fully into the work I was born to do. For the time being, I had completed my learning journey and was able to find joy and love in everything. Since doing the work I needed, I have not had a difficult day or encountered a problem or battle. That's not to say my life has been perfect, I have simply changed my perception.

I continued to work for spirit but with a new openness and without expectation, this improved the clarity of my readings. I stepped into my creativity; I realised my soul is creative. If you have a creative soul, you need to feed it with creative projects both in work and hobbies. I started to paint and draw again, write books, poetry, blogs and prayers. I worked less at becoming a teacher and instead opened myself to inspiring others and leading by example. My intention now is not to heal clients but allow myself to be used as a conduit, so they can heal themselves.

I have always loved music and have an extensive collection. The lyrics and the creative genius behind musicians are my inspiration now. Rather than seeking influences from people like Prince and Madonna who used their provocative and sexual nature to shock, I now observe those who love what they do. When an artist loves what they do, they are simply finding the joy in it, rather than seeking fame and money. People like Pavarotti, Bob Marley, Johnny Lee Hooker, k.d lang and the occasional busker on the street have this quality. This is what inspires me now.

I am open and indulgent to travel, experiences and people. Not so absorbed in my decisions and opinions but finding appeal in allowing the flow of life to guide me. Having no desire to be right, win an argument or be competitive has taken away pain and stress.

Maybe one day I will find a relationship that will add value to my life. If I do or don't it is of no consequence because I can never receive more love from another, than I have in my soul. I am unconditional love, so is every person in this physical experience. Relationships serve as healing experiences and life lessons. As the illusion continues to astound and amaze me, I continue to connect to the real world. The spirit. The place where all life is.

"Thousands of candles can be lit from a single candle, and the life of that candle will not be shortened. Happiness never decreases by being shared."

~ The Buddha

29.
Perspectives

For many years I sat in my story of abuse, shame and guilt. I thought that by sharing my story, it made me a survivor, that I was helping people by saying to them, "hey I understand, that happened to me", I thought that by telling people of my brokenness I was helping them to heal. The truth is to tell people of your 'brokenness' is to stay broken, because you need to stay broke to keeping telling the story. Writing this book is the last time I will tell my story.

The reason I manifested the worst relationship I ever had with Daniel, (even after I had found spirit) was to show me that I hadn't healed (I needed Vim). I was just staying broken so I could stick to my story; the narrative I had created in my mind. This is what we do as broken humans, we take on the story of the adults around us in our childhood and we make that story 'ours'. It's only when we can sit in the truth of what happened and our reactions to it, that we change our lives and ultimately our perception.

All healers give to others what they need themselves because they think it's helping, in truth it's just a subconscious way of showing yourself you have a lot of work to do. I spent years working as a psychic, a healer and a coach before I sat in my truths. It doesn't mean I wasn't good at what I was doing, I was always good at being an instrument for God, but I hadn't fully completed the work I needed to do on myself to become a *truly great* instrument for God's work.

I don't believe children manifest abuse, but I do believe as souls we understand that we will be born into a specific family pathology. For me, I was born of the fear and abuse of my great grandmother and grandmother, and the abandonment and loss of my mother. This created a broken child who was a vibrational match to the experiences of my childhood abuse and the years of dysfunction which occurred while the adults around me worked through their truths. What followed was a series of self-destructive patterns which were created by the pathology of my bloodline. The generations of women that had lived before me. It was in the most dysfunctional of relationships that the penny finally dropped. It was time to let go of 'the story' and start living my fullest, most functional life. I needed to step into my authenticity, awareness of my actions and accountability for my own life.

Having sex with men and women who didn't honour, respect and lift me, drinking myself into oblivion and dressing up in ridiculous outfits for attention were the symptoms of my deep lack of self-worth and self-awareness. Regardless of which self-sabotaging afflictions we choose to indulge in, the process is still the same. Acknowledge what's going on, take personal responsibility for your own life and do the work to take your power back.

I believe we have two toolkits; one is a toolkit created by the ego which contains our survival mechanisms of self-sabotage, the other is the toolkit created by our authentic self. This toolkit contains our survival kit of love, a place where we can honour and respect our feelings. During my time in Portugal, I delved deep into my self-love toolkit and found that I had some deep-rooted issues that would require me to first discover and acknowledge what they were, then to forgive myself and others, to let go of 'my story' and create a new narrative. Only by following this process would I be able to create a new perspective on the experience I was having.

Perception is everything, it creates your reality. No one can see inside your mind and see what you see, the way you see it. It says in A Course in Miracles that, *"when perception shifts from fear to love, at that moment a miracle occurs"*. I had read that line without fully understanding its meaning until I started to move into my spirit. Glyn Edwards was the first person I heard say "spirituality is having a relationship with your spirit", I thought spirituality was communicating with and believing in 'spirit'. It was only when I stopped to listen to my spirit that I understood how profound it was to develop that relationship. To hear your spirit is to understand everything. It's the opposite of living in ego, it's a place where there is only love. It was when I shifted my perception from ego, from self-sabotage, from self-indulgence to a place of love, healing and connection to something higher, that my miracle occurred. My miracle showed up as a deep sense of peace. My peace is to know that regardless of what may or may not be happening within or around me, I am still filled with love and grace and creative life force energy, that is my miracle. It's my wish, that every person who is reading this book, can shift their perception from fear to love and experience their own miracle.

You can only gain clarity in your own life by changing your inner world. Your inner world creates your experience of life, to read a book and have an intellectual understanding of something is not the same as having a spiritual experience. You can't create that shift from fear to love without knowing and understanding your patterns and where they came from. Love is peace and when you find it, it will never go away, dilute or disappear. You may dip in and out of fear occasionally, that is part of the human experience. There may be times when you are unsure and call upon your higher self or God for guidance, but be sure once discovered, love will always set you free. It may be that you had a baby, got married, held a person's hand before they made their transition back home, it may be in those moments, you felt sure that you had experienced the ultimate love. But, let me tell you, the greatest love you will ever experience is the love you hold within your own heart, your own soul because that love is the connection to oneness. Loving yourself ricochets out to all, like ever decreasing circles.

If you are feeling stressed, anxious, lonely, ill, worthless, lost, distressed or angry, no measure of drugs, alcohol, cigarettes, cannabis oil, diet shakes, vitamin drinks, sex, fame, material objects or turmeric will heal you. You've got to change your perception. Nothing external will ever create peace in your life and there is no quick fix. Healing the past to create a better life for yourself, starts and ends in the mind through a connection to God (your heart).

Acknowledging your own patterns, your own patterns, not what other people have done to you, or what other people say or do, only by acknowledging your own patterns, can you start to unlearn these patterns. Changing your debilitating habits to create habits which serve you and bring you to the door of your authentic self is the starting point. Look back at your childhood, your family and how you created the things in your life. Then accept them. Take personal responsibility for your own life. Stopping passing the buck of your own pain and start looking in the mirror. The person who shows up in the mirror is the person you must work with to move forward.

Once you've accepted and acknowledged who you have been, you can start to forgive and let go. Forgiveness is the key to all the suffering you have created in your life. It's the thing that will stop you from holding on to the past because we don't forgive in the present or the future, we only forgive the past. In other words, all that requires forgiveness has gone. Don't you think it's crazy that situations that have gone and are never coming back, are the very things that are holding you down? Like the 'Lady With The Sack', you need to stop carrying around the past, because that is back-breaking work, and you don't need it. Start to learn to love instead of hate, to be kind instead of angry, start to 'Be' instead of 'Do'.

The beautiful and inspiring Wayne Dyer said, "change the way you see things and the things you see change", what a wonderful way to sum up 'Perspectives'. Changing the way you perceive things creates a different view of the world. If you choose to see things with love, you can understand that all is within the laws of 'cause and effect'. With this knowledge, you can start to mind your own business and take personal responsibility. Before you try to fix the world, fix yourself. If you can change your perception from an emotion which is within the category of fear to any emotion that is in the category of love, your world will show you more of the same. Miracles occur in the light, take your mind to the light to see the miracle, if you stay in the dark, you will see only darkness.

Since moving forward in my own life, I have been able to help others, not by telling them what I know, but by helping them to discover their truths. There are no healers in the world because all healing occurs internally. As a spiritual teacher, healer or life coach, or whatever name I put on my business card, I can only help a person to do their work. I can hold their hand when it gets scary and they want to give up, congratulate them when they have a breakthrough moment and explain the tools, I used to heal my crazy, but each client I have ever worked with, did the work themselves.

I hope by revealing my patterns and vulnerability, you can fully submerge in the patterns and stories you have created. Learn who you are, don't let anyone tell you, you're not good enough and never fight the flow of life. Always go with what feels good for you, because that's your heart speaking to you. God and your heart are the same thing, they help you connect to your authentic self and create that essential trust that is required to be happy. Be proud of who you are because this is being authentic. Anyone who knows me or who has worked with me, knows that I strongly dislike labels. Whether it's about mental health, sexuality, race or beliefs, I feel society sticks labels on people and then we categorise them. You can't decompartmentalise life because its constantly in the flow of change. Everyone needs to be free of the confines of social judgment and detach themselves from other people's thoughts and opinions. Only in this truth can you recognise that you are unique and individual. Learn that individuality is what makes you special. If you feel weird or a freak, it's essential that you embrace it, it's your authentic self. Don't ever define yourself with societies labels, just be you.

Trust yourself, your spirit and the oneness of all. Allow yourself to fully experience all aspects of life and don't be afraid to make mistakes, for mistakes are life's way of showing you how to love more deeply. Allow yourself to be inspired, be creative and let abundance flow through you and all around you. May peace, love and miracles find you, cherish you and bless you.

"The deeper that sorrow carves into your being, the more joy you can contain."

~Kahlil Gibran

30.
Shifting From Self-Sabotage to Self-love

Ready to do the work? This chapter will show you how.

Our Toolkits

I believe we have two toolkits; one is a toolkit created by the ego which contains our survival mechanisms of self-sabotage, the other is the toolkit which is created by our authentic self. This toolkit contains our survival kit of love, a place where we can honour and respect our feelings.

Ego Toolkit (self-sabotage)	Authentic-self Toolkit (self-love)
• Excessive Alcohol • Abuse of Drugs (illegal & prescription) • Smoking Tobacco • Sex with the absence of love • Self-harm • Negative mind-talk • Procrastination • Excessive shopping • Gambling • Obsessive Compulsive Disorder	• Kindly mind-talk • Exercise • Loving relationships • Sex only within a loving relationship • Positive thinking • Prayer • Gratitude • Meditation • Nutrition Awareness

• Anorexia • Bulimia • Excessive eating • Dysfunctional relationships • Seeking external validation • Attachment to Drama • Judging yourself and others	(eating light foods) • Feeding your mind with positive information • Practising non-judgment (of yourself and others) • Practising non-attachment • Practising life without expectation • Internal validation
Ego Toolkit Leads to: ↓ Depression Anxiety Low Self-esteem	**Authentic-self Toolkit** Leads to: ↓ Inspiration/creativity Self-love Peace

Natural human survival means we automatically reach into our toolkits. When times get hard and you are feeling crazy and overwhelmed, ask yourself, "which toolkit am I using right now"? First, we must examine our pathology and patterns to acknowledge who you are. Next, it's important to be aware of when you are delving into self-sabotaging behaviour (s), which is both a habit and an addiction. For me it was alcohol, bad relationships and over-spending, what are yours?

Acknowledgement is the first step to healing. To help you release and let go of past limiting perspectives are seven practices to implement into your life. These seven practices will help you to overcome the long-term behaviours of oppression and self-destruct enabling you to move forward into a better life. Remember to stand in your truths and look within, not at other people or situations. It starts and ends with you, for you are the only person in YOUR life.

Study Your Pathology
If you were brought up by both of your parents (even if they split) then start with mothers' side first and then dad's side of the family. Take a pen and paper and write down the story of your grandparents first, looking at the emotions that may have existed in their lives. Then look at the emotions that would have filled your parent's childhood and then those emotions around the time of your conception and birth. If there were times of distress or if one or more parents were absent, make a note of it. Absence does not make the heart grow fonder when it's between a parent and child. Look at the patterns that existed and look where these showed up in your own life. Look

also, at primary caregivers, if your parents were absent during your childhood. If you have children, it's of paramount importance to heal the line of pathology now, the future generations are in your hands.

For me, there was a deep level of shame and guilt that existed in my mothers' side of the family. By becoming a vibrational match to and agreeing to take on the assignment pre-birth, I manifested my guilt and shame in the form of sexual abuse and not speaking up. The feelings of abandonment my mother suffered were directly related to her grandmothers and mothers' fears created by World War I and World War II. This abandonment showed up in my mothers' life by her parents' total rejection of her and the rejection she suffered from Tom. My interpretation of this was exhibited in my relationships. I chose men and women who were insecure and emotionally damaged, thus creating situations where they were unable to absorb my affections, ending in feelings of unworthiness and rejection. Examining your pathology will help you to understand the bloodline you were born into. The healing work you do will affect all future generations. When a woman gives birth, she passes on more than her DNA, she passes on her consciousness and the consciousness of those who have lived before her.

Examine Your Patterns
Look at your relationships, your friendships, career and finances. Look at where repeated patterns have occurred, these patterns are the key to demonstrating where love, forgiveness and release must take place.

For the most part, I chose to create learning experiences within my relationships with men. Men showed up as frightening sexual encounters at first, followed by needy, insecure lovers. My relationship with Emily mirrored those insecurities but awakened me to my masculine energy.

Again, and again, I allowed myself to be used in relationships, seeking external validation. All I needed was to understand I was worthy and to love myself unconditionally. Another pattern which occurred in my life was the friendships I developed with gay men. They showed me how to embrace my feminine energy and that sexuality could be playful and fun. They allowed me to learn to be lighter and carefree.

Examine your patterns and then use prayer, meditation and gratitude to release and let go.

7 Practices to Live Your Most Fulfilled and Peaceful Life

I have written down for you here, seven practices that will have a huge positive impact on your life IF, you use them. There are no miracle cures, healing is hard work. What I can promise you, is that if you do these seven practices and continue to use them in your life, you will create a life of peace, contentment and ultimately happiness.

1. **Spiritual Practices**

Making spiritual practices part of your routine is essential to helping all the other practices work. There are 3 essential spiritual practices which will help to massively improve your minds activity, which are:

Meditation – start with 10 mins per day and gradually work up to 1 hour. This should become as normal as brushing your teeth. Meditation can be done anytime but keep it consistent – everyday. Check out the toolkit resources section for meditation ideas. There is also a good free app called: Stop, Breathe, Think, which you may wish to check out. You may also wish to study Buddhism, Hinduism or Shamanism, which all use meditation practices. Experiment and have fun with different methods until you find what works for you.

Prayer – Do this every day, talk to God, the universe, your higher self, what you call it is not important; ask for guidance (especially if you are struggling with something), prayer is the most powerful tool in your box. Prayer is best done in the morning to start your day. Check out the toolkit resources section for more ideas.

Gratitude – create a gratitude journal and write down 5 things you are grateful for every day, this is best done at night. Keep your book and pen by your bed. Gratitude is the single most important tool for manifesting a better life. We can always find things to be grateful for in our lives, what we give out, we get more of. Start small, be grateful for having clothes, a place to live, food. Then progress into things that are desires but assume they are already manifested.

2. Practice Non-attachment

The second principle may be completely alien to you because you may have been taught as a child that certain things are 'yours'. The practise of non-attachment is essential to those who find life difficult.

"The root of suffering is attachment" ~ Buddha

The most important thing to let go of is drama, your drama and other people's drama. Drama is when we create mayhem around a situation when it's entirely unnecessary, and not to get sucked into other people's reactions to things. Another words, mind your OWN business.

Let go of material possessions, no one owns anything, and you will take nothing from the material world with you when you go home to the realm of spirit. If you lose something, let it go, if someone steals something from you, let it go, if something breaks, let it go. Holding on to things that are never coming back, will only cause you pain.

Practice non-attachment to people and places. Understand that everything is perfect, if someone needs to go in a different direction, just allow that to happen, knowing that they will be back when you need them (not when you think you need them). If a person leaves your life for good, know that you moved out of that energy vibration and they are no longer needed.

3. Let go of Expectation

Letting go of expectation is learning to trust in the natural process of life. Expectation is limitation. When we have no expectation of an outcome, we can never be disappointed.

Think about it, when a relationship ends badly, be it a love relationship, friendship or family member, it's usually because you had an expectation of how a person was supposed to behave. An expectation from a person that they were unable or unwilling to fulfil causes disappointment.

Going into a relationship or situation without any expectation whatsoever will open the door for miracles to occur. Live by the philosophy that maybe 'God has a better idea'. If we allow, rather than push, the universe can deliver beyond our wildest dreams. So, let go and let live!

4. Understand the Illusion

The whole of the physical experience is an illusion. In the illusion is the ego, and creates fear. There are only two states of 'being'; love and fear, everything fits into these two categories. At all times you are either living in a state of fear or love, all that is fear is an illusion, all that is love is real.

"What God did not create does not exist. And everything that does exist exists as He created it. The

---

337

world you see has nothing to do with reality. It is of your own making, and it does not exist." ~ A Course in Miracles

Pain might seem real at the time, suffering may feel real at the time but if you can step into a place of love, all fear will be diminished. So how do we apply this in real-time? Easy, never react with anger or aggression (fear-based illusion), always act with kindness (love). Forgive and be unwilling to accept fear, illness, lack or need. Always send love to yourself, others and anything which seems unbalanced (it's not unbalanced, it's an illusionary perception created in your mind). In every situation be not in a state of ego, but a state of love.

"EGO – Edging God Out" ~ Wayne Dyer

5. Live in the Present

Living in the present moment means switching off the mind talk and just simply 'being fully present'. The mind is where the illusion is created it's the only place where it exists, for it is the only place where fear can live (fear: false evidence appearing real).

Living fully present means using the past and the future as reference points only. Use past experiences to serve the present moment and if you are practising all of the above, the future will be irrelevant (unless you are planning an event).

Letting go of the past is understanding that it is never coming back, that it has gone, over. Just forget it. Not anticipating what will come (letting go of the negative mind talk) will create a stress-free life in itself.

6. Know You're Not Alone

We live on a planet with approximately 7 billion people. This should tell you that you're not alone, but quite often we feel we must do everything for ourselves. So, if you are unable to feel the love of your 7 billion brothers and sisters, try this instead.

Know and call upon your guides, angels and loved ones who have passed away. If you want you can speak to God, source, the universal life force, what you call it makes no difference to the power and presence of love which is available to all from the non-physical realms. Meditation and prayer will help you with this practice.

Just ask, either aloud or in your mind, "help me, I need guidance today" or "I'm lost, help me get back on track…..show me the way out of the illusion and into a place of my true being…love". Once you start calling upon your guides and angels, you can know that you are not alone.

7. Take Care of Your Body

The body houses the soul, it's important. Love it, honour it, respect it. Be kind to your body and treat it like an expensive car, maintenance is super important. Give it the best you can; the best food and exercise, don't give it poisons like; processed foods, cigarettes, drugs and alcohol.

Know that the body is sacred and with sexual activity only use it with someone who you love and trust, you wouldn't lend your Bentley to the irresponsible driver next door, so don't give away your body to anyone who doesn't deserve it. Sex can be another form of external validation and can be viewed as seeking God outside of yourself (God is within). No one 'needs' sex, that's just a false belief that society has created. However, when you are in a loving and mutually beneficial relationship, sex can be the blending of two souls in the physical. It's in this moment that the miracle of life can occur and the awakening of the soul to pleasures of the physical. It may also seek to reaffirm that all in the physical experience is nothing more than an illusion. It's possible to experience the same euphoria in meditation that you can in an orgasm.

Take part in some physical exercise that makes you happy, every single day. Walking, swimming, dancing, weight training, yoga, Tai Chi…. whatever works for you. I like to listen to something motivational whilst I walk or workout. Spiritual books on Audible or podcasts from Oprah's Super Soul Conversations or Hay House are wonderful ways to feed your mind whilst loving your body. You can listen to sections of The Pali Canon, The Bhagavad Gita and great inspirational teachings on Audible. I highly recommend studying all religion and philosophy to expand your mind and awareness but remember, your truths will only be found in meditation.

Lastly, remember this: you don't have to be a saint, you just have to understand the principles of spiritualism and try to apply them to your daily life.

Online One to One Coaching Internationally with Beverley Anne Freeman is available at www.beverleyannefreeman.com

Tool Kit Resources
You can find free meditations here: https://www.beverleyannefreeman.com/free-meditations-hypnosis

And on my YouTube Channel: https://www.youtube.com/channel/UC3qYTCb4qvBnr8jmj2FmC1g
Try this morning prayer to help you get into the routine of morning prayer, at time goes on you can develop your prayer:

A Morning Prayer

Dear God, I love you,
How may I serve you today?
Lead me towards the highest place in Self,
That I may spread love and kindness wherever I go.
Let's create miracles today;
Allowing all perception to shift from fear to love.
Lead the way in creating love and kindness within me and all around me.
Enable me to give love and receive love in equal measure,
In doing so, I will always have enough love in me to serve the world with you as my guide.
Let me recognise that the holy spirit lives in me and that in this physical world I am an expression of your love.

I send loving healing thoughts out to all mankind, recognising
that all are my brothers and sisters.
Allow my ego to reside in a quiet place, so that my divinity may
take centre stage in this life.
I love you, God. Amen

About The Author

Beverley Anne Freeman is a psychic, healer, author and coach. She was born in Bolton, Lancashire and prides herself in her good northern humor and a down to earth approach. She attempted many careers before understanding her true gifts including; fashion retail, bar work, recruitment consultancy and modelling. She now works internationally, inspiring people all over the world to find their true selves and live a life without fear.

Find Out More:
www.beverleyannefreeman.com
www.psychiccoursesonline.com
Contact me: beverleyanefreeman@live.co.uk

More Books By Beverley Anne Freeman
Available on Amazon Worldwide in Paperback and Kindle

How To Make a Living As A Psychic Or Healer
Are you passionate about using your psychic and mediumistic gifts to help others? Perhaps you are a blessed healer or lightworker? Would you like to earn a living doing what you love and using your divine talents? Read on...

Beverley Anne Freeman has been a successful psychic, medium, healer and life coach for over 15 years, developing both high street and online businesses. She has met countless individuals who have been passionate, gifted and highly skilled in the field of holistic healing and intuitive guidance counselling. Many of these individuals have all the love and will in the world to give but have been clueless about to set-up and run a successful business in this arena.

Whether you wish to offer psychic readings, healing treatments or life coaching; from home, the high street or online, this practical guide will give you all the tools you require to create a successful business. From setting up, web design, marketing, legal guidance, insurance, customer care and creating the right space. As well as tools for making sure your business excels in your current marketplace.

The Lady With The Sack, Written & Illustrated by Beverley Anne Freeman

Once upon a time, there was a lady with a sack, where it came from nobody knew and why she had it nobody could tell... Anyone reading this book will soon begin to recognise their own story and identify with the main character in this book. Quirky illustrations tell the all too familiar story of those of us who carry around baggage and get weighted down by the past... only to discover that if they lighten their load happiness will soon prevail. Told with humorous and quirky illustrations and a down to earth approach to self-help.

Titles Coming In 2020
Paradox: What's After Self Love? by Beverley Anne Freeman

Malcolm & Mitch, A Story Through Grief
Written & Illustrated by Beverley Anne Freeman

The Adventures of Raj, Being Different and Learning To Love Yourself
Written & Illustrated by Beverley Anne Freeman

Printed in Great Britain
by Amazon

39349709R00197